Leadership Coaching provides convincing arguments for more brave leadership within corporate structures, and is filled with compelling evidence-based insights, conceptual frameworks, and practical examples on how to develop brave leaders. It is a must-read for anyone involved in coaching executives, leaders, and managers who wish to enhance their leadership effectiveness.

Bob Hamlin, Emeritus Professor and Chair of Human Resource Development, University of Wolverhampton, UK

Leadership Coaching is essential and powerful reading for coaches and leaders who seek not only high performance, but to lead from the bravery agenda of their moral purpose to address key issues such as equality, sustainability, and environmental justice. This text will not only deepen practice, but also enable critical reflection on what it means to be a brave coach today.

Jan Robertson, International consultant in coaching and leadership development in education, New Zealand

This book comes at an opportune time for developing leaders in our VUCA (volatility, uncertainty, complexity and ambiguity) world. Brilliantly written with academic rigour, this book comes with specific and practical examples in guiding anyone who wants to develop their new generation of brave leaders.

Derrick Kon, Director, The Conference Board, USA

LEADERSHIP COACHING

Leadership Coaching offers a new model of coaching for leadership development. It explains how the brave model extends existing leadership theories, and includes specific coaching processes and sense-making techniques to allow the reader to understand how the model would work in practice.

The book begins by asking why it is important for leaders to be brave. It provides an overview of existing leadership theories, and their limitations, as well as introducing the brave coaching approach and the elements that comprise the model. The book includes practical case studies that provide insights into the range of applications for the brave leadership coaching framework.

Based on academic research, and written in an accessible scholarly style, this book shows how coaching can assist in decision making, leading to a different, braver form of personal and corporate leadership. It should be of interest to students of management, leadership, coaching and mentoring, as well as professional coaches and leaders.

Mike McLaughlin works in both the public and private sectors as a coach and consultant, specializing in leadership development.

Elaine Cox is director of the coaching and mentoring programs at Oxford Brookes University, UK. She has authored many journal articles and books, including *Goal-focused Coaching* published by Routledge. She is editor of the *International Journal of Evidence Based Coaching and Mentoring*.

LEADERSHIP COACHING

Developing braver leaders

Mike McLaughlin and Elaine Cox

Routledge
Taylor & Francis Group
NEW YORK AND LONDON

First published 2016
by Routledge
711 Third Avenue, New York, NY 10017

and by Routledge
2 Park Square, Milton Park, Abingdon, Oxon OX14 4RN

Routledge is an imprint of the Taylor & Francis Group, an informa business

© 2016 Mike McLaughlin and Elaine Cox

The right of Mike McLaughlin and Elaine Cox to be identified as authors of this work has been asserted by them in accordance with sections 77 and 78 of the Copyright, Designs and Patents Act 1988.

All rights reserved. No part of this book may be reprinted or reproduced or utilised in any form or by any electronic, mechanical, or other means, now known or hereafter invented, including photocopying and recording, or in any information storage or retrieval system, without permission in writing from the publishers.

Trademark notice: Product or corporate names may be trademarks or registered trademarks, and are used only for identification and explanation without intent to infringe.

British Library Cataloguing in Publication Data
A catalogue record for this book is available from the British Library

Library of Congress Cataloging in Publication Data
McLaughlin, Mike (Executive coach)
  Leadership coaching : developing braver leaders / Mike McLaughlin and Elaine Cox. – 1 Edition.
    pages cm
  Includes bibliographical references and index.
  1. Leadership–Study and teaching. 2. Executives–Training of. 3. Mentoring in business. 4. Business consultants. I. Title.
    HD30.4.M4255 2015
    658.4'092–dc23
              2015011645

ISBN: 978-1-138-78600-4 (hbk)
ISBN: 978-1-138-78602-8 (pbk)
ISBN: 978-1-315-76746-8 (ebk)

Typeset in Bembo
by Taylor & Francis Books

From Mike.
For Lucy, Luisa and Annabelle.

From Elaine.
For my grandchildren: Leo, Molly, Xavier and Charlotte—and the longer term.

CONTENTS

List of illustrations   *viii*
Acknowledgements   *ix*
Foreword   *x*

1 Introduction: The challenge of brave leadership   1
2 The Brave Story   23
3 Pulling Factors   41
4 Gravitational Factors   59
5 Finding Balance: Emotional and moral self-awareness   86
6 The Brave Sphere   105
7 The Brave Decision   126
8 The Brave Action   156
9 The Trust Factor   182
10 Positioning Braver Leadership Coaching   199
11 The Brave Agenda   221

References   *228*
Index   *247*

ILLUSTRATIONS

Figures

1.1	Leader development and leadership development—an inside-outside process	15
1.2	The brave leadership coaching model	17
3.1	John's initial pulling factors diagram	50
3.2	Matt's "evolved" pulling factors diagram	53
3.3	Relationship between pulling factors, gravitational factors and brave action	58
4.1	The gravitational factors	61
4.2	Doing the right thing	77
4.3	The retroductive analysis process	83
6.1	The three functions of the brave sphere	107
7.1	The brave decision-making process	127
7.2	Classification of problems facing leaders	130
7.3	Rich picture of a complex adaptive problem	142
7.4	Light boxes: Collating options and holding them lightly for discussion and selection	150
8.1	Coaching with System 1 and System 2	166
10.1	A continuum of leadership theories	201
10.2	Brave leadership spans all leadership approaches	217

Box

4.1	Six core virtues and 24 character strengths	68

ACKNOWLEDGEMENTS

We would like to thank the following people for their help and encouragement during the research and writing of this book: Tim Cobbold, Roland Carter, Chris Surch, Jo Chidley, G. McGeehan, Rob McLoughlin, John Langston, Stuart Chidley, P.C. Paul, Mark Crompton, Peter Steel, Sheena McColl, Lee Baker, Mal Maginnis, Adrian Hussey and S. Green.

We would also like to thank our friends and family for their wonderful and ongoing support and also for their understanding about how long and time consuming this process has been, and had to be. There are people who are not included here for reasons of anonymity. You know who you are, and thank you so very much.

FOREWORD

Leadership Coaching: Developing Braver Leaders addresses a topic of growing urgency. The global financial and geopolitical calamities of the past decade are, in major part, failures of leadership. As key influencers of leaders' values, identities, abilities to act for the long term and for the wider good, coaches are, like it or not, close to the front line in terms of social and commercial change. That position requires them to have both an awareness of their potential to influence for good and the skills to help leaders take and live with brave decisions.

Over the years, I have often thought about what it means to be brave—usually when I have just been through a physically demanding and potentially dangerous escapade, such as a first skydive or skiing off a mountainside with a parachute, but also sometimes when I have had to make a decision with complex ethical dimensions. Among the factors I observe from such experiences are that:

- the fear that is there to be overcome relates particularly to the unknown—to the instinct to imagine the worst that might happen;
- one of the key mechanisms to overcome fear is trust—both trust in other people, such as an experienced guide, and trust in oneself; and
- when bravery is required, it is important to become "centered" and achieve at least some level of inner calm.

I have been fortunate to meet some very courageous leaders. They have all impressed me with their curiosity (willingness to explore new ideas and perspectives, and to entertain the idea that they might be wrong), with their ability to take ownership of ideas that run counter to the mainstream and to be personally accountable for the outcomes of decisions that they make. They are often highly self-aware, recognizing that to manage complex situations, you must first manage yourself, and they have coping mechanisms that make them less inclined than other people to avoid the difficult issues.

One of my favorite examples is the former CEO of one of the UK's largest retailers. Why, I asked him in an interview, did he step down at the peak of his success in the role? His response was straightforward. At the beginning of his time as CEO, he had some complex and tough decisions to make. These had paid off in terms of growth and profits, as well as other measures, such as employee engagement. Eventually, however, some of these decisions needed to be revisited in the light of changes in markets and technology. The tough question he posed himself was: Is the person who took these original decisions really the best person to lead the decision making this time around? After considerable reflection and self-examination, he concluded that he would bring too much baggage and too many status quo-oriented assumptions. He tendered his resignation, was persuaded to stay another year to assure a smooth transition, and began to look for new challenges.

How this contrasts with leaders who regard their tenure in the role as a personal right! In my studies over recent years of how organizations manage talent, a recurring theme has been that selection and promotion processes encourage the advancement of mediocre managers—people who make few, if any, mistakes because they are risk averse. As these people rise in the organization, they lack the experience of managing failure and of making brave decisions, yet this experience and learning from failure is a core attribute of resilient, courageous leadership.

For executive coaches, helping leaders discover and nurture their bravery is a significant challenge. It requires bravery and risk taking by the coach. It requires a deep insight into how people self-motivate to do what is moral and difficult, and how they self-justify and obfuscate when they lack courage. As the authors of this book explain, the coach sometimes needs to be a mirror to the soul; sometimes an external conscience; sometimes someone who provides a context and space for high-quality reflection about the relationship between internal (client) and external (organizational) values; sometimes a sounding board; and sometimes simply there to provide a structure through which the leader can process his or her thinking.

The coach can help the leader find the courage to address difficult issues, to take decisions that are authentic to their values and identity, to follow through, and to cope with the fallout that comes from being the instigator of unpopular but essential change. Bravery is infectious. So effective coaches support the leader in linking with others who share their concerns and passion for change, and with whom the leader can build a collective sense of shared courage and determination. We might go so far as to call this "systemic bravery."

While it is clear that bravery comes ultimately from within, the authors also make a cogent and coherent case for bravery as a quality that can be built over time. They set out a model for developing braver leaders that has validity and implications not just for organizations, but for coaches, too. Without brave coaches, an organization's capacity to nurture brave leaders will be severely limited. This book therefore raises difficult but timely questions both for executive coaches and for those who train and educate coaches. Indeed, coaches who cannot be brave themselves may be part of the problem, not part of the solution, for many of the ills of poor decision making that undermine organizational performance.

Professor David Clutterbuck
March 2015

1

INTRODUCTION

The challenge of brave leadership

Introduction

Martin Luther King Jr. notably argued that "The ultimate measure of a man is not where he stands in moments of comfort and convenience, but where he stands at times of challenge and controversy. The true neighbor will risk his position, his prestige and even his life for the welfare of others" (King, 1963, p.25). This focus on risk and standing up for others in the face of disagreement presupposes a certain bravery. This book introduces a framework that describes how coaching can help leaders think about where they stand in times of challenge and how they position themselves in relation to their followers and their organization. It suggests that the world needs leaders to be courageous and act bravely in the face of the challenges they encounter in order to create not only successful, but also sustainable businesses. This book then is about coaching leaders to be braver, helping them understand themselves and their organizations better so that they can create and uphold brave solutions to present-day and future problems.

In this introduction we first define leadership coaching and what we mean by bravery, and suggest how a new approach to coaching leaders can help them to develop and operate in ways that will better meet the needs of their organizations and society. The chapter discusses why it is important for leaders to be brave and examines the apparent dysfunction in leadership practice that appears to underpin the current "malaise around financial crisis, climate control and ethical debacles" (Ladegard & Gjerde,

2014, p.631), frequent organizational failures (Gardner et al., 2010) and occasional "public fiascos" (Brewer, 2014, p.1). Such disquiet, in our view, points to a gap in expectation and leadership development. Toward the end of the chapter we introduce a leadership coaching framework that can be used to try and recover this situation through heightened awareness of context, understanding of self and, since we consider decision making as the key aspect of leadership, the decision-making and implementation process in an organizational context.

What do we mean by leadership coaching?

Burns defined leadership as "... the reciprocal process of mobilizing, by persons with certain motives and values, various economic, political and other resources, in a context of competition and conflict, in order to realize goals independently or mutually held by both leaders and followers" (Burns, 1978, p.425).

When we talk about leadership coaching we use Burns's definition of leadership as a benchmark, but we are also guided by Riddle's definition of coaching as a formal process whereby "a qualified coach works with an organizational leader in a series of dynamic, private sessions designed to establish and achieve clear goals that will result in improved business effectiveness for the individual, as well as his or her team and organization" (Riddle, 2008, p.7). Our definition of coaching also aligns with one proposed by Bachkirova, Cox and Clutterbuck (2014, p.1): "Coaching is a human development process that involves structured, focused interaction and the use of appropriate strategies, tools and techniques to promote desirable and sustainable change for the benefit of the client and potentially for other stakeholders."

We also like Edgar Schein's (2006, p.18, emphasis in original) distinction between coaching in practice and other interventions:

- a coach "does not *necessarily* have in mind a pre-determined direction or outcome";
- a coach does not have power over the client; and
- a client volunteers for coaching and is motivated to learn.

Schein argues that the ultimate skill of the coach is to "assess the moment to moment reality that will enable him or her to be in the appropriate role" (Schein, 2006, p.24). This suggests an immediacy that will enable two things for the leader: for the coaching to be absolutely relevant to the current situation; but more importantly, for the coaching to be appropriate for the level of development needed by the leader. This implies that the coach may have recourse to use a framework, model, or some other type of tool to guide the coaching relationship.

Ladegard and Gjerde (2014, p.632) describe leadership coaching as involving "one-on-one counselling of executives, leaders, and managers about work-related issues with the purpose of improving their leadership effectiveness." They say that one of the benefits of coaching is that it provides "custom-tailored development," and so it can take account of individual needs and starting points.

These definitions support the purpose of this book, where we are focusing on coaching to promote change for the benefit of the leader, the organization and beyond. Our definition of leadership coaching, therefore, draws on all these characterizations and explanations and can be summarized as follows:

> Leadership coaching is a one-to-one adult development process that uses appropriate strategies and techniques to optimize, enhance and transform individual leader understanding for the benefit of leaders themselves, their organizations and, ultimately, the society in which they operate.

What Do We Mean By "Brave"?

To define what we mean by brave, it is probably best to compare it to another word that is often used interchangeably with it: courage. The origin of the word courage is given in the *Oxford English Dictionary* as "middle English, denoting the heart as the seat of feelings, from old French, *corage*, from the Latin, 'cor,' 'heart'." Courage, it would seem, is closely connected to how we feel—specifically to overcoming emotions such as fear. Courage does not necessarily mean that any action is taken, but rather that a change in feeling is generated; that the "ability" to overcome adversity is there.

Hannah, Sweeney and Lester (2007) suggested that courageous actions require emotional and cognitive skills, not will alone. These authors also theorized that building positive emotional skills to reduce associations of fears may be an essential step before demonstrating courageous actions and autonomous motivation. Similarly, according to Pury and Kowalski (2007), courageous actions reflect individual readiness to: i) initiate the process, ii) show vulnerability and confront fears, iii) reflect on personal values and goals, and iv) understand potential consequences of actions based on values other than social expectations. On the other hand, being "brave" is defined as being ready to face and endure danger or pain; and showing courage is enduring or facing unpleasant conditions or behavior without showing fear. The word "brave" is also connected to action, to confronting a situation, to "face," to "endure." It could be argued, therefore, that courage is a necessary forerunner of bravery: the internal change from a state of fear to that of managing this emotion is courage, and that courage is a precursor to a brave action, or indeed a brave action through inaction.

Courage, then, is the capacity to overcome fear or pain. It is a state of mind—which can be mustered, plucked up and galvanized in order to enable us ultimately to face problems if we so choose, despite the fact that we may feel frightened. Courage is the determined choice to face problems, it is a means to an end, whereas bravery, we would argue, goes a step further—it includes the action beyond courage and so is an end in itself. So we would consider a brave leader to be one who has mastered their emotions and is ready and able to take action in the face of likely adversity. The operative word here is *able*. The courageous leader might not follow through with the brave action: s/he has the courage, but has not reached the point of action. The brave leader is one who is able to act in accordance with their courage.

Similarly, Peterson and Seligman (2004, p.232) confirm bravery as "not shrinking from challenge or pain; speaking up, standing up for convictions." Drawing on Shelp's (1984, p.354) definition, these authors cite bravery as "the disposition to voluntarily act, perhaps fearfully, in a dangerous circumstance, where the relevant risks are reasonably appraised, in an effort to obtain or preserve some perceived good for one self or others recognizing that the desired perceived good may not be realized." Peterson and Seligman (2004) also reported how the concept of bravery has shifted over time, gradually changing from an emphasis on physical courage in war, for example, to embracing "the taking of social and economic risks as dictated by conscience" (p.216). Thus the change has been from physical valor on the battlefield towards the ability to act with moral bravery in social and organizational settings. According to Peterson and Seligman (2004, p.214), bravery has a significant rational association involving judgment: "an understanding of risk and an acceptance of the consequences of action." Bravery, they argue, requires "the presence of danger, loss, risk, or potential injury. Without a sense of danger, risk, or vulnerability, there is no bravery in an act. Bravery is valuable because it allows people to dampen their immediate fearful response to danger and evaluate the appropriate course of action. It also involves the mastery of fear, rather than fearlessness" (ibid., p.216).

As an example of bravery in action, Katoch (2013) examined how ethical leadership and effective decision making may be developed effectively in the army. He highlighted how leadership is "the dynamic enabling-constraining process that occurs between people rather than the sole function of the individual leader" (p.164). This implies that followers consent to the leader taking control, especially in defining moments. Katoch goes on to say that "courage and humanity are the predominant emotional and interpersonal characteristics on display when a leader earns the right to lead […] Courage is the emotional strength that involves exercise of will to accomplish goals in the face of opposition, and is defined by the character strengths of bravery, persistence, integrity, and vitality" (ibid., p.164). So the leader's role is to demonstrate bravery in defining moments and not to "shrink from threats, challenges, or difficulties" (ibid., p.164). Brave leaders "stand up for what they think is right, regardless of consequences and persevere in completing challenging tasks. They deal with the unknown and lead despite instability and unpredictability. They also display integrity and take responsibility for their feelings and actions […]" (ibid., p.164). Katoch goes on to explain how courage does not only comprise observable action, but is also reliant on the "cognitions, emotions, motivations and decisions that produce them" (ibid.).

As well as a rational element, Peterson and Seligman (2004, p.214) also suggested that bravery must involve moral judgment: "Bravery is usually considered doing what is right, including confronting the status quo or opposing an unhealthy idea, and as such, it takes on a moral tone." This element of moral virtue is picked up by Annas (2005, p.639) who also proposed that "bravery can be shown in a wide variety of situations which have little or nothing in common with the dangerous and violent ones. Real bravery may be required, for example, in the unexciting context of a committee meeting." We can see how the personal danger involved in bravery in business is less likely to be physical, as in military settings, and probably more likely to involve psychological (overcoming fear, anxiety, potential loss of status) or perhaps professional concerns (demotion, transfer, job loss). These personal and social concerns may sometimes be quite at odds with the organization's values, or at least part of the organization.

Our definition of brave leadership draws on all these definitions of brave and can be described as action that:

- consciously ignores personal danger or personal gain;
- is rooted in significant personal and social values, such as responsibility and virtuousness;

- is grounded by an understanding of personal needs and character strengths or assets; and
- leads to an active decision to change a situation, or an active decision to maintain the status quo.

Bravery can be summarized as the act of facing threat and danger whilst feeling fear, but not being overcome by that fear to the point of immobility or retreat. However, there may be situations where the fear does in fact not need to be overcome in a straightforward sense. Imagine a situation where we notice our child is on the edge of a tall building and there is no barrier between them and the concrete precipice. Our fear of heights is not present in that moment, we do not have to overcome it, it does not exist in the sense that there is nothing to overcome, because something we value so dearly needs our attention. If we are physically capable of reaching that child, we are highly likely to take action. We may feel a dread, or a fear that we may not reach the child in time, but we are unlikely in that moment to be overcome by a fear for our own safety. We are not generally overcome by fear when our values need protecting: we do not have to shovel out the darkness to switch on the light. Our values are the light. Bravery arises from feelings such as passion, love and commitment, and compassion. In some sense it could be argued that bravery requires less energy than courage, which could necessitate finding a way to generate the emotional strength to overcome fear or lack. Bravery can elicit behaviors that may make a leader appear bigger than the crisis at hand.

Throughout the book, when we talk about bravery in the leadership context, we are describing leaders who have courage and who do not allow fear to prevent them from taking brave action and defending their principles, even if this involves risks and conflict.

A friend of ours works in a very challenging role within the police force. He faces dangerous situations regularly. He serves the community; he protects the community, both locally and more widely. He has a high moral and ethical standard, and often for those standards to be met, he has to be brave. This element is essential for him to do his job, to perform his duty. If a police officer can do that, very often thanklessly and often anonymously on our behalf, it is probably not too much to ask that our leaders (who are rarely, if ever, in such potential physical danger) do the same. Of course, it could be argued that facing a physical manifestation of danger can in some ways be easier to deal with than the more pervasive and subtle pressures that leaders have to endure. After all, the human race has evolved some adaptive neural (e.g. amygdalae) and hormonal (e.g.

adrenaline and cortisol) strategies to deal effectively with physical threats. However, for our friend, bravery comes from the threat of having to deal with the psychological pressure of remaining true to his "code," his moral compass, and the potential consequences of doing so, and therefore, there are distinct psychological challenges to be surmounted. So in this way, there are distinct similarities between his pressure and the pressures faced by leaders. Our friend can certainly feel fear, but he has a moral compulsion that allows him to be propelled through that fear, maybe even in some situations not even really feeling fear or thinking about behaviors as being brave, due to a distinct sense of doing what is "right." This inevitably points the spotlight back towards our corporate leaders, and begs the question at least of some: where are our brave corporate leaders?

The Need For Brave Leaders

The ability of people to have access to each other and share information directly, immediately and across continents is a very recent phenomenon. The Internet, for example, has enabled the lives and thoughts of leaders, politicians and other public figures to become instantaneously accessible. This accessibility in turn can allow ordinary individuals to notice patterns and themes, to make more considered judgments on what actually might be taking place and why, and can lead them to expect more accountability from their leaders. Heal (2008) notes how over the last 20 years environmental and social impacts have become of greater concern for corporates, with some leaders taking their responsibilities more seriously. There are potentially a number of reasons for this:

- As mentioned, the idea of accountability, or the desire to see accountability, may stem, at least in part, from the relatively recent technical capability, which enables us to comprehend and/or question the decisions being made by those in roles of influence and power.
- Privatization during the Thatcher/Reagan era resulted in deregulation allowing organizations to direct the kinds of standards and decisions that were previously overseen by state regulatory bodies. Thus leaders needed to make decisions on issues that they did not really face even a few years earlier.
- Globalization has increased exponentially. Organizations operate in many countries across the world, often in areas where there is very little social or environmental regulation. In China, for example, although there is certainly some legislation, implementation is patchy. Western organizations with connections in China have then to decide

whether to implement legislation or not. They can set their own environmental or employment standards. This irregular implementation of standards results in many distressing events, which, again through technology, can be reported instantly on personal media devices almost anywhere in the world.

In many ways the world has become more immediate and "radically transparent" (Laszlo & Zhexembayeva, 2011), resulting in increased questioning of the motives driving specific corporate or political behaviors. With the wealth of information that is available from many disparate sources, the complexity of dots can often be joined more easily and effects linked more tangibly to cause. People are now perhaps more able to view leadership in a different light. Greater awareness calls into question what could, and arguably should, ultimately drive corporations, i.e. not solely financial concern, but customer and employee satisfaction and wellbeing, as well as ethical and environmental issues. Perhaps a new paradigm is emerging that suggests organizations should adopt something that we, the authors, have decided to call a "profit by all means, but not by any means" philosophy. Indeed the theme of the Academy of Management conference in Philadelphia in 2007 was "Doing well by doing good," where indications of performance were measured by the way in which an organization improved the lives of its employees and stakeholders. It is hoped that this important shift in focus might move us away from the "profit by any means" philosophy that seemed to drive business at the end of the 20th century.

Perhaps it should be no real surprise, then, that there is a recent trend towards a different expectation from leaders of organizations and how they conduct themselves. Yet it would also appear that there is an expectation shortfall; a gap between what is expected and what is being observed. For example, several companies have been vilified for avoiding paying their taxes in recent years. One of the most high profile is Starbucks, which has faced boycotts and public criticism for avoiding paying corporation tax in the UK. It is not alone, of course. There are many examples of the media and general public being less than enamored with corporate and political behaviors. Indeed, Copeland (2014, p.105) has pointed out how the "emergence of the 21st century was plagued with extensive, evasive and disheartening leadership failures." Potentially nebulous phrases such as "corporate social responsibility" are thrown into stark and devastating relief when viewed as a subscript to the BP disaster in the Gulf of Mexico or the reported working conditions of, for instance, Apple's Foxconn manufacturing plant in China. This expectation gap is almost certainly connected to the leadership within an organization, and should be an area of immediate concern, warranting urgent and focused attention.

The impact that leaders can have within an organization is immense, and this can be both good and bad. They can weave a fairly hypnotic spell resulting in, as Sekerka suggests, leaders who become engaged in corruption, who then discount their choices: "explaining away their decisions and actions as necessary, or simply part of 'doing business'" (Sekerka, 2011, p.2). The pitfalls of being in the thrall of such a toxic leader is discussed by Lipman-Blumen (2005), who argues that we have a tendency to look for the heroic leader to save us and this makes us vulnerable to trusting whatever seemingly influential leadership is presented to us. Tourish (2012, p.5) went as far as to say that "the first decades of the 21st century have been a boom time for peddlers of illusions, vain hopes and bombastic promises, seeking to capitalise on the uncertainty, economic chaos and disillusionment that has engulfed society."

It would seem logical to conclude that in many cases the "DNA" of organizations has been virally compromised and continues to be so from the leadership level downward. This seems to support the old Chinese proverb and more recently Garratt's (2011) claim that the "fish rots from the head"—i.e. organizations begin to deteriorate from the top. Indeed, in recent years there has been one leadership disgrace after another, culminating in the resignation, for example, of a high-ranking executive in connection to the apparent fixing of the LIBOR lending rate between UK banks (Schaefer Muñoz & Colchester, 2012). Who would have thought at the end of the last millennium that our 21st-century "brave new world" would yield such a motley tangle of distress and corruption?

Whilst there can, of course, be a veritable smorgasbord of reasons for organizations having a toxic quality to them (physical working conditions, poor wages, long hours, hostile customers), one of the biggest influencers of the emotional temperature comes from the leaders within those organizations. Just as pendulums placed in proximity and swinging to and fro in random timing to each other will eventually synchronize (Czołczyński et al., 2011), thus it can be with leadership within organizations. Metronomes tend to synchronize with the largest metronome, and in an organization the largest metronome tends to be the leader. It is s/he who often really sets the beat and pulse of an organization. The leader's internal metronome, moral compass or indeed brave compass will often have a profound effect on those around them.

In addition, the rot can set in, or perhaps never be eradicated, due to the conditioning of newer and potentially excellent managers and leaders being influenced by others within the organization—a type of Pavlovian leadership "groupthink" (Neck & Moorhead, 1995). Coercive and other destructive behaviors can show up, and this can have the effect of individuals and often teams of people jumping at their own shadows and responding to a netherworld of intrigue, innuendo and subterfuge, which may well not actually exist. If transparency does not exist and performance is replaced by politics, morale can be destroyed, staff turnover is increased, innovation is stifled and stress heightened. In our experience and that of our colleagues, this land of shadows often exists at its murkiest and most debilitating at the level directly below that of the leader (who perhaps counter-intuitively can sometimes be blissfully unaware of the toxic landfill site on which s/he is operating) and can extend even further to some middle-management levels. It can also include or be driven by the leader and the board. It would seem, then, that some counteracting force must be generated—an "anti-viral" that can combat whatever destructive meme may be at play. We would argue that coaching can be part of that remedy.

Immediately here it must be said that the majority of leaders in most industries are dedicated, honest, inspirational and trustworthy. These individuals are also often incredibly courageous. On the other hand, there are times when even these leaders may lack the very attributes which should, on a close reading of the leadership research, be a prerequisite for them as leaders. There are several reasons why this can happen: one is that individuals are chosen for leadership positions because they are in some way technically gifted, or they are likely to be able to "achieve targets"; another is that they may have begun their careers full of hope and ambition, but the culture around them, or the challenges they face in the market, or the lack of development, has somehow dimmed and diminished their vision. This sometimes calamitous combination of the less-than-ideal choice of candidate for a role, a challenging company culture and the lack of an effective development program can be quite common. Whilst there are always likely to be challenges in appointing leaders, it does seem that there is a genuine disparity between effective leadership and the amount of leadership training, development and coaching support that is available.

We would argue that there are three key missing components that may account for the disparity between theory and practice in leader development:

- First is our idea that bravery itself should be a key component of leadership, and as we shall discuss later, in Chapter 10, it may also be a "thread" that links several strands of leadership theory.

- Second, there needs to be an available framework within which the idea of bravery can be explored.
- Third, the discipline of coaching has a much more important role to play in leadership development than has perhaps previously been considered the case.

There is, in fact, good reason to suspect that coaching is underused by leaders and this may be because the coaching offered is not supplying exactly what leaders need by way of developmental and practical support. A review of the current literature suggests, for example, that leadership approaches which include strategies and ideas to improve the leadership and follower experience have not been readily translated into coaching models. This missing element is, we believe, something that requires more than merely introducing nascent leaders to ideas and concepts. It is also more than simply plucking out the apparently salient points from a leadership development program and parachuting them into a one-to-one coaching session. These approaches on their own may do little to neutralize the leadership-led toxic landscape; rather, the introduction of coaching for braver leaders would raise self-awareness and organizational awareness, which in turn could enhance decision making.

Although, many leaders will already have a high level of awareness and take account of what might be driving them—i.e. a sense of a lack of control or potentially having to curtail their need for adventure or novelty—our concern is with those leaders who find it hard to be brave, despite a desire to do so. We are also concerned with those who find it difficult to align their values with those of the organization, or those who sometimes lose sight of their personal needs and strengths, and how these can be marshaled for the benefit of the organization through well-considered decision-making strategies. It is for these leaders that coaching is most helpful.

What Does Being Brave Involve?

It is likely that for leaders to enter into the brave arena, they will often, if not always, have to decide to move purposefully against or away from their work or organizational customs or cultural traditions. Robinson and Bennett (1995) describe such "deviance" as involving behaviors that differ from accepted policies, rules and procedures. The term "positive deviance" (Staw & Boettger, 1990; Spreitzer & Sonenshein, 2004) has also been used to describe this move away from the expected. However, more recently, Hannah, Avolio and Walumbwa (2011, p.556) have used the term "pro-social" to refer to behavior that goes beyond ordinary role requirements—behaviors that protect co-workers and the organization, and which involve positive acts to promote the wellbeing of others. The essential ingredients here appear to be that "deviance" is defined as traveling away from what is expected as the norm and that pro-social may include the positive deviance aspect of going beyond the norm, by, for example, not simply being polite, but also being kind. We consider this to be a key aspect of the brave leader, and one that can be encouraged through coaching. It could be summarized as "positive social deviance."

In addition, as Sekerka (2011, p.1) points out, "while a great deal of research has been done to find the causes and conditions for corruption, we still know very little about how to help people sustain their moral strength when working in ethically corrosive environments." Sekerka suggests that people can protect themselves when working in such environments by continuously developing their "moral muscles" through examining "the decision-making strategies that involve a weave between character, thought, choice, and action" (ibid., p.2). She argues that "while whole systems continue to invoke a call for ethical performance standards, individuals are the moral agents who make the decisions and conduct daily activities that create business enterprise" (ibid., p.2).

Often, however, they need support from someone like a coach in order to think through the right course of action, and this would certainly support Sekerka, McCarthy and Bagozzi's (2011) proposal that for those who choose to preserve their integrity, dishonest practices need not be accepted as insurmountable. Sekerka talks about the need for professional moral courage and the processes needed to support it: "people need to be aware of their vulnerabilities and practice cultivating the desire, activation, and execution of moral strength on a daily basis" (Sekerka, 2011, p.3). The maintenance of professional moral courage involves a combination of moral agency, multiple values, endurance of threat, going beyond compliance and having a moral goal. This goal is important, for without a goal we are unable to measure our behaviors. To be positively socially deviant we must deviate away from something but not simply at random: the deviated route must take us somewhere.

Another interesting phenomenon comes from the use of the word "brave" or "bravery" itself. We suggest the very use of the term can begin to allow leaders to make a more considered evaluation of their next move. By using the word "brave," one of the key ideas is to contrast bravery with potential weakness. In an organization, it is often not a question of running away like a coward, or hiding, but it can be an issue of weakness: buckling under pressure, remaining in a comfort zone, falling into groupthink, or even simply wanting to be liked at the expense of taking appropriate action. So bravery incorporates an element of concerted action. The brave leader is the opposite of the weak leader. The brave leader is very likely to be ethical, but may not be seduced into assuming that because some ethical "process" was allegedly being followed, things actually were ethical: indeed, being ethical can often require emotional courage and brave action.

Coaching As Part Of The Leader Development Process

During the last 15 to 20 years there has been a growing trend towards the incorporation of coaching as part of the leader and executive development process. Indeed, there is now a plethora of leadership training and coaching available worldwide, with some organizations and individuals specializing exclusively in the area of leadership coaching. There are also academic institutions and corporate programs of executive and leadership coaching, which offer qualifications in the area. Many MBAs offered at universities across the world also include a coaching element. In addition there is a wide range of leadership texts that mention coaching, although there are fewer that actually focus in depth on explaining leadership coaching. However, despite the availability of resources there still appears to be a disparity between articulated best practice and the reported negative experiences and events caused by leaders who are less than effective.

It could be that the reason good leadership is either stifled or never nurtured in the first place, is because of a lack of properly considered development. Leadership development largely neglects the important aspect of leader self-awareness in favor of communication, performance and organization development. Our argument throughout this book is that coaching can begin to redress that omission and enhance leader development, possibly in ways that have yet to be realized.

A suggested aim of executive and leadership coaching could be to improve the leader's effectiveness in ways that are related to the business strategy of the organization. As mentioned already, coaching can add considerable value to *leadership* development by supporting and promoting the *leader* development aspect as well as the leadership elements. However, despite the range of general coaching models and frameworks available, there are few that are built on leadership theory or that focus specifically on guiding leadership development. One framework that does stand out in the field is Lee's (2003) ACE (Actions, Cognitions, Emotions) FIRST (Focus, Intentions, Results, System, Tension) model, which is built on the theory of authentic leadership. Lee explains how leaders experience two conflicting imperatives: to be authentic and act out of personal conviction, whilst also operating to meet the needs of the organization and others within it. He presents a model aimed at providing an overview of how a leader establishes patterns of behavior in response to organizational situations. Thus Lee's is very much a cognitive model aimed at changing behavior.

Bravery, however, has to be advanced not just through understanding deficiencies and then changing behaviors as in Lee's model. Rather, it is concerned with moral development and stamina built through examples and models; through practice in the organizational context and though the development of particular attributes, for example, awareness, understanding and humility. The brave leadership coaching model is aimed at enhancing self-understanding, organizational awareness and ethical, self-assured decision making in order to help leaders become brave, and incorporates techniques that leaders can use on a daily basis.

However, much existing leadership coaching could be seen as generic and focused on the defensive strategies of what Argyris (2012) calls a "Model I" orientation, rather than addressing issues of moral courage or bravery. We would contend that the moment a leader perceives an approach as just expedient, just something "to tick a box" (e.g. corporate compliance) rather than something intrinsic to their sense of being a leader, then much of the power of leadership coaching can be lost. The leadership coaching approach we propose takes an inside-out approach, drawing on the values and developing emotional and social intelligence of the leader and supporting the transformation necessary to implement values, often against all the odds, in order to promote moral courage and take brave action.

Day, Harrison and Halpin (2009, p.19) have made a useful distinction between leadership development and leader development, stressing that the former focuses on skills for the role, whereas leader development is about individual development crucial for underpinning the role. They suggest that leader development can be accelerated:

> through the application of scientifically based principles derived from theory and research from diverse areas such as developmental psychology, lifespan development, adult learning, Gestalt psychology, expertise and skill acquisition, leadership and growth modelling, as well as training and development.
>
> *(Day et al., 2009, p.19)*

They argue that this process is different from leadership development, which focuses mainly on the skills and attributes necessary to perform the leadership role. Figure 1.1 shows this distinction.

In Figure 1.1 we show the types of inside work needed as part of leader development which have a corresponding impact on the "outside" manifestation of the leadership role. This inside-outside process is inherent in the brave leadership coaching model. The use of the brave coaching model, for example, indicates that coaching can assist in critical thinking, support decision making and thus lead potentially to a different and braver form of personal and corporate leadership. We explain later how coaching might help overcome any focus on expediency and make links more directly to the development of the leader him/herself, encouraging triple-loop learning (Swieringa and Wierdsma, 1992) and considering the principles, including moral principles, that underpin decision making before preparing to take the brave action. Consequently, this model for developing brave leaders extends and operationalizes existing theories of leadership through its inclusion of specific coaching processes and sense-making techniques.

Our definition of a leadership coaching model is a construct to guide clients (leaders) during, between and after coaching sessions to perform their role more effectively. This definition applies to the brave coaching model and yet our model is distinct from the kinds of models that tend to

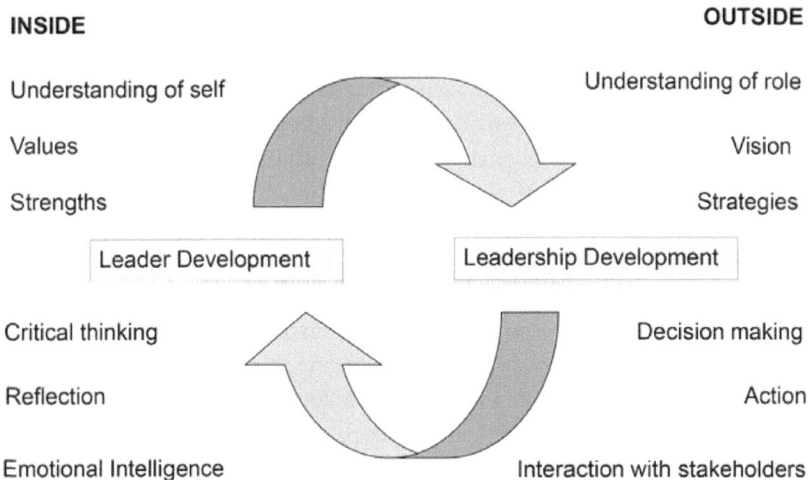

FIGURE 1.1 Leader development and leadership development—an inside-outside process

appear in much of the literature, in that it is a multifaceted framework for working with leaders. It is a process framework rather than a simple flow diagram or mnemonic, with interconnecting parts, each of which represents a real-world coaching activity (see Figure 1.2). It is worth mentioning here that whilst we believe that the model is probably at its most effective when used in conjunction with an experienced coach, there may be situations where a leader may wish to work through the parts of the model on their own, either because they do not have access to a coach or they have, for whatever reason, a requirement to self-coach. It would be foolish to suggest that this might not result in a positive outcome.

The Brave Leadership Coaching Model

In presenting our model, however, we propose that coaching can be important to overcome any short-sighted focus on expediency, or behavioral change, thus making important, more direct links to the development of leaders themselves, encouraging them to think systemically and strategically, and considering the values and principles that underpin action rather than focusing just on actions themselves.

The brave leadership coaching model was initially built as a result of empirical research undertaken with leaders during an action research study. Since then, it has evolved with more input from leaders and coaches. The leaders were all actively involved in contributing to the model's development. This subsequent and ongoing research has deepened our understanding and helped further refine the structure and framework. The model embraces a number of coaching approaches rather than being built on just one—as discussed in Barner and Higgins (2005). It is psychological in that it will help clients bolster or change their self-perceptions through a strengthening of their value and belief systems; it is behavioral to the extent that it aims to help clients alter their behavior to align with values and beliefs. Thus the changes clients make will need to come from inside themselves and yet be observable in their working practices. The model also uses a systems approach since it helps clients consider the patterns of interaction between themselves, their teams and the organizational system. Finally, it incorporates a social constructionist focus on story formation. Clients are encouraged to think about narratives of brave leaders and subsequently about how they "story" themselves (Barner & Higgins, 2005). The elements of the framework are illustrated in Figure 1.2.

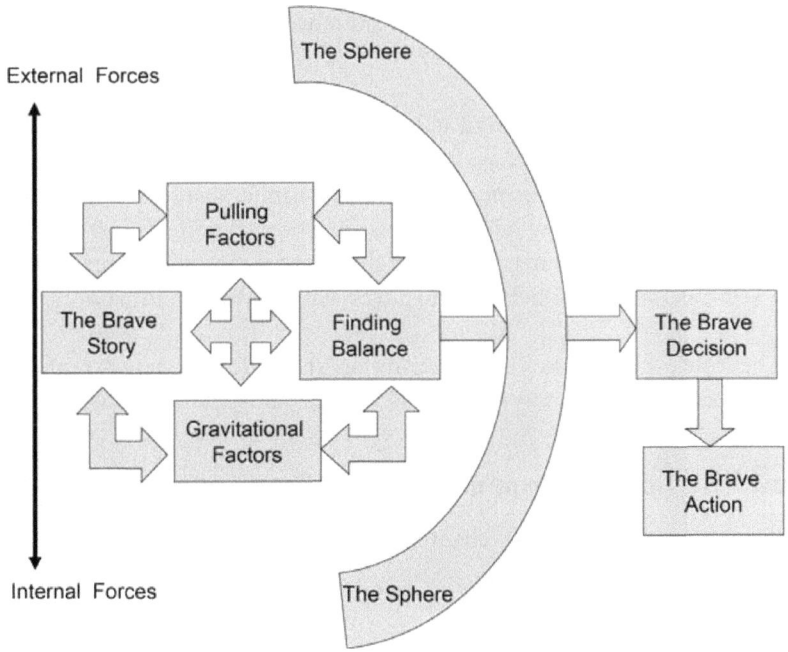

FIGURE 1.2 The brave leadership coaching model

Assumptions

The assumptions that underpin this model are that:

- the leader is ready to change, that s/he is aware of the need to be open to the coaching process and not resistant;
- the model can be used as a framework into which values-based leadership principles that encompass a range of leadership theories, including spiritual and servant leadership, as well as authentic and ethical approaches (Copeland, 2014) may be incorporated; and
- leaders are stewards (and coaches are agents in that stewardship).

April, Kukard and Peters (2013) explain how stewardship is a form of leadership that focuses on others, the community and society. They advocate service over self-interest and provide a road map for developing the next-generation leader. April et al.'s research, which involved interviews with global industry leaders and MBA students, highlighted how many senior leaders move into a stewardship mindset only when they have gained extensive experience and their careers have matured.

We consider that the three most important aspects of steward leadership in relation to brave leadership are:

- shared vision and clarity of vision, which shows commitment to a just and sustainable society;
- risk-taking and experimentation, which implies that successful stewards must display bravery and openness to innovative ideas; and
- vulnerability and maturity, which requires a fundamental shift in self-awareness and behavior to show empathy and compassion.

The steward leader also has to be committed to delivering results responsibly in partnership with empowered others, within a purposeful community.

How The Book Is Organized

Following this introductory chapter there are ten further chapters:

Chapter 2: The Brave Story

In this chapter, the first part of the brave leadership coaching approach is introduced with the challenge to leaders to consider their ideas about bravery in relation to their leadership. They are asked for definitions and stories about people who have been brave and when and where they have been brave. After providing example responses from four leaders—John, Ron, Matt and Christine—the role of values elicitation and links with identity are discussed. The last part of the chapter focuses on how to bring a values approach to the challenges that individual leaders face in their own work. This is done via a four-step process of considering the right thing at the right time.

Chapter 3: Pulling Factors

This chapter sets out the approaches used in the brave leadership coaching model to develop situational awareness and enable the leader to make sense of organizational challenges. The chapter sets out a way of encouraging leaders to consider what is pulling on them in their current environment and to understand the interdependencies and synergies contained within the challenges they face. The pulling factors represent things that are external to the leader, such as company culture or economic factors, and the analysis approach proposed helps them to reflect on their "landscape" and look at the contextual elements that might otherwise polarize and pull them in different directions. Such polarization could potentially influence leaders adversely by causing tension and stress. The chapter provides examples of how the coach can help leaders analyze their pulling factors—an essential step in the brave leadership coaching model.

Chapter 4: Gravitational Factors

In this chapter, leaders are asked to consider the psychological factors that ground them in their work, by way of contrast with the environmental concerns that tended to pull them off course in Chapter 3. The gravitational factors are a key aspect of brave leadership coaching and have their foundation in positive psychology. They comprise the psychological capital and character strengths that leaders can muster to counter the pulling factors and associated tensions. The heightened awareness of personal power that exploring psychological capital creates allows leaders to consider what is most important to them—not only their personal goals and values but also wider family, societal and environmental concerns. The gravitational factors then are the attributes that position leaders in relation to their strengths, virtues and values. In addition, this chapter also introduces coaching approaches to developing psychological capital and includes a retroductive technique as a way of tracing and understanding habits and reducing blind spots.

Chapter 5: Finding Balance: Emotional and moral self-awareness

In Chapter 5 we discuss the need for leaders to find balance using their gravitational factors to ensure that equilibrium is achieved. We stress how factors are frequently in tension: pulling factors create conflicts that test our values and pull us away from ethical or moral courses of action. We maintain that in order to achieve a balance it is necessary to take stock in four key areas that can support a strong "core": emotional awareness, reflective pause, self-regulation and moral preparation. We also examine a useful emotional needs analysis that is part of the Human Givens approach and the practice of mindfulness, which can be key for achieving or preserving balance.

Chapter 6: The Brave Sphere

The brave sphere embraces the notion that it is important for leaders to consider organizational situations and perspectives calmly and from a "safe distance." The ability to reflect in a detached yet focused way enables tensions to be experienced, held and considered, prior to making brave decisions. We might even say that holding the tension calmly requires a certain amount of bravery in itself—our reason for calling it the brave sphere. In this chapter we examine how using a metaphorical sphere performs triple functions for the leader: i) providing a place of calm and sanctuary to reflect on problems (we call this the sphere of sanctuary); ii) enabling a focus on different perspectives and needs within the organizational landscape (the sphere of observation); and iii) the opportunity to analyze feelings in relation to the observations, holding what they find as a resource for sustainable decision making (the sphere of influence).

Chapter 7: The Brave Decision

In this chapter we focus on how the elements of the brave leadership coaching model, with its emphasis on values and emotions as well as situational sense making, facilitate the leader to come to their decision. In Chapter 6 we played with the idea of moving the sphere around each of the pulling factors and testing how moving the sphere towards or away from the gravitational factors feels. In this chapter we examine how the options for problem solving can be identified and formulated into a decision before shifting into a brave course of action. We begin with an overview of different types of problems that are faced in organizations. We then explain how the depth of awareness achieved using brave leadership coaching supports the kind of reflection and decision making necessary to address the kinds of complex, "wicked" problems that leaders encounter, ultimately leading to the best possible decision under the circumstances.

Chapter 8: The Brave Action

In Chapter 8 we complete the brave circle by discussing how coaching can help leaders to action their decisions. Such action invariably also requires bravery in overcoming a number of tensions—some psychological—that mainly affect the leader as an individual, others relating more to the tensions created through the different agendas of stakeholders both within and without the organization. These may arise through existing systems or stakeholder configurations and responsibilities, such as financial teams, trades unions, board members or shareholders. In the chapter we examine these tensions and then provide a range of responses and strategies which, with the help of the coach, leaders can use to begin to address implementation issues and so fulfill their brave actions.

Chapter 9: The Trust Factor

In this chapter we examine some of the trust issues that concern coaches when undertaking leadership coaching. The issue of trust is vital in all coaching but, as we will explain, it is especially crucial for the coach-leader relationship as it is linked to the development of a working coaching alliance, as well as coach credibility and integrity. It is important to recognize that trust issues challenge coaches to consider their own boundaries and ethical positions and point towards the importance of coach supervision for ongoing personal development. We would suggest that it is unlikely that true bravery in organizations can exist without trust, and if that is true, and if we need brave coaches to work with brave leaders, then we must have an extremely high level of trust between leader and coach. We conclude the chapter with a discussion of the tension that can exist between integrity and benevolence in the coaching relationship.

Chapter 10: Positioning Braver Leadership Coaching

This chapter evaluates the brave leadership concept in relation to familiar leadership theories, such as transformational, authentic, situational and relational leadership, suggesting that bravery is essential across these approaches for them to be morally effective. Although there are many leadership programs available, it would seem that executive education often does not translate into the type of leadership with which people in organizations feel comfortable. Toward the end of the chapter, therefore, we synthesize the key arguments for a coaching approach to brave leader development. We reinforce how coaches can support leaders to be braver and to have the resolve to confirm to followers and stakeholders that they are worthy of respect. To support them in this endeavor we argue that coaching is the right development intervention.

Chapter 11: The Brave Agenda

In the conclusion to the book we summarize the brave leadership coaching framework and link this to the need not only for braver leaders, but also braver coaches. Coaching leaders to be brave is not something we can do on every assignment because coaching is all about the client agenda. However, if the leader is stuck in the individualistic paradigm of profit and efficiency, and does not want to focus on taking brave action, it may be that the coach needs to decide whether that coaching assignment is worthwhile. This chapter ends with a challenge to coaches to be brave enough to bring sustainability in all its complexity and guises into the coaching room as a challenge to a new generation of brave leaders.

Case Examples

Throughout each chapter, in order to enhance understanding of the processes being introduced, we draw on case stories and dialogue with four leaders who have experienced the brave coaching model in action. We use the developmental journeys of John, an IT director for an international engineering company; Ron, an HR director for a finance company; Matt, who is the operations director for an aviation company; and Christine, the finance director for a logistics organization. These examples enable us to bring the brave coaching model to life and illustrate its elements in greater detail.

Who Is This Book For?

Leadership Coaching: Developing Braver Leaders is a book aimed at managers, leaders and coaches who work or wish to work toward sound, sustainable corporate structures and to be respected and valued by their followers. The book illustrates how a model of coaching for brave leadership can enhance leader perspectives, contribute to their development, help them explore various factors in their environment and consider the brave thing to do. The content will also have relevance for leadership education, and will be of key interest to coaching students of all orientations, and to academics and researchers in the field of coaching.

2
THE BRAVE STORY

Introduction

At the beginning of this chapter, it is important to point out that there is always a tension between coaching and coaching models. The very introduction of some kind of seemingly linear framework or model seems to most coaches to compromise the open, constructivist nature of the coaching relationship. The same tension exists within our framework for developing brave leaders. Therefore, right at the outset of our coaching with leaders we avoided telling them what bravery was and how to go about attaining it, preferring instead to listen to their accounts and so enable them to arrive at their own ideas of what bravery means.

There were two main reasons for this. First we felt that our view of what bravery is would not necessarily be the same as our leaders and we needed to allow space for them to "show up" in their own unique way. Second, by allowing leaders to identify their own brave role models, they could be making links with their "ideal self" (Boyatzis & Akrivou, 2006). In Chapter 1 of this book we focused on the social/organizational need for brave leaders. We believe that being a leader involves being able to serve society, organization, family, and so each leader has his/her own set of values and the need to be considered brave, part of the leader identity. However, leaders will have their own individual perceptions of what it means to be brave.

In addition there is also a need for leaders to be in touch with their values and beliefs and this prompts the requirement for a process to encourage and support self-awareness. As Kouzes and Posner (2009, p.15) suggest, "leaders are supposed to stand up for their beliefs, so they'd better have some beliefs to stand up for."

There are a number of techniques that coaches can use to encourage leaders to build their understanding and enhance communication of their values. The first that we have identified involves helping leaders to become aware of what it is they truly value so that they can ultimately determine their own governing values, or espoused theories, and theories in use as defined by Senge (1990). It involves asking leaders to define bravery by identifying role models and so construct their own "brave story." The process enables them eventually to uncover their ideals, their passions and their hopes.

In this chapter we propose that identifying their own ideas of what it means to be brave and then linking this to their own leadership practice can guide leaders towards change in the way that Boyatzis and Akrivou (2006) have described. These authors explained the concept of the ideal self as something that is the driver of intentional change in behavior, emotions and attitudes. They clarified how it is this ideal self that is "the core mechanism for self-regulation and intrinsic motivation. It is manifest as a personal vision, or an image of what kind of person one wishes to be" (ibid., p.625). Boyatzis and Akrivou also suggested that cognitive and emotional processes are required for people to articulate an ideal self, but that "it is trait based positive emotion which becomes the driver and the substance of the ideal self overall [...] Once the force of the ideal self is activated it plays an executive or motivational function within the self" by activating the "will" and encouraging self-monitoring (ibid., p.625).

Boyatzis and Akrivou (2006) suggested that there are three elements that unite to create the ideal self: core identity (which includes our values and philosophy), hope (which draws on self-efficacy, optimism and feasibility), and the image of a desired future (which comprises dreams, aspirations and fantasies). They considered that our dreams of a desired future are part of our sense of purpose in life; they are driven in turn by our "passion, values and operating philosophy" (ibid., p.628). Our concern when working with leaders has been that their original dreams for their desired future may be buried or lost during the demands of their work and need a process for re-kindling the passion that drove them to be leaders in the first place. Thinking about the future self as a continuation of the ideal self is an important next step.

This chapter has three main sections. In section one we explain the first stage of the brave framework, where leaders are invited to explore who has been brave in their lives. Here we give examples of brave stories from leaders with whom we have worked. In section two, we highlight the values that the same leaders highlighted as part of their reflection on bravery. We consider the significance of values elicitation and how it can be helpful for leaders to understand what motivates and inspires them. This leads us to section three, where we pause to think about the values of the coach and the coaching profession. We end the chapter with further reflection on the role of the coach in the brave story process.

1 The Idea Of Bravery

In this section we introduce an important element of our model for developing brave leaders. As mentioned, the model does not begin by proposing a predefined structure for the coach and leader to work within, but instead with the coach opening up a conversation in which the leader can begin to consider the idea of bravery, in a totally non-directive way. Thus a conversational approach is suggested. In our experience, leaders do not readily spend time considering concepts like bravery and what that means to them, or how that might translate to their business environment and their leadership. In fact, we have found that as a general rule, leaders do not have the time, or do not appear to take the time to contemplate or reflect on issues such as bravery. This may of course be influenced by the culture of their organization, and may be driven by other factors such as peer or stakeholder expectation. Of course, there are many exceptions to this, but we believe that leaders are an under-utilized resource, due mainly to too great a focus on continuous action which undervalues the significance of pausing, thinking, considering and reflecting. We therefore believe it is important that in this coaching model there should be plenty of spaces for leaders to reflect and consider how they envisage bravery, and for the coach to "coach" around whatever emerges.

Our conversations with business leaders have suggested that bravery can mean many things and that it is also likely to have a contextual element to it, making it quite idiosyncratic. The first part of the brave leadership coaching framework therefore involves an open discussion of how the leader perceives bravery, where he or she has seen examples of bravery, and also who is considered to be brave.

However, asking leaders to think about who has been brave has a far greater benefit than just providing a definition. Asking leaders to consider what bravery might look like, and by implication highlighting how they might behave when they are brave, enables them to consider their ideal brave self, similar to what Boyatzis and Akrivou (2006) refer to when they talk about the "ideal self." In essence this gives them something to measure themselves against. This means that they can begin to generate a "gap" between the current situation and their ideal. There are also aspects here of psychological priming or non-conscious activation (Levy, 2003), which has been shown to influence perception, motivation, evaluation and behavior (Bargh et al., 2001). Exposing leaders to the concept of bravery, partly in relation to a potentially idealized braver version of themselves, and also partly by the simple addition of this word to the business context, begins the process of them "looking within." Benjamin, Choi and Strickland (2010) talked about the relationship between priming and social identity, and demonstrated how priming can have the effect of increasing the strength of a particular social identity—in this case the leader's social identity as a brave leader.

At the point where the coach introduces the idea of bravery, the leader could be described as being in pre-contemplative mode (Prochaska & Velicer, 1997). S/he may not have even considered thinking about bravery in relation to business. By introducing the concept and asking a couple of simple questions about bravery, the coach moves the leader into contemplative mode. This is a subtle but important and potentially powerful phase. It is important to allow leaders to step into the exercise gradually and to consider what different interpretations of bravery might mean to them. This allows them to personalize the coaching experience and to take ownership of the discussion.

So it is our belief that the leader should not be given a checklist of what bravery might look like. Instead we consider that it is vital to approach the idea by engaging with what the leader already knows, what s/he can relatively easily begin to formulate ideas around. Also rather than posing a potentially nebulous question such as "what does bravery mean to you?" we prefer to ask the leader for their own brave stories and to describe who they consider to be brave. The idea of beginning to qualify bravery around an individual or individuals will be potentially useful later on in the coaching process as we call on these role models for inspiration. For instance, Brown and Trevino (2006) have studied how having an ethical role model in one's career is likely to contribute to the development of ethical leadership. Weaver et al. (2005) similarly interviewed individuals who had been influenced by an ethical role model at work, finding that characteristics such as caring, honesty and fairness were important to them.

The brave story—a values elicitation exercise

During our research we spoke to a variety of leaders from a cross-section of organizations and sectors and asked them to think about who they considered to be brave. The usual response to this question from the leaders was "Do they have to be alive?" and "Do they have to be famous?" The answer to those two questions was always, "No." A few people wanted to know if a fictional character was applicable or whether examples had to be connected with business. If fictional characters were mentioned, it was useful to prompt for examples of real people as well. Leaders could also be encouraged to think about what brave acts they have seen, when they themselves have been brave, and also what constitutes bravery. The answers to these types of questions can illicit what we call the "brave story." The brave story is not simply about helping leaders to identify who they think is brave, but also to encourage them to create an internal narrative of bravery that can sustain them through their work.

Below we present four of the brave story responses that we collected. Names and some details have been changed to protect anonymity. The first question that all the leaders were posed was, "Who do you consider to be brave?" Their responses are in their own words.

Leader one: John

For the past three years John, aged 43, has been the UK-based IT director for an engineering company. He has an international role.

I suppose I would immediately think of some sort of physical bravery, like a rugby player or a mountain climber, you know, the ones who climb without ropes and any kind of safety net—although some people might consider that to be slightly mad rather than brave. I know that you haven't said that this has necessarily to be about someone in business, but I'm actually keen to go down that path because you have made me think about considering the idea of bravery in business rather than the obvious physical type of bravery—like putting yourself in harm's way—though I still consider that to be brave.

There are obvious business icons that spring to mind, like Branson and Gates, but I don't know if they actually are brave. I suppose they are, or have been, but what this exercise has made me do is to think about the fact that I don't really know much about them. There are people who pore over biographies looking for clues about what makes people great and of course that is fine, but what I'm really interested in, I'm just realizing, is a more tangible set of examples of bravery, someone that I have been closer to, worked beside or at least in the same organization.

And so on consideration, in answer to your question, I'm thinking about my previous boss, Alison, before I landed this job a couple of years ago. She was a bit of a mentor to me, amongst other things: definitely the inspirational type, larger than life. But one of the things that I thought was particularly brave about her was the way in which she treated everyone the same. I know that might sound odd initially in terms of describing bravery, but what I mean is that she didn't hide behind her status or title. Now bear in mind that this lady was clever, really clever, phenomenal processing power, probably in Mensa, that type of thing, but she never used that intellect as a club to beat others with. You see I think that it is the weaker types who hide behind the mask of their position and perceived authority, but you have to be a whole lot stronger to be nice. And what I mean by that is that she was considerate, she listened, she genuinely had an open-door policy and I think she cared. Now in that particular business at that time, this was a really brave approach to take because everyone or almost everyone seemed to have adopted a dog-eat-dog approach. But what Alison had noticed was that we were living in a fear culture. Some called it just business-like, but I agreed with Alison, it was just full of fear. Now I don't know if she had made a conscious decision to behave the way she did, but she just seemed not to bow to that rigid, hierarchical structure and so treated everyone with respect.

She also wasn't afraid to take on what she thought were improper practices or injustices as well. And when that happened she would be extremely logical in her preparation, and almost like a lawyer preparing for a very important court case, she would seem to know all the possible moves in advance. And so in those situations, we tended to see her not hold back in terms of her focus and drive, and those were the times when we could really see how smart she was. So for me, the "Who do you think is brave?" question is best demonstrated by my ex-boss. She was fair and unbiased but didn't shirk away from conflict. And for her to behave the way she did in that particular environment was for me particularly inspiring.

Leader two: Ron

Ron is in his late 30s, a UK-based HR director of a finance company. Ron has been in this role for five years.

For me bravery can be epitomized by someone I greatly admire, Mahatma Gandhi. I love his phrase which goes along the lines of "be the change that you want to see around you." That is difficult to do, and I think that it is a question of taking each situation at a time, of trying to assess all the variables and then moving forward. Gandhi wasn't violent or aggressive and yet still made a huge impact. It isn't that I don't think that we need to be tough at times, but there is also a toughness about not necessarily jumping to the wrong conclusion, or being mean because things aren't going well.

So in my mind the whole bravery thing is probably about being understated, just sometimes letting go of things, and sometimes grabbing onto something quite firmly and just saying, no. It isn't about pyrotechnics and "showboating"; it is more about having a quiet inner strength that allows you to keep going to look for that sense of the correct step to take, the best route to follow. Someone else I greatly admired was Christopher Reeve, the *Superman* actor. How he not only kept going after his accident, but became a spokesperson for a cause which he believed in was so inspiring. I remember seeing the headline in a newspaper when he died, it said "Superman dies." On one level it was a bit surreal, like something from the movies, like it was a headline from the *Daily Planet* or something. And yet it was the perfect headline, because he really was Superman. I also think people are brave who take the chance to be like a human guinea pig, who "boldly go" like an astronaut, or a submarine commander—pioneers who go out on a limb and people who make brave decisions. Nelson Mandela is also someone I greatly admire. He challenged his own credibility; it was essentially a case of him saying "I'm not going to be as prejudiced as them". So for me it can be physical bravery of course, but so much of it is in the mind.

Leader three: Matt

Matt is in his late 40s, US based and in an international role as operations director for an aviation company. He has been in this role for three years.

My thinking about people who are truly brave, and I'm talking in business terms here, are people who put others first. They end up, or can end up in the firing line because they just want to help; they just want to do the right thing, to get the job done. I know that this might not always be a popular thing to say in business, but I think that it isn't about the leader. It isn't about the cult of the personality. Sure that can work from time it time in certain situations, but it can also be really dangerous. Now don't get me wrong, I'm not saying that we don't need leaders who can do all that charismatic stuff and get the whole cheerleading thing going. Yes, that certainly has its place. But look, behind closed doors, when the pedal hits the metal and you need to really motor along to get things moving, accurately and quickly, you can't have that type of distance between you and who reports to you. By all means be inspiring and motivational, but do it in a real and humble way. You see, I think bravery is about leadership where you can put aside the ego. Yes, of course we probably all need an element of that, but what is at the core of the man or woman? What's going on in their heart? Are they there for themselves, or are they there for others and the business?

In fact, I would say that being truly brave is having no ego; to be in that firing line that I mentioned, but to be there, not just be seen to be there, but to be there with the primary driving factor of wanting to help. It's like those people who help others by doing charity work. And whilst we can talk about who we think might be a great big business hero or heroine, a lot of the time the real heroes are the unsung heroes. I would say that my boss is like that. She has been hugely influential and yet I doubt that too many people know quite how much. I'm not suggesting that someone like Abraham Lincoln didn't have all the qualities that I admire; I strongly suspect that he did. Yet because of his place in history, he is amazingly well known and admired. So sometimes we can think of people like that as being great because it just all kind of "happened" for them, which of course it absolutely didn't. But we know about them because of their pivotal role. Yet I think that there are so many others who have so many great traits, who are also in their own way humble and brave, and who are never heard of.

Leader four: Christine

Christine is in her early 50s and is based in Brussels. She has been in her international role as finance director for a logistics company for four years.

I actually do have ideas about some people who I would consider to be brave, but the classical approach to this might be to name some high-flying business person, or explorer, or entrepreneur, or perhaps even a politician—although these days it might be very difficult to get any sort of consensus on who might be considered to be a brave politician. Certainly in the past there have been some, I think. Perhaps, however, in times of conflict it is easier to pick out the Churchill types. These days it does seem to be a lot murkier and so even though there may be a lot of bravery going on, it is probably very difficult to spot it.

I think that the difficulty today is that there is so much marketing in place between us and some of the more prominent individuals in the public eye, that it is easy to fall for the story rather than what these people actually did or are actually doing. It is a bit like those books which we see at airports, particularly around Christmas time, which are the auto-biographical success stories—the ones which chart the rise of the latest "wunderkind." I often wonder that if we all had books written about ourselves how we might actually fare in print. I think that the particular form of self-aggrandizing which can exist in those types of books, not all of course, and also all over the Internet, can lead us to not only potentially belittle our own achievements, but also to presume that the neatly packaged "sound bite" is reality, when in fact it is much more likely to be an easily digestible morsel of a much more complex story.

I think what I am saying is that it is easy to go for the clichés, the historical figures, the very successful business people, or the people who put up with great hardship, like an ultra distance athlete who raises millions of euros for charity. I'm not suggesting that just because certain individuals might be clichés that they shouldn't be celebrated, but more that we have to look to ourselves. We have to find the extraordinary in the ordinary. Just as it would be interesting if we all had our own "Christmas autobiography" published, it would also be interesting if we could celebrate bravery closer to home. In my opinion bravery is more about a continuing drip feed of behaviors; behaviors which change things. We have changed the culture in this organization, but it has been a continual and ongoing process—evolution not revolution. Yes, of course there have been some very bold moves made by some individuals and those have been inspiring. And we can see from those people who are famous for being brave, like say Amelia Earhart, or Emmeline Pankhurst, that there were certainly moments in time which changed or challenged perceptions and even ultimately the course of history. And far be it from me to diminish any of those. I do think that also bravery is about effecting change whether it be physical and/or perceptual against a system, a regime, a culture which is quite simply wrong, and that whilst there may be tipping points which are reached through certain single events, that for most of us most of the time, it is a continual ongoing process of the smaller things which then eventually tips the scales. And the Earharts and the Pankhursts did that as well, but in this sound bite age it is easy to forget that, and just be seduced by the headline rather than spending the time reading the small print!

And so I tend to see bravery more in the quotidian, and over time. For me therefore there is an element of continuing to travel through adversity, to chip away over a period of time. I think that it was Winston Churchill who said, "when you are going through hell, keep going." I love that saying, not because I want every day to be like "hell," but because of the innate wisdom in the words. For me, people who work with Médecins Sans Frontières are typical of the type of bravery I am talking about. They may of course have to face physical danger, but the psychological strength that they possess must be immense. And we do hear about the headline events they get involved in, but what about the consistent application of effort that they apply on an ongoing basis which is going on when another big headline event is keeping everyone's attention focused elsewhere? Maybe part of bravery is being strong enough not to need the constant limelight.

These are only some examples of the conversations that we have had with leaders. However, they are indicative of the "trends" that we noticed. The initial responses from other leaders in relation to who they thought of as brave tended to include famous people such as: Nelson Mandela, Martin Luther King Jr, Richard Branson, Bill Gates, Steve Jobs, Winston Churchill, Mahatma Gandhi, plus American presidents and explorers. However, as people reflected further, they moved away from the very famous and, whilst still recognizing their various contributions, tended to focus more upon the day-to-day aspects of who might be being brave in a work context. This could be someone who is already in their work constellation or it could be someone outside the workplace, from the present day or from history. It was as if the more widely known and inspirational figures acted as a bridge in their thinking to allow them to begin to consider what being brave might mean for them specifically in their business and/or society. These responses support the point made by Grint (2010) that brave leaders are not necessarily heroic. Brave role models can emerge from any walk of life, but need to be people who inspire by going "out on a limb" and taking a stand against injustice or promoting corporate social responsibility.

In this section, we have seen how the first part of the brave leadership coaching framework has allowed leaders to move into a space of thinking about bravery and begin to make their own connections and distinctions. Our initial question to the leaders was to ask them who they thought of as brave, but we also wanted to know if there was a moral component that "attracted" them, too, and this indeed did seem to be the case: certainly Lincoln and Gandhi would seem to fit that criterion, as did the less famous individuals chosen by our leaders. So each leader was encouraged to reflect and consider who they view as brave.

In our practice, responses are always noted so that they can be played back and the value-rich language unpacked for clues for what the leader considers important aspects of their ideal brave self. We suggest that the emphasis on the ideal self through the brave story exercise can be invigorating for leaders, especially those who may be stressed or close to "burnout." Boyatzis and Akrivou (2006, p.633) have pointed out that the power of the ideal self is not only emotional, arousing just the parasympathetic nervous system, but is also physical, involving "neuro-endocrine processes that allow the body to renew itself, while ameliorating the ravages caused by chronic stress."

2 Values Elicitation

Values are defined by the *Oxford English Dictionary* as "principles or standards of behaviour" and these principles in turn guide our judgment of what is important in life.

In order for people to value something, they therefore need to be responsive to its relative importance, worth or utility. They need to make an appraisal dependent upon individual or specific points of view or in individual or social situations. A value, then, is something intrinsically valuable or advantageous to the individual, or indeed a group of individuals, if there is a consensus on importance, worth or utility.

Following discussions about who is brave, a question about what values are important in a leadership role helped leaders make a link between the brave people they had identified earlier and some of the qualities that are important at a more practical level. When John was asked what values he thought were important to him in his leadership role, he replied: "What I value is openness, transparency, honesty, resilience and a sense of decency." This was reflected in his brave story, where he explained how he valued the fact that his ex-boss had disregarded her status and treated everyone the same. John values the fact that Alison was open, honest and fair, that she listened and that she ignored the hierarchical structure of the organization, treating everyone with the same respect.

Ron cares about people and has a strong sense of right and wrong. His reply to the same question also emphasized resilience:

> I value a strong mindset: the type of quality in an individual which shows up when they meet resistance. To be determined, to push through and stand up for what they value and what they see as right. Like Martin Luther King Jr—anyone who carries on believing in something, knowing there is an injustice.

Matt's response highlighted a certain inherent toughness, which might reflect his need for greater flexibility:

> I think that I value people who grasp the crazy situations and businesses and departments with both hands and just wrestle them into submission. I think also that I value people who put their money into things, who put something of theirs into the game—maybe they take risks, but it is a calculated risk. I value people who leave good alone, and do not let perfect get in the way of good. And despite the

outcome, I value people who do things for the right reasons, not the wrong reasons.

Similarly, Christine identified honesty as well as perseverance. Her values echo her mission to generate corporate accountability and social responsibility:

> I think that I value perseverance—the Churchill quote, to keep on going. I value an unflinching pursuit of justice and truth. That may sound idealistic, but I do think that we can make organizations better. Through the financial lens, as far as my organization is concerned, I can see many things which need to be improved, and I really hate to see wasted resource and money squandered—but most of the time that is down to ignorance, a lack of awareness or training, or both. However, what really makes my blood boil is dishonesty and things done for short-term personal gain. So I suppose I also value the opposite of those!

John's response is interesting and highlights the relationship between personal values and professional values. The ex-boss to whom he refers seemed to have brought her personal value of fairness (something John admired) into the professional environment and used it to begin to alter the culture of the organization. Initially this might have been perceived as deviant in some way, but as others in the organization, like John, begin to admire her, they would begin to emulate her approach and so the culture would change and become more acceptable to people like John and his ex-boss. Organizational culture could be seen as comprising a complex set of values, assumptions and beliefs that define the ways in which business is carried out. Hofstede (1980) even suggested that a kind of professional socialization occurs within organizational cultures which results in homogenization of values and a collapsing of individual differences.

Usefully in this regard, Dolan (2011, p.8) has presented a triaxial model for understanding the complexity of organizational value systems, which it is also helpful for us to consider because it incorporates both individual and group values. The model comprises three interconnected values: economic-pragmatic, ethical-social, and emotional-spiritual. The model suggests, first, that economic-pragmatic values are necessary to maintain and bring together organizational sub-systems. These values relate to efficiency, performance standards and discipline, and guide activities such as planning, quality assurance and accounting. Second, that ethical-social values are those that group members share, and emerge from beliefs held about how people should conduct themselves in public, at work and in relationships. They are associated with values such as honesty, congruence, respect and loyalty. Third, emotional-spiritual values are those that relate to intrinsic motivation and what makes people excited and passionate. Optimism, energy, freedom and happiness are examples of this category of values. Without these values people do not become creative or highly committed. Dolan went on to examine the relationship between the three axes in the model and identified important organizational concerns that result from tensions between value systems: sensitivity (social responsibility), survival (the bottom line), and innovation (creativity and new ideas).

An interesting exercise would be to encourage leaders to examine the values inherent in their brave story against Dolan's trichotomy and to look for the tensions that Dolan has suggested exist. The aim would be initially to identify some balance in individual values and then to see where tensions arise between individuals, teams and the organization. For example, one of the leaders in our study, Christine, appeared to be espousing her own values about what she considered right, and suggested that she would stick to them come what may. This conviction could be linked to her ethical-social values or to her emotional-spiritual values. Unpacking the values would help Christine with her coaching agenda, which was to consider where she should head in her future career and whether she was truly aligned with the organization. Christine was therefore deeply involved in considering what bravery meant for her.

The desired dynamic ultimately is the alignment of values between the organization and the leader. The leader and the organization should, if possible, have a shared value set, but if the leader feels strongly enough that some specific misalignment cannot be tolerated, then it could be that the brave thing to do is to deviate from those organizational values and in some circumstances it might mean leaving the organization.

In the leadership literature itself, Burns (1978, p.43) explained the role of values in the theory of transformational leadership:

> The essence of leadership in any polity is the recognition of real need, the uncovering and exploiting of contradictions among values and between values and practice, the realigning of values [...] The leader's fundamental act is to induce people to be aware or conscious of what they feel—to feel their true needs so strongly, to define their values so meaningfully, that they can be moved to purposeful action.

The idea of values-based-leadership (Copeland, 2014) suggests that when aligned with the organizational mission, individual values lead to value congruence, which research has shown to yield positive outcomes for individuals and their organizations. In order to achieve such congruence leaders need to ensure that what they value is rewarded accordingly in the organization. Intriguingly, Graber and Kilpatrick (2008) argue that organizations often fail to reward those who uphold or enact the values of an organization, highlighting Mayer's (2005) suggestion that there is "a pervasive attitude in the business community that ethics and values are all about restraint and denial, not about active and productive investments" (Graber & Kilpatrick, 2008, p.194).

Similarly, thinkers such as Covey (1992) have argued that values need to be correctly aligned in order to ensure effective leadership, and Senge (1990), for example, suggested that we need to note the difference between the values that we communicate (our espoused theories) and the values that we act upon (theories in use). The relational approach to leadership has also gathered strength over the past few years, as will be discussed further in Chapter 10. This approach ensures that employees are involved in developing a shared vision and principles, thus bringing people together in the organization. Indeed, Blanchard and O'Connor (1997) considered deep shared values to be fundamental to a successful organization.

Another outcome of the values elicitation that the brave story activity provides is that it helps leaders to think about what first drew them to their work and helps them to live by those principles again. The coach might ask leaders to explore to what extent they themselves are similar to their brave role model. What values do they each share?

For example, in one session another leader, Peter, was asked to talk about someone who he considered to be brave. His answer was his mother. She had been a single parent and had three children to bring up on her own for quite significant parts of Peter's childhood. He had been in awe of her ability to work so hard, to fight their corner, so that they could have every benefit that she could possibly give them, and yet still maintain a happy and positive demeanor. In conversation with Peter it became apparent that this upbringing had, perhaps unsurprisingly, had a huge impact on him. Bravery for him was about putting oneself in potential harm's way for those who you care about, challenging the system, and remaining mentally strong and positive.

During a discussion about his current role as the chief executive of a relatively high-profile charity, Peter then began to describe how the journey to his current role via a relatively traditional corporate career had not as far as he was aware been a conscious decision. He had simply found himself gravitating to that area. Whilst discussing his mother he began to wonder whether his childhood had had more of an impact than he had realized:

> As obvious as it may seem when I sit here and talk this through with you, I had genuinely not considered that some of my later career choices had been quite so driven by the values instilled in me from childhood. Yes, of course I have always been aware that things had been a little challenging in the past, but as to how much that may have been quietly influencing my journey along the way to this present role, I simply had not considered. The pragmatist in me says that this could simply be coincidence, but I find myself feeling something falling into place here. Like a subtle little puzzle that has lurked at the back of my mind has just been solved.

An interesting outcome from a subsequent conversation with Peter was that he said he felt as though he had been treading water recently in his current role, and had now decided to alter radically his and the organization's approach towards acting more congruently with its espoused values.

Role models then are important for eliciting values, and with the help of the coach they can also enable leaders to recognize where they may be similar to or different from their role model, especially in relation to the values they hold. So role models become symbols of possibility, which not only offer inspiration but may also remove uncertainty: the very fact that the role model has achieved what we admire in the leadership world means that it is possible to do so (Chung, 2000).

3 Implementing Values

In the first part of this chapter we discussed the process of values elicitation through identifying brave role models. We now want to highlight the importance of leaders implementing their values within their organizations. In addition, we introduce the more controversial idea that coaches might also have strong values, which they might want to uphold in their coaching work. Goleman (1998) proposed that personal values are not "lofty abstractions," "but intimate credos that we may never quite articulate in words so much as feel." Our values, he suggests "translate into what has emotional power or resonance for us, whether negative or positive" (p.115).

When we, the authors, think of the values that leaders may hold, we want to include personal values such as openness, fairness, believing that the family is of fundamental importance, understanding that trust and honesty are vital and that maintaining a healthy work/life balance is essential. However, we would also want to include some social and environmental values. We believe that responsibility and sustainability are also key and are fundamentally what motivated us to write this book.

Leadership, we believe, is about more than personal and social values; it is also about the challenges of a mature society which, as Vinkhuyzen and Karlsson-Vinkhuyzen (2012, p.2) argue, asks "different qualities of leaders than what has been sufficient in societies before." They point out, however, how research rarely focuses on why some individuals "step up to promote sustainability or if and how it would be possible to actively nurture the development of such leaders" (ibid., p.3). Indeed, these authors argue, and we tend to agree, that "for the next stage of the evolution of humanity, it will be necessary for people to take more responsibility for the condition of the planet and the species inhabiting it" (ibid., p.4). This would necessitate changing the view that values are fixed and largely unchangeable, and adopting the view that humans have a capacity for greater, expanded value sets. Later in this book we examine the types of leadership that might help us get there.

However, for now we propose that leaders are accountable for the culture of their organizations and have the responsibility to promote the best possible values in their organizations. Cameron (2011, p.25) explains how responsibility is associated with freedom of action and empowerment, and that leaders are "more likely to be accountable and dependable if they are able to act freely and to feel empowered to perform." He says that responsibility means being "response-able," or possessing "the capability and the capacity needed to respond." In this sense our brave model is a response model. According to Cameron (2011), behaving responsibly means being good or doing good, and involves standards of rightness, correctness and virtuousness.

Vinkhuyzen and Karlsson-Vinkhuyzen's (2012, p.1) starting point is that values are formed by "a range of factors (cultural, political, social, religious) and are thus subject to change," so we can see that the standards of behavior of all within the organization are dependent on the leader. If values are subject to change in this way, then individual leaders such as Christine, who we introduced earlier, who internalize values that are supportive of sustainability, are most likely to be those who manifest values-based leadership and manage to change organizational culture and the values of the people. If more leaders who hold those values have specific moral capabilities that enable personal transformation, improved interpersonal relationships and social transformation, they might begin to exemplify the necessary paradigm shift towards sustainable consumption and production and lead the wider society towards it (Vinkhuyzen & Karlsson-Vinkhuyzen, 2012), and so overcome the value–action gap identified by Kollmuss and Agyeman (2002).

However, leaders like Christine are quite rare. Of the leaders we have worked with she is in a minority and many do not overtly share concerns about the moral need to transform patterns of consumption towards more sustainable ones.

There remains, therefore, one further question for us to consider. Vinkhuyzen and Karlsson-Vinkhuyzen (2012, p.11) suggest that a new strain of moral leaders is necessary who are "willing to change their values and design new institutions." If such leaders are rare, as suggested, we want to ask to what extent coaches should be moral leaders themselves and so overtly encourage the leaders they coach to become more morally conscious. We do not have an answer to this, as it would require coaches to hold a specific agenda for the coaching assignment, which is a difficult notion for most non-directive coaches to accept. Perhaps here is an opportunity to see how these two opposing values might be reconciled.

Summary

In this chapter we have introduced a values elicitation exercise aimed at allowing leaders to articulate their brave role models and to consider how this augments their definition of bravery and emphasizes their values in relation to their work and to future situations. We also highlighted the stories of leaders where values had been identified and subsequently linked to their leadership roles.

The use of stories has been widely discussed in the coaching literature. For example, Brockbank and McGill (2006, p.156) have suggested that stories are an "authentic self-disclosure—an attempt to reveal the self as a person and to reach the listener," and a "signal of invitation" through which the client can open a door to his or her self. Similarly, Echols, Gravenstine and Mobley (2008, p.112) suggest that "we are the keeper of our own stories, telling over and over again those that define who we are," while Drake suggests that one role for the coach could be to help clients "forge new connections between their stories, their identity and their behaviours in order to generate and embody new options" (Drake, 2010, p.120). He describes how there is a close connection between how people view themselves, how they describe their daily lives, and how they subsequently behave. Thus stories are a way of exploring connections and providing material that can guide opportunities for inner development.

The role of the coach then is one of co-editor. The coach must listen and relate back to the leader the lens through which they detect the leader's world is being viewed. Cox (2013) argues that coaching is different from everyday conversation because there is a focus on clients telling their stories "without the coaches' interjections and interpretations" (p.32). Cox suggests that the benefits are far reaching, "not least because when coaches are not focused on exchanging their own narratives, they can focus on helping the client to see as many different perspectives and interpretations in their story as possible" (ibid., p.32).

We have found that introducing the idea of bravery to leaders and having them discuss it can lead them to consider change and what that might mean, before any other part of the brave coaching model has been discussed. For example, the "brave story" conversation might have resulted in the leader deciding to begin an initiative with her or his immediate team to get them to discuss who they consider to be brave. It is important to realize that if that happens, it is something to be embraced. Whilst our coaching model necessarily appears to have a structure and a sequence, the idea that everything will flow along in succession is likely to be incorrect, perhaps for much of the time. The fact that the coaching relationship has already begun will help leaders to generate the space to contemplate and reflect on all aspects of their work and so the coach needs to temper expectation and guard against the idea that this is a model at all. We call it a model, but it could equally be called a framework. It is a shelter, a place to organize ideas. Coaching is not a cookie-cutter exercise. Instead, it is an evolutionary process—one within which the leader and the coach, it is hoped, can evolve and gain greater understanding of themselves and their environment. Consequently, some coaches may dip in and out of this framework, although some may wish to follow it through, step by step. Even within the steps, however, the coach and client may veer off at a tangent to explore something that has been uncovered, or has become quite pressing, to return later to the next "stage." Within each of the "stages," therefore, there is much scope for the coach and leader to do things in a way that is familiar to them. Some leaders may read this book and become excited by some of the ideas, which they in turn may wish to share, or even coach in their own organizations.

3
PULLING FACTORS

Introduction

Lofting's (1922) story of Dr. Dolittle introduces an animal called a pushmi-pullyu, which is a cross between a unicorn and a gazelle. The pushmi-pullyu has two heads, one at each end of its body, and when it tries to move, both heads try to move the body in opposite directions.

Leaders may well empathize with the image this conjures. In their roles, leaders are frequently pulled in several different directions at once: they have to juggle a huge range of complex tasks and demands at the same time. Problems arise if they only ever respond reactively and they have not had the opportunity really to consider what is pulling them or pushing them.

The next stage of the brave leadership coaching model provides a way of exploring the range of factors that might be pulling on the leader. These pulling factors are likely to derive from complex and "wicked" (Rittell & Webber, 1973) problems—the kinds of problems that are messy, quite difficult to define and lack a single solution. The routine problems of the organization are managerial and tend to be dealt with efficiently lower down the organization, whereas these more complex problems do not have a right or wrong answer. Often it is difficult for leaders to determine where the problem lies or exactly what the problem is, and so careful diagnostic work is necessary. Also, as well as being complex, the problems are sometimes novel and also tend to be interdependent, like corporate social responsibility for instance. Mumford et al.

(2000, p.14) explain how leadership becomes critical when there is a need to develop and implement "adaptive responses to new or changing situations."

Thus we can begin to see how novelty and complexity in problem solving might require a more sophisticated approach to analysis. The pulling factors process enables leaders to consider the various forces on them from a position of calm reflection in order ultimately to be more effective. In an environment of "information ambiguity" (Mumford et al., 2000, p.14), and without the space to think, leaders are likely to find it difficult to locate what the course of action might be in their current situation, and particularly the brave course of action.

Pull-push theory is used in marketing to assess motivation of purchasers of services or products (Dowling, 2004). However, the way we are using the term is different. We are not concerned with how pulling factors motivate the leader, but with: i) how exploration of factors can help expand the leader's boundaries and perspectives; ii) whether the factors are pulling the leader "off balance"; and iii) how they impact decision making. The process is therefore more akin to Lewin's (1996) force field analysis which provides a way of examining factors (or *forces*) that influence a situation. Lewin's theory looks at the strength of forces that are either hindering or helping the movement towards a certain goal. Examining the force field (or "life space," as Lewin termed it) helps to understand not only a person's motives, but also their values, needs, moods, goals, anxieties and ideals. Lewin argued that any changes in an individual's life space, including their development as individuals, relied on the internalization of external stimuli (from the physical and social world) into the life space.

The difference between force field analysis and the pulling factors analysis described here is that in pulling factor analysis the relationships between factors are identified and their ever present, but potentially evolving, impact is considered. Although we might want to consider the weight of the force a pulling factor is having on the leader at any one time, the pulling factors are also viewed as having interdependencies and synergies. The analysis is about creating initial awareness of different types of connection between factors, rather than promoting recognition of strength of impact and priority, at least in the first instance. We also view pulling factors as external forces and not things that are generally internalized. It is possible that a pulling factor may align directly with an individual's value set, for example. In that case it is not likely to pull and is in fact more likely to "center" and strengthen. Lewin also discusses, amongst other things, values, moods and anxieties. Once again, these are distinct from pulling factors, although they may be impacted by the pulling factors, and we deal with them quite separately in Chapter 4 on gravitational factors.

In this chapter we discuss the idea of pulling factors and provide examples of the analysis in action. This part of the brave coaching model enables leaders to begin to take stock of their environment and the competing forces and demands within it. Whilst the "brave story" allowed leaders to consider what their own ideas of bravery are and who they might consider to be brave, the discussion of the pulling factors is likely to be the first time that the coach and the leader have begun to turn their attention to the detailed dynamic of the issues that concern the leader within the organization.

1 What Are Pulling Factors?

Our research suggests that the reason that leaders have a sense of being pulled in different directions is because they have a need to fulfill some obligations in each of these areas. Everyone will probably have used the phrase, "I feel like I am being pulled in so many different directions." Sometimes leaders might say: "there are so many competing factors which I'm trying to consider, I don't know which way is up," or "the biggest challenge I have at the moment is knowing where to begin: I walk down a corridor and feel myself being drawn in different directions as I think through the different demands of the key people here." There are many other examples of these "pulls" on our attention, but it is likely that there will be a common thread running through all of them—that is, that we are almost certainly dealing with complexity.

Often there is an emotional component to the sense of being pulled in a particular direction. This emotion can manifest in a feeling of not wanting to be pulled towards an element in the environment, or indeed from a sense that something is pulling us that we feel is important from a loyalty perspective, or a sense of obligation, but which might not be aligned with our values. It may even be that this compelling force invokes a sense of fear, or even anger. The key is that for some, if not all of these pulling factors, there is likely to be emotion involved. When that is the case, it is often difficult to think rationally; and with conflicting emotions, confusion, short-term thinking, hesitant decision making, and a sense of being overwhelmed can frequently be the order of the day. If we also consider how isolated leaders can sometimes feel, a fresh and more dispassionate approach to helping them consider situations from different perspectives can be useful.

Johnson (2014) has explained the polarities and dichotomies that seemingly conflicting organizational concerns can produce within an organization. He calls these "interdependent pairs" and suggests that "the more we understand about the elements of this phenomenon and the dynamics by which it functions, the more effective we can be at leveraging its energy" (p.207). Interdependent pairs are aspects of our existence that seem to be opposites or poles, but which are actually dependent on each other. Johnson gives the simple example of inhaling and exhaling. Other examples identified by Glunk and Follini (2011) are: long-term *and* short-term thinking; keeping control *and* being able to delegate; focusing on relationships *and* results; and, what we are perhaps most concerned with in this book, combining internal *and* external focus.

Within an organization, factors such as cost effectiveness and service excellence might form a similar pair, where one is not possible without the other: for example, service excellence cannot be provided if an organization goes into receivership because it failed to take account of costs. Johnson explains how an energy system flows between and around the two factors forming an infinity loop with upsides and downsides. For example, customers may be attracted to a product based on competitive pricing, but they may also be attracted to a company because of a reputation for service excellence; equally customers can be lost because of poor service and because of high prices. Such conflicts produce a tension that every organization and every leader needs to resolve. The poles (pricing and service in this instance) must both be pursued because both are of benefit to the organization.

Drawing on Heracleous and Wirtz's (2014) case study of Singapore Airlines, Johnson goes on to explain that "because the phenomenon of interdependent pairs is so ubiquitous, we all have an experiential base in dealing with it" (Johnson, 2014, p.211). Similarly, he argues that our training in solving problems leads us to deal with the tensions inherent in interdependent pairs by seeking the "right" or "best" answer as a "solution." However, he suggests that rather than look for a right answer on one side of the polarity, that we should explore the upsides and downsides to each factor:

> When we make explicit the two poles and the fact that there is an upside and downside to each, any group within an organization can readily identify what those upsides and downsides are. They can also identify, with a "Dual Strategy" orientation, what Action Steps would

help maximise both upsides and what Early Warnings would let you know you are getting into the downsides.

(Johnson, 2014, p.211)

Glunk and Follini (2011) have also focused on the idea of interdependent opposites in their discussion of leadership coaching. They explored how the coach can support clients in overcoming the polarity traps that Johnson has warned against, arguing that "a coach who is able to hold interdependent opposites with ease in the coaching encounter will allow clients to experience transformation on a deeper level" (p.222). However, they also point out how the "obscured interrelatedness" of certain polarities makes it difficult for people to manage the paradoxical tensions that arise in daily life. As a result they suggest that people tend to fall into one of three polarity traps:

- Overemphasizing one pole and repressing the other. Leaders in particular often take a long-term view and forget to look at short-term impact.
- Fluctuating between emphasizing one pole or the other, causing confusion for all involved. This might, for example, result in knee-jerk oscillation between an urgent need for results when in fact relationship issues might be in need of attention.
- Advocating a half-hearted compromise between the two poles, resulting in lack of impetus for either. Such an outcome could be disastrous when applied, for example, to maintaining leadership control vs. delegating.

Experienced coaches may be familiar with leaders or managers who fall into these traps, instead of working to expand their boundaries and embracing what Collins and Porras (2005, p.44) call "the genius of the AND." The genius of the AND involves embracing both ends of any continuum or polarity, rather than the either/or. Thus we could think about how to preserve our core values AND begin to invest in new initiatives. The creative dynamic that this kind of thinking generates can enable novel solutions to ongoing problems.

Glunk and Follini (2011) argue that there is a role for coaching in fostering meaningful change that will enable the deeper understanding required to accept and resolve interdependent opposites. Such coaching, they argue, creates space for understanding and accepting polarity tensions. Interestingly, before support of this kind can be tackled with clients, these authors recommend that coaches explore their own work for tensions between: creating safety *and* providing challenge; encouraging self-acceptance *and* promoting change; deepening learning *and* forwarding the action. As Glunk and Follini suggest, coaching that fails to tolerate the recognition of such opposites risks becoming shallow and humdrum.

2 Pulling Factor Analysis

Pulling factor analysis involves three levels of discussion:

1. identifying the pulling factors;
2. thinking about polarities, interdependences and synergies between factors; and
3. exploring the potential of factors to disrupt equilibrium and pull the leader off course.

Identifying the pulling factors

When beginning to discuss the pulling factors, the coach invites the leader to describe those external factors that s/he considers relevant and important at this point in time, remembering that whatever the leader brings to the coaching session will be the right thing to discuss in relation to pulling factors. To introduce the pulling factors, the coach could use a phrase such as:

> We have begun to consider the idea of bravery and before we go further with that, it might be useful to explore the environment within which you are currently working, in terms of what might be impacting on or restricting your thinking and/or decision making just now.

The coach might also ask:

> So, what decisions are you having to consider within your business environment right now?

or:

> Of all the things going on right now, are there any areas where you feel that you are being pulled in different directions?

It might seem that this approach is quite directive or that it drills down to a fairly granular level right away and does not necessarily leave much scope for a more leader-led exploration. However, we have to consider here why the coach has been employed. Has the coach been employed to challenge thinking, or to help the leader think more broadly? Has the coach been employed to get the leader to think about the different leadership approaches that could be taken, or specifically to help the leader think about bravery? The original contract will have a bearing on the direction the coach takes during each session.

The most likely engagement, in our experience, would be one in which the coach has been commissioned by the organization or the leader to assist with the leader's general development. This development could take many forms, and through dialogue and exploration it may become apparent to the coach and/or the leader that the idea of bravery should be explored. This may come about because there are decision-making challenges that the leader is facing in the organization, or there may be some crisis in individual confidence. In any event the coach needs to pay particular attention to the broader context of the engagement with the client and how that may affect their "speed of descent" into some of the detailed discussions about pulling factors.

It must also be remembered that the pulling factors that leaders encounter are real-time issues taking place in a real environment and that they are likely to be the issues with which the leader is really struggling. So in that sense these particular issues may have more immanence and meaning than any other agenda that the leader may bring. They may be issues that concern: leadership or influencing style; decisions relating to organizational change; investment and expansion possibilities; market competition; or even more personal issues, such as career choice.

What follows is an extract from a dialogue between coach and client using the very first strand of the pulling factors structure. The leader in question, John, worked for a finance company in an IT director role. He was one level below board membership and was considered a good candidate for succession planning. The managing director had asked for him to receive coaching as part of his overall development, as in her opinion, John was likeable, conscientious, very bright and had much to offer, but perhaps needed to have more of a sense of purpose and have slightly more conviction about issues that he actually cared about. The coach and leader had already discussed the "brave story" before this meeting.

COACH: What would you say is pulling you right now, in your environment? What I mean by that is, imagine that you have five minutes' "down time" during the day. Perhaps you are traveling to a meeting, or walking down a corridor. If you find yourself thinking about work, what do you feel is pulling on your attention, your energy?

JOHN: You mean right now, or what is likely to come up?
COACH: As a starting point, let's just think about right now. Imagine that if we drew you as a circle on this piece of paper, what would currently be taking up your attention, what is "shouting" for your attention? You may not be doing anything about it, but you know it is there, niggling at the back of your mind. Or in fact it might not be a niggle; it might be that you feel this thing is lassoing you in!
JOHN: Ha! That is definitely what things tend to do around here! I have to say that your questions are making me think of a myriad of things. How long have we got? Do you mean everything that is going on, or everything that is going on in relation to one issue? And I just need to understand a bit more about what we are talking about here, in terms of what is pulling me. I could get down to quite a lot of level of detail, let me tell you!
COACH: I think it might be best to think about one issue for the moment. And in terms of the types of things that might be pulling on you, let's call them pulling factors. It may be useful to sketch out a few ideas on this bit of paper, to get the creative juices flowing. Would that be okay with you?
JOHN: Absolutely, I'm keen to understand this a little better, although I have to say that just simply thinking about what these things might be has certainly got my adrenaline flowing, and if I'm not careful, my head starting to spin!
COACH: Ha! Well, hopefully we can find a way to help you navigate through some of these issues. Could you pick one thing at the moment that you feel has got you being pulled in different directions, and that is likely to result in you having to make a stance or take a decision in the days, weeks or even months ahead please?
JOHN: Mmm. Well, there are a couple of what I would describe as "biggies" coming up. But just so I understand, would this process or discussion we're about to have work with other stuff as well, the less than big stuff?
COACH: Well of course, ultimately you will be the judge of that, but I'm not going to dodge the question as I suspect that you are asking for a more direct answer. In my opinion, yes it does. I want to answer your question as fully as I can, but please bear in mind that I'm also attempting not to bias your opinion about the usefulness or not of this exercise. What I will say is that in my experience, stepping through these ideas with, as you call it, the big stuff, tends to permeate by a form of osmosis to the smaller stuff.
JOHN: Okay, thank you, let's see what happens then. I am intrigued. And let me then choose the topic of the company suddenly deciding that

we need to overhaul our information technology systems. Well, I say suddenly, but there have been rumblings for six months or so.
COACH: What is your opinion on that?
JOHN: I think that it is premature, and foolish. There is nothing inherently wrong with our system; it isn't the best but it isn't the worst. It is on a stable platform, it is upgradable and it isn't broken.
COACH: Okay, thank you for that. If you don't mind then, I'd like to go back to the drawing with "you" represented as a circle here in the center. What I'm going to do is to draw some other circles at a bit of a distance from you, just to get us started. So this one might be called "company values," this one might be "company culture," this one "company economics," and this one, "other," which we could perhaps leave as other for the moment.
JOHN: Does the distance away from the circles or the size of the circle have any bearing?
COACH: That is a good question. It can do if you think that that would help?
JOHN: Hmmm. Let's leave it as it is at the moment until I see where you are going with this.

One way of capturing what is emerging from the pulling factors conversation and to crystallize what is pulling the leader at any point in time is to draw a diagram. An example is shown in Figure 3.1. In this example John has agreed that economic factors, company values and company culture are specific issues to consider. There may also be other issues, such as the expectations of peers or stakeholders.

Thinking about polarities, interdependences and synergies between factors

As the pulling factors discussion evolves over one or more sessions, the coach will support the leader to consider each of the factors in turn. This exploration phase might include a discussion of just how company economics is pulling the leader and may be facilitated by questions such as:

- What is the issue here?
- Who are the people who are pulling on you as far as this factor is concerned?
- In which part of the organization is this tension most evident?
- What does this mean to you and your values?

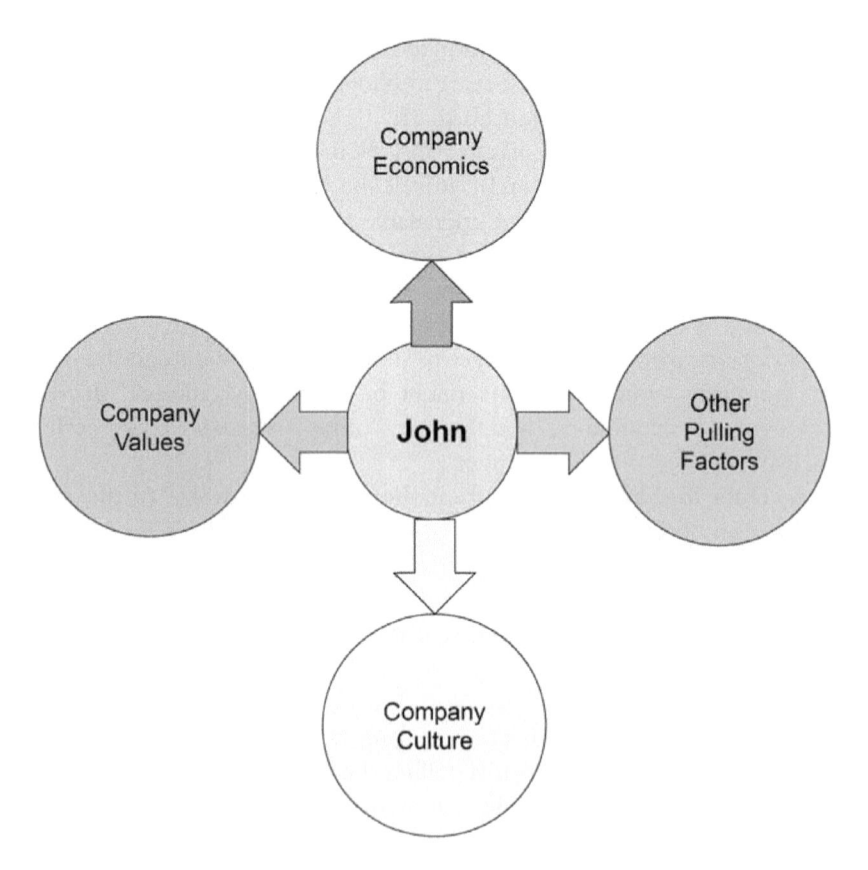

FIGURE 3.1 John's initial pulling factors diagram

The discussion of company culture can be initiated with similar questions. Company culture can be a major issue for leaders in the sense that there are myriad issues involving the dynamic interplay between the leader and the culture within which s/he works. For example, the leader may be trying to change the culture, or they may feel that the culture is corrosive to them, or that certain behaviors that are being reinforced are influencing the culture. It may be that the conversation about culture sparks another idea about something else, and of course if this is the case then the conversation would head in that direction and begin to examine the interdependence between the two.

Company culture could be a real-time dynamic in the work of the leader, whereas company values might tend towards the more aspirational. One possible dynamic between culture and values may be that the culture needs to be moved closer to the aspirational values. However, in our experience, one of the main challenges with organizational value or mission statements is that they do not engage employees. They are frequently seen as somewhat ethereal, not connected to the real world, and existing only in print on a poster in a dining room. So the leader's issue may not be that there are no values to aspire to, but more that there is a disconnect between the behavioral average (the current culture) and the desired collective value set. Two other leaders with whom we worked talked about the complicated pull that corporate and individual values can create. The first sees a tension between compliance with ethical and other directives by the organization and concerns that employees have on the shop floor:

> Going into a corporate headquarters you will see the environmental document, the social ethics document, you'll see the community plan, and I sit there and think: "most of this is compliance nonsense." The bit that the workforce actually values is a different issue because they want to see you as a leader. The pull from them is that they want to hear why I, as leader, think we're going to be successful: they want to hear that they are not being closed; they want to hear there are growth opportunities; they want to know about their training, their development, and whether they will have a job next year. They are all the values that pull on me every day because every time I walk the floor, that's what they ask me. They couldn't care less about the corporate ethics policy but they're really interested about whether we are closing the factory: a workforce value issue they ask me about is "are we on a wage freeze for another year?"

The second identifies a situation where decision making is undermined in the organization without real justification:

> Two and a half years ago we had a reorganization, big reorganization with departments changing, the whole structure changing. Not that many people were leaving but just reporting structures were changing. As a result people were not sitting with their teams. Two and a half years later and I'm responsible for making it happen—at last getting everybody sitting within their teams. Two and a half years later that hasn't happened because the company has kept pulling the move because it costs too much or it's too difficult or there's some other change coming up. So we have our people—and this is the most important thing to our people—what they desperately want is to sit

within their team. They come to work; they want to be in a team environment, they want to enjoy coming to work. At the moment this is the biggest thing that is preventing them from doing that, and yet we won't sign off moving people. Worse than that we say "yes, it's going to happen," and I personally communicate this is happening, but two weeks later it gets pulled again so it makes me look like an idiot and it completely goes against my values and my belief that this is the right thing to do, this is the right time—and there is no real business justification why we don't do it.

Another of the leaders introduced in Chapter 2, Matt, was inspired by the idea of the pulling factors as planets, each with their own ability to attract. Matt has worked in operations for three years and described a potential forthcoming conflict within the senior team in terms of the size of the pulling factor:

Important people who are already a long time in the business and very strong people—if they say something then it's the size of a big planet. I mean it's not realistic to have all the bubbles of the planets the same size: there are ones that are things that are pulling me further away than others. So I don't know how to put it exactly and we can talk about it later, but items like managing all those staff members, including my boss, is a big planet. I mean, if you have to stand up against people who have already been 25 years in the business saying, well, we'll go in that direction while you believe the other direction is better, then it's not so easy.

Matt is gradually beginning to talk about making a brave decision, although there is still an element of confusion: thus in exploring the pulling factors it is useful for him to have time for reflection between sessions in order to generate and position their pulling potential. For example, Matt's situation may be further complicated by the fact that there is an ethical component that he did not consider when initially discussing the conflict issues with the coach, or there may be team dynamics to consider. It should also be noted that even after consolidation the pulling factors are not static and will change. They need therefore to be revisited periodically. This "multi-pass" approach to the pulling factors continues to support the fact that the use of any coaching model can never be completely linear. Figure 3.2 shows one example of how the pulling factors map may evolve when the leader reflects over several sessions.

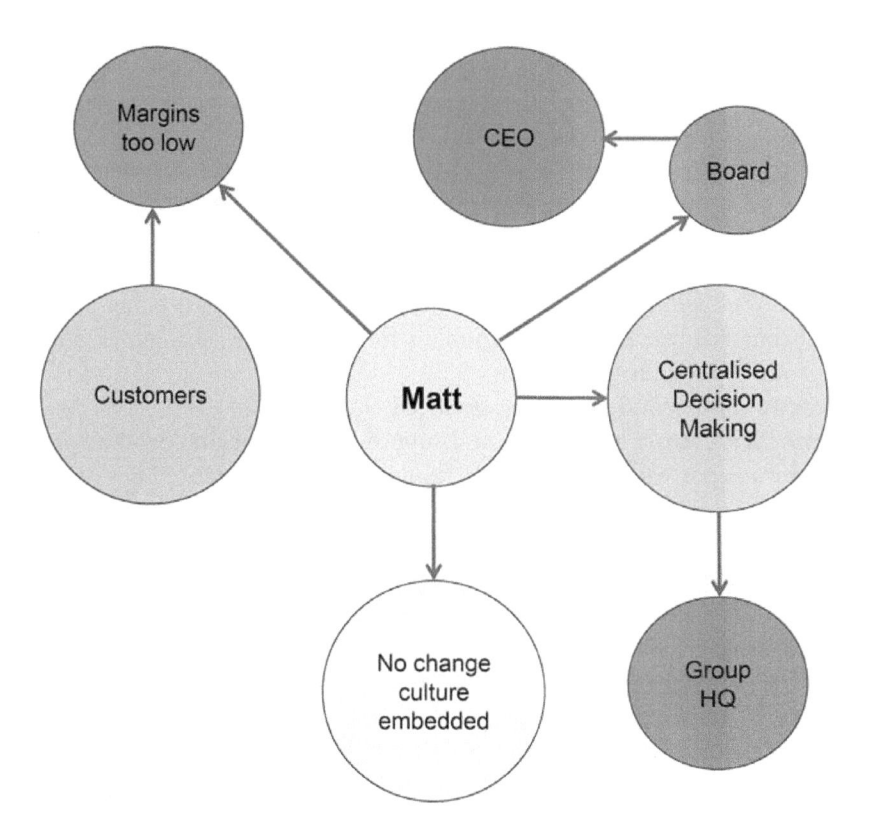

FIGURE 3.2 Matt's "evolved" pulling factors diagram

Exploring the potential of factors to disrupt equilibrium and pull the leader off course

The final stage of the pulling factors discussion is a more in-depth analysis of the tensions between factors, which might highlight seemingly irreconcilable poles or suggest interdependencies and even synergies between factors. This stage involves the leader in starting to understand upsides and downsides of each of the pulling factors and the boundaries that might be in place in certain areas, maintained by boundary keepers (Glunk & Follini, 2011) who may yet be polarized in their thinking. Thinking about pulling factors in this way helps the leader to explore, question and integrate the positives and negatives within each factor and ultimately to develop a more "ambidextrous mindset" (Guttel & Konlechner, 2009).

Picking up on our earlier coaching conversation with John, we can see how the analysis develops in the dialogue, and how it begins to explore John's values:

COACH: Okay, well maybe one way to do this is to look at each of these areas in turn. So, in relation to this possible change to the IT system, can you think of anything which is having an impact on you, pulling you, from a company values perspective?
JOHN: Well yes, right away—because that is exactly what is being used by some managers as a big argument for making the change, as one of our "values" is innovation.
COACH: You sound less than convinced.
JOHN: Well, it is a laudable value I suppose, but it is being bandied about by people who are often the least innovative I know. They are just using the innovation value to give them more visibility.
COACH: What would you say is actually driving their behaviors then?
JOHN: I will tell you exactly what it is. In my opinion they are shouting about innovation because they want the existing IT system overhauled because it will keep them occupied for the next five years!
COACH: All right. For the moment, then, let's look at the company culture. Is there anything there which you feel is an important part of the landscape that we are exploring?
JOHN: Yes. Interestingly, the culture is quite dynamic and we do pride ourselves as being quick and nimble and able to embrace change. That had gotten me thinking.
COACH: What about the company economics? Is there anything significant there?
JOHN: Again, yes. If this new IT system can be seen to make us more efficient, then there would be a strong financial case for doing it, although I would say that it will also be costly in the first instance.
COACH: Is your financial director for or against this proposal?
JOHN: At the moment she is waiting to get some updated figures. And so I would say that she is open minded at the moment, but I think veering towards a decision to go with the change.
COACH: Thank you. Having stepped through that, is there anything else which you think might be significant and pulling your energy and attention regarding this issue?
JOHN: Yes there is. There is the whole people impact issue.
COACH: Ah. Right, I wasn't sure if that type of thing would come up here, or where it would come up. Could I ask that we please come back to that particular area later on? I'd like to look at issues that

involve your values under a different "heading." In terms of the pulling factors and your current environment, I would describe them as being things "external to you." They are outside influences, rather than those you might wish to champion or that you feel passionate about.

JOHN: But I feel passionate about innovation, so I don't quite understand.

COACH: Yes, that is a very good point, and I need to explain that in a little more detail. If we look at what we have been sketching out so far, you will see that the note I have written on the page as an aide-memoire to refer to later, says "innovation as a club"? And what I mean by that, and let me also check your understanding, is that this particular value is pulling you "off center." It is a value which you can subscribe to, but which in this case is simply not what you agree with. So imagine for a moment that you were a child's spinning top. You know the type of thing?

JOHN: Yes, centrifugal force and all that.

COACH: Yes, exactly, well imagine that the spinning top's upright position is its optimum state, and let's ignore the other forces like friction and air resistance at least for the moment. Let's simply imagine that the spinning top is at its happiest spinning in an upright position. But if we apply a force to it, by nudging it, it begins to wobble and tries to get back to its "happiest" state of spinning upright. At the risk of taking the analogy too far, another way to think about it is that the spinning top is made of metal, the type of metal that can be influenced by a magnet, and that the pulling factors are like magnets which the top attempts to resist, and get back to its "happiest" state of spinning upright.

JOHN: No, no, that's not taking the analogy too far at all. I like that, I think I get that. So what you're saying is that anything which keeps me "upright," which centers me, which feels right to me, is not a pulling factor.

COACH: Exactly. I quite like that analogy. Maybe I should have used it earlier! And so if you don't mind, I'll come back to the people impact bit later. Is there anything else that is pulling, that is impacting on your ability to stay centered or grounded?

JOHN: Well, yes, there is one more thing, and that is the impact of this on our customers and that's an interesting one, based on what you just said. You see, I care about our customers, and yet they can be incredibly demanding. So caring is part of me, at my "center," but the customer can sometimes be the beast that has to be fed. So is this a pulling factor or something different?

COACH: Again, that is a very good question. I would suggest, and please have a think about this, that the caring is part of who you are. It may drive many of your decisions, but we can possibly separate out the customer in terms of the pulling factor component. So, for example, one way to think about the customer as a pulling factor is to have a think about where you may have a conflict of interest, for example.

JOHN: Okay, I can see that there may be a customer need to have us able to drive the cost of some of our services down, and if they heard that some new IT system was likely to do that, which I'm not convinced it would, they would be clamoring for it.

COACH: Have they heard about it?

JOHN: Not as far as I'm aware, but there is another thing that probably fits into this customer pulling factor category, which I've just thought of. As you know, we provide a wide range of services in what could be described as the financial area, and we have even been diversifying into physical products as well. But essentially the better our information, the more accurately, efficiently and quickly we can pull things together, the more successful we are. Some of our customers have been complaining that we aren't fast and accurate enough, and that we are too expensive—and that is a bit of a headache for all of us.

COACH: And would this new IT system provide that?

JOHN: Well, you have kind of hit on the nub of the issue. On paper, this system is the best thing since sliced bread, it probably even toasts your bread, according to its exponents at least—and so yes, of course it is being claimed that the system will improve on our reporting, all our reporting.

COACH: And what do you think is likely to actually happen?

JOHN: I am pretty convinced that we might get there, but only eventually. I have spoken to several people in different organizations who have gone down a similar route and they have said that it was absolute chaos. It is a different operating system from normal, and that causes fundamental challenges, and the claimed ability to be able to link it to other stand-alone packages is just fantasy. The company who are selling it talk a good game and obviously have some people who will say good things about them, but that doesn't tally with other people's experience, in my opinion. We would be better waiting 18 months until the 2.0 version of our current system is available. What is starting to happen is that people are focusing on perceived shorter-term gain, and I think that they are just totally wrong. And so, in terms of your question, the customer is also a pulling factor because they have demands on us and although they don't know about this potential IT change, as far as I am aware, they are a "pull" because there is a natural tension there.

COACH: Is there anything else that springs to mind regarding these pulling factors?

JOHN: No, not at the moment, thanks, but this has really got me thinking. This is really useful. I'm beginning to see the power in taking the time to lay things out like this.

In our discussion of pulling factors above we have seen how the organizational issues that leaders such as John and Matt have identified each have the potential to knock them off course. The role of the coach, therefore, has been to help leaders to identify factors within the organization that have the potential to trap or even derail them. In addition, without understanding what is having an impact on the leader, it is likely that decisions would be made with a lesser awareness of all important factors, which may well then reduce the usefulness of the decision-making process.

Summary

In Bandura's (1991) theory of social cognition, it is argued that our environment influences our cognitions and personal responses in two main ways: i) by affecting the operation of the self-system; and ii) by providing support for adherence to moral standards. This reciprocal process suggests that environmental factors, such as those identified by John and Matt, have an impact on the leader as a person, and by implication on the behavior that s/he exhibits. In Figure 3.3 we show this interplay between the environment, the person and behavior.

It could be argued that to actually be brave, we must have a sense of the "peril" that we face, as the act of bravery implies experiencing a feeling of courage in the face of adversity and/or fear. If an action is taken arbitrarily or with no thought of the consequences involved, then there can be no recognition of courage or bravery by the individual. An act itself may be considered by others to be brave on occasion, but without the main protagonist having a sense of context, consequence and conviction, there can be no sense of a brave decision and/or action. We would suggest, therefore, that the pulling factors are not only an essential part of the leader's decision-making process, but also that without taking cognizance of them, where they are relevant to the decision at hand, the element of bravery is inconsistent, reduced or perhaps even negated entirely. Instead of a brave leader we may get a weak—or at best a blissfully unaware—leader.

58 Pulling Factors

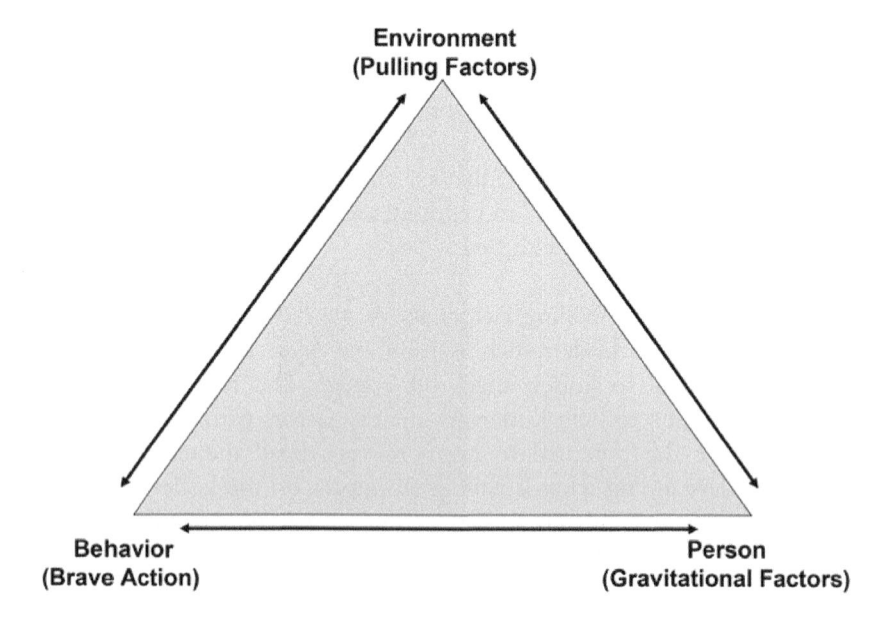

```
                    Environment
                  (Pulling Factors)


                         △


     Behavior              ←→              Person
  (Brave Action)                    (Gravitational Factors)
```

FIGURE 3.3 Relationship between pulling factors, gravitational factors and brave action

In this chapter we examined how the different contexts within which leaders operate and their interactions with others, which they themselves initiate and negotiate, constitute the environmental or "pulling" factors that impact their work. In the next chapter we examine other more personal, gravitational factors that can be seen as grounding the leader and providing a touchstone to help inform brave action. The fact that pulling factors are pulling in one way or another, as seen in the dialogues with leaders in this chapter, implies that they have the energy to lead the leader away from a balanced or centered position. This in turn suggests that there is a sense of normalcy or equilibrium, an axis from which the leader can be potentially dislodged: for the leader to experience a sense of being pulled in one direction, they have to be pulled away from something. In the next chapter, therefore, we focus on what makes up the center of gravity that guides the leader on their brave quest.

4
GRAVITATIONAL FACTORS

Introduction

The initial elements of the brave leadership coaching model will have enabled the coach and the leader to explore the idea of bravery and to recognize individuals whom the leader identifies as being brave. The external pulling factors will also have been identified. Leaders will therefore have begun to consider what bravery means for them and in what context. They will have given thought to where the pressures are within the environment in which they operate, and the forces that are pulling on them, some of which may be useful, others not. At this stage the leader and coach may well have drawn up a visual map, perhaps in a similar style to the examples shown in Chapter 3. It is at this point that attention shifts to what we describe as the gravitational factors.

In the film *Gravity* (2013), Dr Ryan Stone, played by Sandra Bullock, is pushed and pulled around by a field of space debris whilst undertaking her first spacewalk. After losing contact with mission control, we watch her struggle to find a way of reaching a relatively safe and functioning craft so that she can get close enough to the Earth's gravitational field to get back home. For leaders under attack from organizational "debris," similar efforts are needed to become grounded. From a safe place, they need to be aware of different core psychological aspects of themselves and find ways to build and maintain the self-awareness that in turbulent times will ground them and bring them back down to Earth. We call these psychological aspects "gravitational factors" for the simple reason that paying attention to the factors can help the leader feel centered: they are the areas the leader will gravitate towards in times of challenge or stress in order to keep on track.

In this chapter we will therefore be examining what we consider to be the "gravitational factors" that can help leaders to remain grounded despite the organizational demands made on them. As already discussed, leaders and their organizations face immense challenges in the wake of new technologies and global competition. It is difficult for leaders to try to navigate through these challenges without stable and reliable points of reference. Cameron (2011) uses the metaphor of an airplane pilot flying with no visual or instrumentational contact, where it is not possible to steer a course. He says that:

> the same disorientation afflicts individuals and organizations in situations where there are no unchanging referents. When nothing is stable—no clear fixed points or undisputed guiding principles exist—leaders are left with nothing by which to steer. It becomes impossible to tell up from down or progress from regress.
>
> *(Cameron, 2011, p.29)*

In situations like these, leaders are compelled to invent their own rules, and then to make their choices based on past experiences, anticipated rewards, listening to those with the loudest voices or paying attention to the most pressing external demands.

Our contention in this chapter is that the gravitational factors, which include psychological capital, virtues and character strengths, act as regulators that can help steer leaders when they face extreme challenge or organizational turbulence. Their function is therefore to "ground," center and recharge. Just as it is important to be in contact with nature, to walk barefoot on soft lush grass, or along a sandy beach, it is also important to be psychologically grounded. (This is different from being in balance, which we will discuss later.) Grounding is more akin to having a firm foundation. If we decide that we are going to walk along a tightrope, we will need to ensure that the rope is anchored and secured to firm foundations, for no matter how good we are at balancing, we are unlikely to succeed in our endeavor if the foundations that support our structure are not firm. We will also be highlighting in this chapter some ways in which gravitational factors can be developed, supported or challenged through coaching, in order to ground the leader.

We begin the chapter by looking at the three main gravitational factors and their development: first, we explore the positive psychology concepts of hope, optimism, self-efficacy and resilience, which collectively form what has been termed "psychological capital" (Avey et al., 2009); second, we add a discussion of virtues and character strengths, which we argue are also a part of the psychological capital mix; and third, we expand the discussion of virtuousness to show that it also has an important part to play in the gravitational dynamic. These three factors are shown in Figure 4.1 as grounding the leader, keeping him or her centered and in touch with what is important despite all that is going on around.

1 Psychological Capital

According to Luthans et al. (Luthans, Luthans & Luthans, 2004; Luthans, Youssef & Avolio, 2007), psychological capital comprises four positive psychological concepts: hope, optimism, efficacy and resilience, which enable people to respond positively to workplace challenges. These authors position psychological capital as part of a continuum from traditional economic capital (what you have), through human capital (what you know) and social capital (who you know), toward positive psychological capital (who you are).

The concept of psychological capital as a set of important intrapersonal resources appears to have its origins in Seligman's (2002) work on

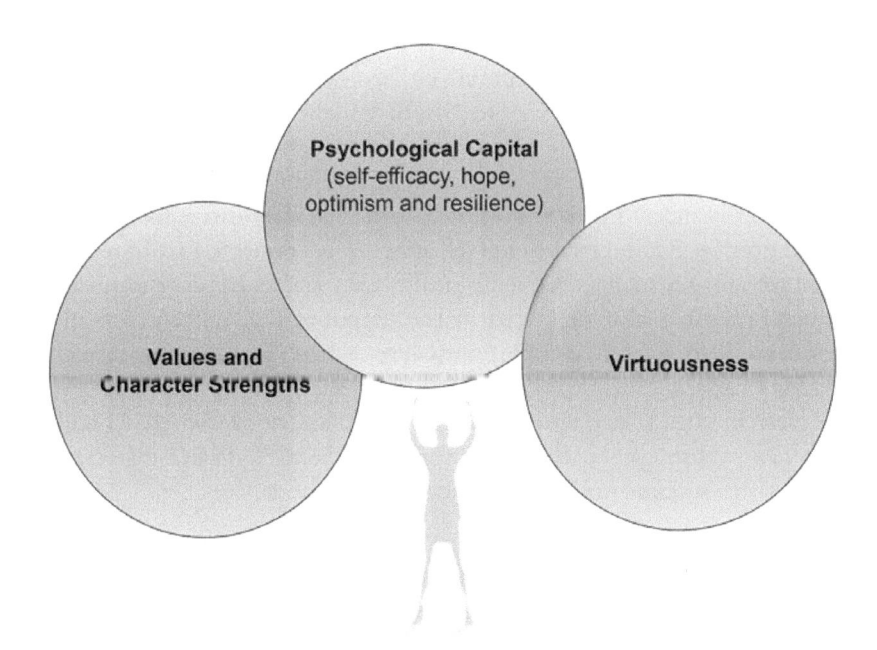

FIGURE 4.1 The gravitational factors

authentic happiness, where he proposed that it could be built through engagement in flow-type activities. It was also used by Stajkovic (2003) to explain core confidence factors in work motivation. Luthans et al. (2007) provide a more recent definition of psychological capital, suggesting that a person's positive psychological state of development is characterized by:

> (1) having confidence (efficacy) to take on and put in the necessary effort to succeed at challenging tasks; (2) making a positive attribution (optimism) about succeeding now and in the future; (3) persevering toward goals and, when necessary, redirecting paths to goals (hope) in order to succeed; and (4) when beset by problems and adversity, sustaining and bouncing back and even beyond (resilience) to attain success.
> *(Luthans et al., 2007, p.3)*

Luthans et al. (2007) also suggest that these four constructs have a positive impact on our attitudes, behaviors and performance. Various definitions of the constructs are available:

Self-efficacy/confidence

Drawing from Bandura (1991), efficacy is viewed as the conviction (or confidence) a person has about his or her abilities that enable them to complete tasks successfully: "to mobilize the motivation, cognitive resources, and courses of action needed to successfully execute a specific task within a given context" (Stajkovic & Luthans, 1998, p.66). People's motivation is affected if they do not believe that they can achieve success. In addition, as Bandura explains, self-efficacy is connected to other functional advantages such as reducing health risks and enhancing innovation. Interestingly, it is also suggested in the literature that self-efficacy affects the degree to which people persevere when faced with challenge (Maddux, 2002).

Research (e.g. Ladegard & Gjerde, 2014) has suggested that building self-efficacy through coaching reinforces a client's efficacy expectations and that this sustains further self-efficacy and confidence.

Hope

Hope has been defined by Dufault and Martocchio (1985) as a dynamic life force that embodies positive expectations of a realistically possible, but as yet uncertain future. Such future also needs to be of personal significance to the individual. More recently, hope has been described as a strength that helps overcome uncertainty (Peterson & Park, 2006, p.1151) and has been defined as a positive motivational state involving an interactively derived sense of successful agency (or goal-directed energy) and pathways (the plans necessary to meet those goals) (Snyder et al., 1991, p.287). Snyder et al. (2002) described hope as having the motivation necessary to move toward identified goals (agency), together with ways to achieve them (pathways). Hope is therefore seen as linked to a set of cognitive processes that aims at attaining specific goals even when beset with obstacles.

Over the last few years, research into hope and workplace stress has suggested that hope provides a certain protection against perceptions of loss of control and vulnerability (Snyder, 2000). Peterson and Park (2006) cite their study of cadets at a US military academy where the strength of hope predicts who stays in the service: indeed, the strength of hope is seen as being "associated with good health, long life, and freedom from 'accidents'" (p.1151).

Optimism

In positive psychology, optimism is depicted as both a positive future expectation that is open to development (Carver & Scheier, 2011) and an explanatory/attribution style, interpreting negative events as external, temporary and situation specific, and positive events as having opposite causes (i.e. personal, permanent and pervasive) (Seligman, 2002). When discussing hope and optimism, Snyder (2002, p.257) notes that similar to hope, "optimism is a goal-based cognitive process that operates whenever an outcome is perceived as having substantial value." Thus optimism is defined as the expectation that the future will bring good outcomes. Optimistic people expect to experience good things, whereas those who lack optimism assume they will encounter bad things in life (Scheier & Carver, 2009). Optimism thus involves reacting to setbacks from a "presumption of personal power" (Bayramoğlu & Şahin, 2015, p.155). Setbacks are not seen as permanent but are restricted to particular circumstances and so can be overcome by effort and ability.

Bandura (1998, p.56) confirms that: "evidence shows that human accomplishments and positive well-being require an optimistic sense of personal efficacy to override the numerous impediments to success." He goes on to state that "[s]uccess usually comes through renewed effort after failed attempts. It is resiliency of personal efficacy that counts" (ibid., p.62).

Resilience

Resilience is described by Luthans (2002, p.702) as "the capacity to rebound or bounce back from adversity, conflict, failure, or even positive events, progress, and increased responsibility." Resilience therefore refers to a process of adaptation, usually under difficult circumstances.

According to Coutu (2002), the common characteristics of resilient people are: "a staunch acceptance of reality; a deep belief, often buttressed by strongly held values, that life is meaningful; and an uncanny ability to improvise." Coutu argues that all three are needed for resilience, but emphasizes the last of the three—what she calls "ritualized ingenuity" (ibid., p.6).

This ability to improvise involves the ability to make the best of whatever is to hand, something Lévi-Strauss (1966) called "bricolage," which is defined as a type of inventiveness that arises from an ability to improvise a solution to a problem without proper or obvious tools or materials. Weick (1993) linked the idea of bricolage to the resilience that enables people to bounce back from a crisis by "maintaining both a coherence of identity and the capacity to act" (Duymedjian & Rüling, 2010, p.135).

Various associated research has focused on resilience as: the ability to function well during times of extreme hardship (stress resistance); recovery from traumatic or disturbing experiences (bouncing back); or adaptation as adverse conditions improve (normalization) (Cutuli & Masten, 2009). Research also suggests that resilient people experience positive emotions sometimes even during stressful events, illustrating a certain capacity to bounce back successfully in spite of difficulties (Tugade et al., 2004). Stephens et al. (2013, p.14) even argue that resilience is "an important facilitator in becoming virtuous."

Developing psychological capital

Luthans et al. (2007) and Avey, Luthans and Jensen (2009) have described how psychological capital can be developed in organizational settings using a cognitive behavioral approach. They explain how goals are used to guide the process and how the coach explains a need for:

- Concrete end points to measure success.
- An approach, rather than avoidance, framework that allows clients to work towards desired goals rather than away from them (for example, focusing on quality targets, rather than avoiding product rejects).
- Using the "stepping" method of identifying sub-goals (Snyder, 2000) in order to build efficacy along the way to the larger goal. Clients are

supported in generating multiple proactive pathways towards the goal, discussing and reflecting on any realistic (and unrealistic) options identified.*(Avey et al., 2009; Ives & Cox, 2012)*

Luthans et al. (2007) similarly describe the development of self-efficacy as involving five activities: goal setting, being open to challenging tasks, high self-motivation, application of effort towards goal accomplishment and perseverance through adversity. This process for developing psychological capital has been described by Avey et al. (2009, p.287) as enabling participants to take ownership of any "personally valuable and realistically challenging goal." Although essentially focused on solutions, during the development of self-efficacy, participants are prepared for obstacles that might arise and are primed to implement contingency plans or alternate pathways to attain their goals: "The facilitator and other participants serve as role models for the realistic optimism and efficacy-building processes that elicit these positive states and build employees' confidence to generate and implement plans to attain goals" (ibid., p.287).

An important aspect of this integrated strategy for developing psychological capital is that it enables participants to consider the impact of setbacks and to discuss what might be outside their control or to see where their sphere of influence might lie. So, integral to this developmental approach are discussions of hope and optimism, efficacy and resilience. The example dialogue below illustrates this:

COACH: Let's then explore the resources of hope, optimism, efficacy and resilience. If it's okay with you, I'd like to begin with hope.
CHRISTINE: Yes, that's fine with me.
COACH: Okay. In relation to your goal to change the opinion of the board, how hopeful are you?
CHRISTINE: Actually I am pretty hopeful, and perhaps even a little excited at the prospect.
COACH: What about optimism?
CHRISTINE: Well, I suppose as I'm hopeful that I can make the change, I'm also optimistic about that I can change their opinion.
COACH: Is that realistic?
CHRISTINE: Mmm. Yes, I think so. Were you thinking that I was being too unrealistic in my expectations—that I was somehow riding along on the crest of a wave of hope?
COACH: No, not at all, but how confident are you in your argument, what you are bringing to the table? Is there room for maneuver, to allow you to adapt, to still drive the idea home, convincingly?

66 Gravitational Factors

CHRISTINE: That's a good question. I think that I have a good argument, but just as you were talking there, I've had a slight niggling little feeling, probably doubting myself a bit, that maybe I haven't really thought through enough what else I need to do as a backup. What other moves could I make if I don't strike gold with the first pitch? And just thinking about that has left me feeling a little less confident than I was ... and actually that question you asked about me being realistic has made me think that maybe I was going to throw that idea out there and hope for the best. I was too high on the hope and optimism scale.

COACH: So maybe we might need to explore that?

CHRISTINE: Yes, I think that would be a good idea. Am I right in thinking that this would be connected to self-efficacy?

COACH: Yes that's it. And I'm also thinking that if we look at what you might do if you are thrown a curveball by the board, that this might help with your confidence before approaching them, and having contingency plans might also help with your residence, should the need for you to weather any kind of storm.

CHRISTINE: You think that there might be a storm? That's not helping my confidence much!

COACH: Ah! Perhaps that is the case right this second, but would you rather that we work on things now, deconstruct them a bit, and then put them back together so that you are familiar with all the pieces of the puzzle? Or shall we continue to surf that wave of hope and optimism?

CHRISTINE: [laughs] That's a bit harsh.

COACH: Remember, our focus is on realistic optimism, not optimism just for the sake of it.

CHRISTINE: Okay, let's look at the possible responses to my opening gambit.

From this discussion with Christine, we begin to see how it is possible to supplement the goal-oriented approach by identifying reactions to setbacks and using mental simulations to visualize success. Ives and Cox (2012, p.45) describe how in a goal-focused approach the coach can help the client by encouraging "efficacious goals, which will feed back into more optimistic expectancies thereby creating a cycle of improvement." These authors argue that by raising self-efficacy indirectly through helping with the achievement of successful outcomes, it creates a more accurate self-perception—one that is founded on actual performance results.

2 Virtues And Character Strengths

The second key aspect of building psychological capital is the identification and development of character strengths (Peterson & Park, 2006). Although character strengths are not included explicitly in Luthans et al.'s (2007) definition of psychological capital, we consider they could be a key contributor to the other core psychological capital constructs and so should be part of that discussion. Indeed, a number of researchers (e.g. Govindji & Linley, 2007; Pritchard, 2009) have suggested that understanding our strengths and using them appropriately links significantly to our self-efficacy and can potentially lead to increased resilience. In addition, as Elston and Boniwell (2011) found, developing and using specific strengths results in an increase in positive emotions, such as hope and optimism. Similarly, Peterson and Park (2006, p.1151) have identified hope as a character strength and associate it with both life and work satisfaction across a complete range of occupations, including leadership.

Peterson and Seligman's (2004) work on virtues and strengths combines in an inventory of virtues in action. In that inventory they define virtues as "the core characteristics valued by moral philosophers and religious thinkers," and strengths as "the psychological ingredients—processes or mechanisms—that define the virtues" (p.13). The concept of a virtue, which encompasses hope, empathy, compassion and forgiveness is, according to Peterson and Seligman, accepted as the standard for the best of the human condition, and according to Cameron (2011) it has no negative connotation; it cannot be exceeded. The psychological "ingredients" that make up the strengths include our values, which might vary depending on with which culture or organization we align. The virtues could be described as thematic or categorical concepts that encompass the habits, values and strengths that people possess and which produce social good (Gowri, 2007), whilst the values or strengths are a sub-set of these. Peterson and Seligman (2004, p.18) described strengths as akin to personal traits: "strengths of character that a person owns, celebrates, and frequently exercises." Similarly, Ruch et al. (2010) suggested that each person possesses all of the character strengths in varying degrees, thus creating a distinct individual profile.

Ruch et al. (2010) provide a useful taxonomy of the six core virtues and 24 character strengths that make up the commonly used "values in action" (VIA) classification (see Box 4.1). The VIA survey (an online test is freely available on the VIA Institute website) can be a useful tool for executive coaches to suggest to their clients, and the resulting conversations can focus on how core values and character strengths can be used or strengthened.

BOX 4.1 SIX CORE VIRTUES AND 24 CHARACTER STRENGTHS

1 Wisdom

Creativity (originality, ingenuity)
Curiosity (interest, novelty seeking, openness to experience)
Judgment (critical thinking)
Love of learning (mastering new skills, topics and bodies of knowledge)
Perspective (wisdom)

2 Courage

Bravery (valor, speaking up for what is right even if there is opposition, acting on convictions even if unpopular)
Perseverance (persistence, industriousness)
Honesty (authenticity, integrity)
Zest (vitality, enthusiasm, vigor, energy)

3 Humanity

Love (valuing close relations with others)
Kindness (generosity, nurturance, care, compassion, altruistic love)
Social intelligence (emotional intelligence, personal intelligence)

4 Justice: Civic strengths that underlie healthy community life

Teamwork (citizenship, social responsibility, loyalty; working well as a member of a group or team; being loyal to the group; doing one's share)
Fairness (treating all people the same according to notions of fairness and justice; not letting personal feelings bias decisions about others; giving everyone a fair chance)
Leadership (encouraging a group of which one is a member to get things done, and at the same time maintaining good relations within the group; organizing group activities and seeing that they happen)

5 Temperance: Strengths that protect against excess

Forgiveness (forgiving those who have done wrong; accepting the shortcomings of others; giving people a second chance; not being vengeful)
Humility (letting one's accomplishments speak for themselves; not regarding oneself as more special than one is)

> *Prudence* (being careful about one's choices; not taking undue risks; not saying or doing things that might later be regretted)
> *Self-regulation* (self-control; regulating what one feels and does; being disciplined; controlling one's appetites and emotions)
>
> **6 Transcendence: Strengths that forge connections to the larger universe and provide meaning**
>
> *Appreciation of beauty and excellence* (awe, wonder, elevation; noticing and appreciating beauty, excellence and/or skilled performance in various domains of life, from nature to art to mathematics to science to everyday experience)
> *Gratitude* (being aware of and thankful for the good things that happen; taking time to express thanks)
> *Hope* (optimism, future-mindedness, future orientation)
> *Humor* (playfulness)
> *Spirituality* (having coherent beliefs about the higher purpose and meaning of the universe)
>
> *(Adapted from Ruch et al., 2010)*

Peterson and Park (2006) have explained how particular character strengths are associated with different life contexts. For example, they suggest that both life satisfaction and work satisfaction include gratitude, hope, zest, curiosity and love, with hope being the strength that "allows people to overcome uncertainty and to stay the course" (ibid., p.1151). They go on to suggest a link between love and accomplishments as a leader: their research showed how the "capacity to love and be loved" predicted their cadets' accomplishments as leaders.

Dahlsgaard, Peterson and Seligman (2005) have shown that the six virtues of wisdom, courage, humanity, justice, temperance and transcendence identified in Box 4.1 are valued by the majority of world cultures in the West and in the East. More recently, Lanctot and Irving (2010, p.33) have suggested that "values tend to define cultures or characteristics of roles within an organization or social construct, while virtues transcend cultures and other socially-embedded constructs." Universally accepted virtues such as courage might involve different value sets in different countries, but still remain a desirable virtue.

The core virtues are in turn made up of a number of character strengths, such as perseverance, honesty, love, gratitude, hope and kindness, each of which gains in value as we identify it in others and exercise it to a greater or lesser extent ourselves. Linley (2008, p.9) describes a strength as "a preexisting capacity for a particular way of behaving, thinking, or feeling that is authentic and energising to the user, and enables optimal functioning, development and performance."

Descriptions such as Linley's which attribute virtues to the individual and identify them as "pre-existing" character "traits" that are sustained over time are misleading. An alternative view is provided by situational psychologists such as Annas (2003), who provides a counter-argument that is important to us in this book. She argues that virtues like courage are situational and that "our actions are explained to a far greater extent than we believe by situations that we are in, sometimes features of situations of which we are not even aware" (Annas, 2003, n.p.). For example, if a leader takes the seemingly courageous decision to make 50 people redundant next week in order to secure the future of the organization and ensure jobs for the remaining 150 people in the workforce, this does not mean that he will make a similar "brave" decision in a different set of circumstances. At another time and with different information to inform the decision, this same leader may decide to take a different course of action, which may or may not be considered brave.

Hannah et al. (2011, p.560) have argued that based on Bandura's social cognitive theory, people will "develop moral courage as they act or 'say no' and assess the impact of those choices and feedback from others." Miller (2002, p.26) earlier summarized this succinctly, saying: "courage is one of those things that can only be properly attained by doing it. To get courage, be courageous." This suggests that not only are virtues, like courage, situational, but they can also only be developed through situations. Annas described how, "if we are in familiar, repeated situations, then we can build up a local trait of acting in a certain way, but these traits do not have 'cross-situational consistency'; if we predict that people will act consistently with that trait in a different situation, most people will let us down" (Annas, 2003, n.p.). If this is so, and leaders have the potential for "local traits" (ibid.), which are encouraged by repeatable situations, then the support of a coach to encourage understanding of the situations seems indispensible.

Doris (2005, p.633) has further argued that virtues are also typical instances of such traits. He argues that if we have courage, we are expected consistently to behave courageously, despite possible inducements to do otherwise. However, he cautions:

> Here's the trouble: There exist quantities of empirical evidence indicating that behavior varies quite radically with slight situational variations, such as whether the actor is in a hurry, has enjoyed a modest

bit of good fortune, or observes an emergency in a group or alone. Given this situational variability, people's behavior is likely to be quite *inconsistent* with regard to the patterns expected on familiar trait categories, such as those embodied in philosophical writing on the virtues.

(Doris, 2005, p.633, original emphasis)

Annas (2003) also points out that Doris believes character to be "fragmented" and so we cannot count on the brave tendencies we develop in one kind of situation to carry over to others. Doris (2002, pp.62–64) thus appears to have a "localist" account of traits, arguing that we are "all fragmented selves." Indeed, we tend to agree, since if as coaches we thought of the self as a pre-existing integrated whole, then there would be little work that we, as coaches, could do to help clients develop and change. The work would belong to the psychologist trying to make the client whole again. We agree with Doris that the idealized psychology of character, of which strengths are a part, is best thought of as a heuristic, a mechanism that is useful for helping us "get along in the world, and with each other" (Doris, 2005, p.633).

According to Doris, then, local traits are all we have; thinking of ourselves as having global traits which unify our practical reasoning is a mistake and we cannot expect the tendency we have developed in one situation to be carried over to another. In addition, as Annas (2003) points out, rather than continuing to be reinforced, a trait might be destabilized by features of a new situation, features such as being in a rush, being in a group, or features of which we might not even be aware. It could be, therefore, that our attitude to life needs to be more a matter of strategy and becoming, being in search of or avoiding particular situations, rather than falling back on possessing a unified character. Doris (2002) also argues that personality typically has a quite weak effect on moral behavior compared with the massive effects that situations can have.

This situationalist approach chimes with a developmental coaching philosophy and suggests that the role of the coach is to encourage the leader to use tools and strategies to analyze situations to arrive at brave solutions. It is more a matter of developing strategy, than developing traits, although we do suggest that discussion of strengths can be illuminating starting points for a developmental conversation. However, as Annas (2003) also suggests, we should not rely too much on superficial, conventional understandings of virtues. Supporting this situationalist argument, we would suggest that understanding the potential of character strengths can be an important part of developing and performing as a brave leader, as long as we don't view them as static.

As another example, we can see that whereas some researchers have described courage as a core virtue comprising a number of emotional strengths that involve "the exercise of will to accomplish goals in the face of opposition" (Peterson & Seligman, 2004, p.1150), others suggest that challenging environments actually encourage personal agency so that when people are faced with ethical challenges their moral courage is created right there in that environment (Sekerka & Bagozzi, 2007). Both positions can be seen to be correct, if we think of character strengths as part of a dynamic self system that adapts according to different situations (see Hill & Roberts, 2010). So courage can be built. Indeed, Luthans et al. (2007) confirm that rather than being static, traits such as character strengths are more temporary and "state-like," and are open to development.

Developing character strengths

A focus on character strengths and virtues is congruent with most people's ideas of human flourishing and how to provide solutions to life's challenges. Many clients might also find the explicit goals of being more courageous, caring or honest more inspiring than those of simply solving problems or engaging in more positive thoughts or actions.

Kaiser and Overfield (2011) have suggested that one of the ways of augmenting discussions of strengths with the leader would be to incorporate a 360° feedback process. Following the use of any personality tool, such as the VIA strength survey, co-worker feedback can be elicited to provide feedback on how the leader is perceived in the workplace. Such feedback could ask questions such as, "Does the leader balance control and delegation?" or "Does the leader pay too much attention to detail, or to the loudest voices?" The combination of these two methods of awareness raising (a strengths inventory and 360° feedback) could be very powerful for developing the leader and provide useful material in the coaching session. We would caution, however, that whilst 360° feedback can be informative, it should not be considered as empirical evidence. It is a tool like any other, and it does have its limitations. There are many factors that can skew the findings of this type of approach, including: how the questions were worded; how they were interpreted; how confidential the exercise was perceived to be; if the leader had just done something unpopular; if someone had an "axe to grind"; and if the leader had just done something really brave!

Buckingham and Clifton (2004) cites deep concentration as a potential pathway for the benefits derived from strengths use. This model claims that greater cognitive activity is responsible for the increased achievement associated with strengths use. In most models of development of character strengths, problems are reframed into specific opportunities to develop (Peterson & Seligman, 2004; Buckingham & Clifton, 2004). For example, courage could be enhanced through refusing to give in to social or peer pressure, taking a stand on unpopular suggestions or decisions, acting against abuses of power or unethical practices, identifying the values that have served us well in previous challenging situations, confronting difficult and challenging situations despite our fears.

In the following extract from a coaching session with John, strengths are discussed. Although a strengths conversation is distinct from a values elicitation conversation, we chose this example because there is an overlap here between values and strengths. This does not always happen, of course, but when it does, it illustrates the non-linear aspect of coaching models and how both coach and client can be flexible in sequence and approach.

COACH: I thought that in exploring these strengths that we could begin by focusing on one which you have mentioned several times during our conversations.

JOHN: Is it fairness by any chance?

COACH: [laughs] Yes, it is as a matter of fact. Fairness is viewed as a character strength, and you seem to view it as being very important.

JOHN: I really do think that it is very important.

COACH: I'm curious, do you view fairness as important at this point in time because of all that is going on and all that you want to achieve, or is it less situational for you than that?

JOHN: Do you know, that is an interesting question, because it has been coming more and more into my mind about how important it is, and I think this is because of a few issues that I'm having to deal with right now. However, I'm beginning to suspect that it is something that's been bubbling away under the surface for quite some time, and may in fact have been something that has always been important to me, at least since school. In fact, I think that recent events have simply reconnected me to that feeling of the need for fairness.

COACH: And so is fairness something you would consider impacts your decision making?

JOHN: Well once again, your question is curiously pertinent. When I said that it had been bubbling away under the surface, I also realized that it had been literally under the surface.

COACH: In what sense?

JOHN: In the sense that I had become accustomed to the organization's habits—perhaps even a little institutionalized. And putting it bluntly, I think there are times when I let my sense of fair play be swept under the carpet, both by others and by my own lack of conviction.
COACH: Lack of conviction to what?
JOHN: Lack of conviction to doing the right thing in certain situations. Not acting on what was fair. Going along with the others.
COACH: And yet I thought that it was a strength of yours.
JOHN: I think that it used to be. I want it back. I've missed it. I feel I haven't been being true to myself.
COACH: Is it back now?
JOHN: It is definitely much more in my awareness.
COACH: How can we get it to be more of a "go to" virtue for you then?
JOHN: Well, simply talking about it really helps, and having the time to reflect has also been very useful. And so I think that I need to reflect more on this. You also mentioned a while back that when we go on our decision-making journey, I would be encouraged to think about what I value and that it might be useful to draw up a list. Well, if I was to make a list then fairness should definitely be near the top.
COACH: Of course.
JOHN: I know that this might sound a little like one of those "road to Damascus" moments, but I realize that I haven't even included it in my set of values. I'm genuinely shocked by that. I think that it was early on in our relationship, and being brutally honest with myself, I was too busy at playing the corporate game, imagining how what I was saying might sound to the board. Hence I talked about flexibility, intellect, decisiveness, etc.—nothing wrong with them, except that I had lost a bit of me at that point. I can't believe I did that.
COACH: Don't be too hard on yourself. We did discuss this as being a journey, an evolution. The great news is that you have realized this now. So not only are we going to be able to redefine your values to truly reflect who you are, we can work on fairness as one of your key strengths. And when we get to the decision-making part, I suspect that you will want to access that strength.

3 Virtuousness

In the previous section we explored the related concepts of virtues and strengths as proposed by Peterson and Seligman (2004). In this section we want to focus in more detail on the notion of virtuousness, which we claim forms a key part of the gravitational dynamic. Virtuousness is closely linked with values and the concept of psychological capital, providing an anchoring point as well as being associated with increased performance and wellbeing (Cameron, 2011).

To begin, rather than adopt Peterson and Seligman's seemingly one-dimensional definition of virtues we prefer to recognize Lanctot and Irving's more nuanced definition which takes account of the situationalist argument:

> A set of related personal attributes or dispositions that (a) is universal and not contextual (MacIntyre, 1981; Peterson & Seligman, 2004), (b) has moral implications that extend beyond the individual (Ciulla, 2001), (c) has recognition that possessing it without excess is considered good and lacking it is considered harmful (Koehn, 1998), and (d) can be attained through practice (Strang, 2005).
> *(Lanctot & Irving, 2010, p.32)*

In particular we like the inclusion of a moral imperative extending beyond individual concerns and the recognition that virtues are open to development through practice. This last point supports the contention that virtues are "contextual, learned habits that reflect and involve discriminating moral judgment and deliberation, activities that form part of an interdependent narrative of what it is to be virtuous" (Cunha et al., 2013, p.455).

The idea of virtuousness is discussed by Bright, Cameron and Caza (2006), who explain how it is different from ethics in that "choices are made, not only from the standpoint of living within the constraints of ethical rules, but also from the perspective of building personal and communal excellence" (p.249). According to them, virtuousness has its roots in a Latin word, "virtus," meaning "excellence," and was described by Plato and Aristotle as the action producing "personal and social good" (ibid., p.251). It encompasses the best of the human condition and there is the assumption that human beings naturally incline towards moral goodness and that virtuousness is inherent; developing in the brain even before language (Cameron, 2011; Haidt, 2006), so that we are genetically disposed to being virtuous.

Thus an ethics of virtuousness within an organization relates to "the pursuit of the highest aspirations in the human condition" and is characterized by its human impact, moral goodness, and unconditional societal betterment (Bright et al., 2006, p.249). In as much as it seeks the high point of human endeavor, virtuousness deviates away from the normal standards of just being healthy and effective and moves instead towards positive attention on wellness and excellence. This process is described by

Bright et al. as a form of "positive deviance" (ibid., p.250), which is concerned with the development of excellence in human and organizational character and virtue. There is also later research that confirms that a virtuous leader creates an upward spiral of positive forces: Fredrickson (2009) found that all aspects of organizations as well as individual social, intellectual and emotional capacities, were expanded and increased by a positive approach. Both coaching and leadership can be seen as professions that closely follow that philosophy.

Being virtuous is also different from being ethical. As suggested in the introduction to this book, ethical behavior focuses on duty: "avoiding harm, fulfilling contracts, ensuring compliance and obeying rules and laws" (Cameron, 2011, p.26). Ethical acts are those that reach "some minimal moral standard and are therefore not unethical, such as honesty or obeying the law" (Treviño et al., 2006, p. 952). Virtuousness, on the other hand, has a positive bias, focusing on flourishing and enriching. Cameron describes how virtuousness "does not stand in opposition to concepts such as citizenship, social responsibility, or ethics, but it extends beyond them." According to Cameron, it is a "universal and stable standard of the good" (Cameron, 2011, p.26): decisions are made for the purpose of building individual and organizational excellence.

In addition, we want to stress that being virtuous does not involve the pursuit of reward. Rather, it is doing things for the right reasons. If a leader or employee is being virtuous in order to manipulate some kind of payback, then that self-interest negates the claim to being virtuous.

However, although anticipation of reward is not a part of virtuousness, virtue does bring its own rewards: research is beginning to show that an organizational culture characterized by virtuousness amongst leaders and employees actually increases performance and economic outcomes (Cameron et al., 2011). This ties in with a comment made by a financial director we know: "Profit is an outcome of getting the people bit right."

This difference between ethical behavior and virtuousness is, we believe, one of the key differentiators between ethical leadership and brave leadership. We initially struggled with the question, "if we have ethical leaders, why do we need braver leaders?" Later in the book, in Chapter 10, we discuss how brave leadership links to some other leadership schools of thought, and we make some important observations there. However, if we were to summarize just one of the important differences between brave leadership and ethical leadership, we would say that although both ethical leaders and brave leaders need to be conscious of ethical practice, brave leaders will go beyond what has to be done to comply; they do what must be done to fly.

Developing virtuousness

In this section on developing virtuousness, we illustrate how present and future challenges can be approached using two models that emerged from our research. The first we call "doing the right thing" (Figure 4.2). The second is the retroductive analysis of outcomes and antecedents (Figure 4.3).

Doing the right thing

In "doing the right thing" there are four interrelated aspects which reflect the moral imperative of "doing right," which can each be practiced and learned.

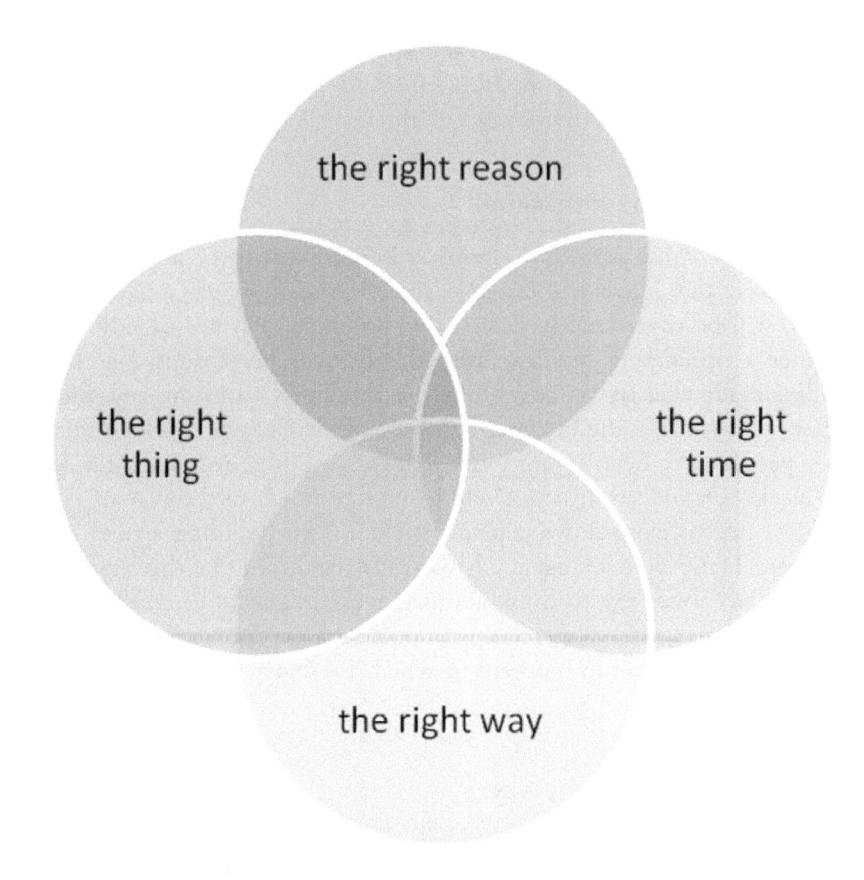

FIGURE 4.2 Doing the right thing

Doing the right thing:

The idea of doing the "right thing" is used by the Chartered Institute of Purchasing and Supply (2007), which emphasizes the logistical importance of getting the right goods, at the right time, etc. We think that there is something inherently powerful about using the phrase "doing the right thing," as this links with recent calls for virtuousness in organizations (Cameron, 2011).

Doing things for the right reason:

Doing things for the right reason links directly to ethics and values, but these need to be wider than personal or organizational values—they need to have a social, ecological or wider moral value. If the reason for doing a thing is not "right" —i.e. it clashes and is misaligned with either the values of the leader and/or the organization—then it is unlikely that a longer-term successful outcome will ultimately be achieved.

Doing things at the right time:

Doing things at the right time involves being attuned to situations. It is highly likely that bravery in business, just as in its more physical manifestations, will be connected to timing. For example, it is not exactly brave to enter a smoldering building after the fire has been doused and the building made safe. By the same token, it is unlikely to be the epitome of bravery to challenge the bullying behavior of a colleague if several dozen other people have been saying exactly the same thing, every day, for several weeks. Or indeed, it is unlikely to require much in the way of positive deviance to close down a plant that has been polluting a river if an environmental protection agency has already instructed that this should be done. In fact, one way to think about bravery might be to consider that the height of bravery is inversely proportional to distance, in terms of time, from the optimum moment at which the brave action should have been taken.

Doing things in the right way:

Doing things in the right way is also a key element of the brave leadership process. We can imagine how a leader might use the idea of bravery and doing the right thing as an excuse to drive through an agenda in a way that is simply not ideal. In some ways we could draw an analogy here between a government needing to raise taxes, and invoking the ire of the population by the mechanism by which those taxes are raised. In a broad sense an organization needs to make a profit, but how it makes that profit can send a pulse though the organization which signals not only to customers but also to employees what the true culture is.

An example will illustrate how the model has worked in practice. We discussed the idea of "doing the right thing" with Christine, the financial director of a multimillion-dollar organization in the transport sector. It should be said at the outset that Christine firmly believes that bravery is a hugely important component in being successful in business, but also that the "people stuff" is not the "soft stuff" but the "hard stuff"—hard because it is easy to get it wrong if the wrong leadership is in place, and hard also because getting the people bit right can deliver some hard numbers, some real business improvement.

Christine had been talking to her immediate senior team about doing the right thing and being brave within the organization, and whilst she was the first to admit that what she had witnessed could hardly be called a scientific study, she believes that using the language of "braver" and "doing the right thing" has significantly transformed the culture in that team. She knows that there is still a long way to go, but cites an example where a big financial risk had to be taken, which it ultimately was, emphasizing that if it had not been taken, the organization would have quickly become competitively unviable. Her conviction is that if the idea of bravery and rightness had not become the new "buzzwords" for the senior team, this would never have been allowed to happen.

The "doing the right thing" process encourages a discussion around how both past and upcoming challenges may be approached from different angles to ensure a brave outcome. Used as a focus for discussion, scenario planning and subsequent action, the process can be useful to refine definitions and point towards a preferred outcome: "the hypothetical preparation involved in creating potential scenarios alerts [leaders] to critical information that they might otherwise have missed" (Cox, 2013, p.152).

Developing insight: Retroductive analysis

In this section we want to show how retroductive analysis can be used as a powerful coaching tool. It can be used in many ways, but there are probably two distinct uses as far as braver leadership coaching is concerned.

First, much is made in the coaching literature of the distinction that coaching tends to look forward whilst some therapeutic approaches delve into the past to attempt to ascertain the root causes of certain present-day behaviors (Bluckert, 2005). However, it is also important for coaches and their clients to gain insights into why certain outcomes happened, for without this knowledge, learning can be diminished. Coaches and clients need to have an idea of goals and preferred outcomes and so coaching cannot function in an environment where there is no thought at all of the past. So whilst we absolutely would not advocate the coach developing a conversation about the formative childhood years of the client, as some forms of therapy might, we would suggest that a retroductive understanding of the connection between performance effect and behavioral cause could be extremely beneficial. In fact, retroductive analysis could well be a significant addition to the successful coach's toolkit.

Retroductive analysis provides a helpful method for tracking back through previous experience to examine how current situations or outcomes have been arrived at. The process involves taking a visible and tangible end point and then reasoning backwards by examining where earlier in the process or experience there were indications (antecedents) of the eventual outcome. This technique is a useful way of understanding habits and reducing blind spots for individuals, but could also be useful for leaders when considering previous successful or brave outcomes and what led up to those.

A second use for a retroductive approach in coaching, and one that is most applicable to a braver leadership context is that it can help uncover where values have been overlooked and/or where a brave opportunity was missed. This insight may illustrate where a gravitational factor, for instance, had been ignored and/or a pulling factor inappropriately favored. It may also uncover where the leader has actually been brave in the past.

Although it may be used discretely at any point in the coaching alliance, we include retroductive analysis at this point in the coaching model because gravitational factors are unique to each individual and may in some instances need to be teased out. Through the use of a retroductive approach an important gravitational factor, for example, may be accidentally elicited.

Although we are suggesting that the use of retroduction may be an elegant addition to the coaching approach, it is probably useful to set out some broad red flag indicators that may suggest reasoning backwards has entered into therapeutic territory:

- the discussion veers towards traumatic, painful, disturbing or emotionally upsetting memories, particularly those from a formative time;
- particularly odd behaviors are uncovered;

- the coach begins to suggest reasons for these strange behaviors; or
- the discussion deviates away from organizational and career cause and effect.

This list is far from exhaustive. Much has been written about the differences between coaching and therapy, and it is not our intention to duplicate that work here. What we would say is that retroduction can yield great rewards, and it should be approached by the coach and client with the same mindset that they would use to solve a puzzle: an enquiring mind, a light touch, a genuine intrigue about what may lie behind the particular outcome being considered.

Some key things to remember about retroductive analysis in relation to coaching are:

- it deals with a known tangible outcome;
- this outcome is not simply presumed or guessed at—it exists;
- the outcome or end point is not being debated;
- there should be distinct and traceable steps backward from the end point; and
- the coach is helping the client to explore, and is not interpreting events for them.

Jessop (2005) suggests that retroduction involves asking what the real world must be like for a specific outcome to be actualized. This differs from an inductive approach, which seeks to generalize from a number of cases to something broader, and deduction, which seeks to make sense of a case or cases from a pre-ordained theory. Retroduction is concerned with checking our working hypotheses against our observations—"the logic of discovery" (Rosental, 1993). In Jessop's (2005, p.43) words, knowledge is produced through a continuing process of confrontation between "retroductive theoretical hypotheses about intransitive objects and evidential statements generated in and through transitive enquiry." A retroductive approach is therefore useful because it gets at the factual reality behind subjective and shifting evidential statements: it tests what happened in reality to arrive at the current reported situation.

Retroduction involves moving from the level of observations and lived experience to postulating about the underlying structures and mechanisms that account for the phenomenon or change involved (Mingers, 2003). Doval (2008, p.504) uses the example of Sherlock Holmes explaining his methods to Dr Watson in "A Study in Scarlet" (Conan Doyle, 1887, p.86): "there are a few people, however, who, if you told them the result, would be able to evolve from their own inner consciousness what the steps were which led up to that result." Conan Doyle had Holmes describe this as "reasoning backwards." So whilst Sherlock Holmes used deductive logic, he almost certainly at certain points also used a retroductive process.

The process involves taking a visible and tangible end point and then reasoning backwards by examining where earlier in the leader's experience there were indications of the eventual outcome. This is demonstrated in a coaching meeting with Christine, where retroduction was used to gain insight into a previous decision:

COACH: And so, what was the decision?
CHRISTINE: Well, the decision was to change the packaging to something biodegradable—and it wasn't easy, I can tell you, particularly as it is going to be more expensive, at least in the short term.
COACH: I wasn't sure that you were going to go down that route.
CHRISTINE: Neither was I, in fact I can't quite believe that we agreed on it, and I really can't believe that I decided to pursue this with the board.
COACH: What changed?
CHRISTINE: I'm not sure. And I think I'd like to think about that.
COACH: Well, when did you begin to seriously consider this as a viable idea?
CHRISTINE: About three months ago.
COACH: What happened?
CHRISTINE: I was watching a wildlife program and marveling at how every scrap of nutrient can be harvested out of a sometimes very barren environment, how generally nothing goes to waste, how everything is utilized. Now there right away is an example of nature's version of something being biodegradable. I knew all about that, of course, but what really struck me was the balance, the beauty, the almost clockwork-like efficiency, but particularly the balance.
COACH: Is that something that is important to you?
CHRISTINE: Actually, yes, it is, when I think about it. I love balance in life, in sport, in energy conservation. There is such a beauty and elegance in balance.
COACH: And was it at this point that you decided to tackle the board with the biodegradable packaging idea?
CHRISTINE: Actually, no. I remember now that the actual point was when I was taking my sister's children out to the park. It was about four weeks later. I thought about the wildlife in that situation, about

Gravitational Factors 83

how self-contained and in balance that little ecosystem was, right in the center of a city. And then I looked at the children and realized that they deserved to be in the center of a balanced ecosystem, and that businesses, like leaders, are at their best when they are in balance. And then it really struck me that our business was actually out of balance, and that businesses are part of a much, much bigger ecosystem. And that the name of the game had to be sustainability. Businesses must have a sustainability conscience and take active steps to promote this.

Figure 4.3 shows the retroductive process undertaken by Christine following her successful decision-making outcome with her senior team.

In this example, we have seen how Christine, through looking at the evolution of her thinking, has uncovered two important personal values: balance and sustainability. She also uncovered two values that were an enabler in her making a brave decision and taking a brave action.

Some further questions that the coach might use to prompt retroductive thinking are:

- At what points in the last five years have you felt strongly about events?
- Starting from where you are now, where have there been tensions or unusually low or high energy in the previous six months of board meetings?
- How has your brave role model influenced how you got here?
- What preceded that behavior?
- What was compelling you to do that?

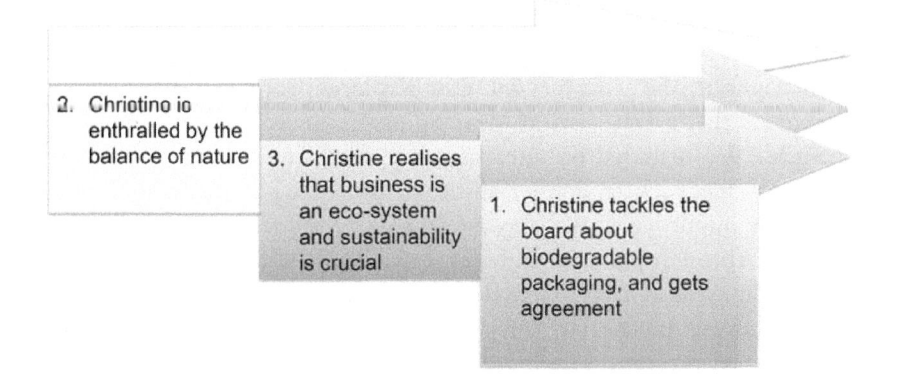

2. Christine is enthralled by the balance of nature
3. Christine realises that business is an eco-system and sustainability is crucial
1. Christine tackles the board about biodegradable packaging, and gets agreement

FIGURE 4.3 The retroductive analysis process

- What was behind that?
- What was the event before that?

There could also be a third use for retroductive analysis in the evaluation of coaching. Coaching has the advantage of producing distinct end points and outcomes, and these outcomes can be used as a "lens" or filter through which to analyze the coaching process that has occurred—the interpretation of the events in time which led up to that outcome. We would suggest, therefore, that the kind of reasoning backwards that retroduction involves could also be a useful tool for reflection on the outcomes of coaching. In coaching there will normally be an end point—a conclusion to the assignment with some tangible outcome. At a practical level there may be observable actions taken. At a causal level the picture is less clear and this is where a retroductive analysis can provide insight.

Summary

In this chapter we have examined the psychological features that ground leaders in their work.

We called these features "gravitational factors," proposing that these are the areas that ground or "center" leaders when they are being pulled off course by the tensions of the organization. These are the concepts of self-efficacy, hope, optimism and resilience, as well as the virtues and strengths that help leaders to position or site themselves, especially at times when they may be being pulled off course.

We also included a discussion of virtuousness as a way of being that provides another anchoring point for the leader. In our research, leaders suggested that "doing the right thing" was part of being brave. This idea of "rightness" also includes timeliness, doing things in the right way and for the right reason.

Throughout the chapter we also explored some of the coaching approaches that can be used to develop psychological capital and enhance strengths. We included the idea of using strengths inventories combined with 360° feedback to get a realistic picture of what gravitational needs the leader might have. We also introduced retroduction as a way of tracing back through previous experience, and indeed through the coaching experience itself, as a way of understanding how the present outcome has been achieved. In fact, we suggested that the discussion of virtues and strengths and the retroductive analysis should be considered as important processes in the quest for brave leadership and should not be overlooked. They are key to enhancing the leader's self-understanding, which in turn underpins bravery. We consider that these two tools are vital in building the "brave muscle" needed to tackle leadership tasks well.

In Chapter 5 we begin to explore in more depth how coaching can help leaders to find a balance between the organizational tensions and their gravitational factors.

5

FINDING BALANCE

Emotional and moral self-awareness

Introduction

Leaders, we would argue, are like dancers and athletes in that they need a strong "core"; not necessarily a strong physical core, but a strong emotional core. A strong physical core is centered in the upper body and allows other parts of the body to perform quality movements. In physical terms, then, a strong core is necessary for dancers and anyone who wants to enjoy stability and independence in movement; with a weak core our power in movement is reduced. This "core" idea is linked to the notion of finding balance or centering, and involves "working with traits such as physical grounding, center of gravity, alignment, stance and posture, confidence, strength, and endurance" (Robbins, 2014, p.2). Robbins explains how core centering can help people deal with pressure and achieve equilibrium. He also suggests that there are more subtle adaptations arising from core centering, which can include "intuition, the flow state, gut feelings, sixth sense, premonition or precognition, seeing from the center, the unitive experience, and oneness with the world" (ibid., p.2). In combination, he claims, these transformative practices can be the basis for a breakthrough in performance, as well as in life.

By analogy, a strong, balanced core would seem vital for brave leaders too. Leaders frequently face situations where pulling factors such as policy, organizational norms and peer pressures thrust them out of alignment. Such competing values can not only threaten effective decision making, making shortcuts more attractive, but can also be a menace to the stability of leadership direction. The leadership role can also be enormously stressful and it is recognized that too much stress and pressure can diminish rational thinking and decision-making capability. This chapter therefore looks at ways in which the leader and the coach can explore and balance the very normal needs and emotions of being a leader as a way of starting to develop a stronger core and a more integrated/inter-individual way of being, deciding and acting. Some coaches use a cognitive behavioral approach to explore the links between emotional reactions and behaviors (Neenan & Palmer, 2013). However, there is often little emphasis on calibrating the client's current emotional landscape, in order to balance thinking and behaviors.

In this chapter we introduce the part of the brave coaching model that is concerned with finding balance, and examine how the pulling factors and the gravitational factors are often in tension, resulting in unwelcome emotions or stress, thus impacting wellbeing. Pulling factors can create disturbances that conflict with prime values, needs and emotions and pull leaders in directions that they know are not ethically, environmentally or morally sustainable. Yet sometimes the tensions appear to satisfy some real needs, including material needs necessary to provide for the family, or work goals that satisfy our sense of achievement. In some extreme cases indulgence of these needs could be classified as ego gratification, megalomania or greed.

For the brave enterprise to succeed, it is therefore important for the leader to take stock of a number of areas that can support a strong, balanced emotional core. We have already mentioned in Chapter 4, a number of skills and processes that could be seen as maintaining a balanced core, such as building resilience which acts in the same way as resistance training—to strengthen the core. There are a number of other ways of strengthening that core and finding the balance needed to support a brave stance. Sekerka (2010, p.6) suggests that our initial reactions, particularly to ethical challenges, need an understanding of emotional responses and time for reflection. She argues that "to habitually pursue right action and to manage and address tough ethical decisions, individuals must balance their reactions, knowing how to manage responsibilities along side of their own personal desires" (ibid., p.6). Sekerka (2010) and Sekerka, McCarthy and Bagozzi (2011) have also noted four specific areas that can be strengthened in order to increase moral courage, and these are also useful to guide development of courageous responses to tackling challenges. These are: emotional awareness, reflective pause, self-regulation and moral preparation. We shall expand on these four core balancing competencies in more detail in the rest of this chapter.

1 Emotional Awareness

Boyatzis et al. (2013, p.21) have pointed out how emotional competencies enable leaders to generate "a sense of shared hope and vision with others, shared compassion and shared mindfulness." They have explained that to be an effective leader "a person needs to understand and skillfully manage his emotions appropriately based on each person or situation and understand the emotional cues of others in order to effectively interact with others" (ibid., p.2).

Sekerka et al. (2011) have also suggested how emotional awareness helps individuals attend to the way in which emotions are expressed. For example, they consider that people with professional moral courage do not ignore, repress or sublimate negative feelings, such as confusion or helplessness. They use this affective information instead as a signal to reflect and then to proceed with caution and care towards better coping and self-regulation. Positive feelings are also important to be aware of. Garland et al. (2010) have suggested that the "broaden and build" effect of positive emotions can help counter states such as fear. Fundamentally, the broaden and build theory suggests that it is highly likely that we can become more resourceful and resilient when faced with different situations when we are experiencing positive emotions. So, as Sekerka et al. (2011, p.9) confirm, "when emotions are not viewed as distractions or suppressed, they can serve as agents in promoting [courage] and facilitating effective moral decisions."

Our own research suggests that for bravery to be enhanced, leaders should begin from a position of as much understanding of their own emotions as possible in order to facilitate emotional balance. To kick-start this process in coaching an emotional needs audit, such as that incorporated in the Human Givens approach to emotional health (Griffin & Tyrrell, 2004, 2008), can be useful.

The emotional needs audit (ENA)

According to Andrews et al. (2011, p.2), Human Givens can best be understood as an "integrative bio/psycho/social approach," where clients can begin to understand how to get their emotional and physical needs met in balance through the use of their own innate resources, which include those "given" through genetics and those that are developed through life experience. Griffin and Tyrrell (2004) confirmed that having our needs met allows us to be emotionally healthy, arguing that if any of our needs remain unmet for a considerable period, or our resources are not made best use of, then mental and/or physical ill health can occur. Thus the Human Givens approach is based on the idea that we all have needs and resources and that we flourish when the needs are met. The needs are seen as motivators in the sense that we are motivated to have them met, and also that we can suffer stress when they are not met in balance.

The Human Givens website (www.hgi.org.uk/index.htm) lists the "givens" as the ability to develop complex, long-term memory; the ability to build rapport, empathize and connect with others; to learn, problem solve, remember and plan; to use our imagination productively; and to step back and take an objective look at our circumstances.

The Human Givens process usually begins with completion of an ENA, a tool developed by Griffin and Tyrrell (2004) based on the work of Abraham Maslow and Alfred Adler, which identifies emotional needs and unhelpful emotions by asking questions such as:

- Do you feel secure in all major areas of your life (work, home, environment)?
- Do you feel you receive enough attention?
- Do you think you give other people enough attention?
- Do you feel in control of your life most of the time?
- Can you obtain privacy when you need to?
- Do you feel an emotional connection to others?
- Are you mentally and/or physically stretched in ways that give you a sense of meaning and purpose?

The questions are scored from one (No) through to seven (Yes), with any scores below three likely to suggest areas that are major causes of stress.

The ENA has been shown to be a valid and reliable instrument for measuring wellbeing and quality of life (Tsaroucha et al., 2012), and also provides a useful discussion tool for coaches (McLaughlin, 2010). We introduce it in the brave coaching model to explore any areas that may not be in equilibrium and, most importantly, to raise emotional awareness. The ENA enables the coach and leader to generate a conversation so that important work can be done in relation to the key areas identified. The scores are used as an opening for discussion about balance, rather than as diagnostics, the idea being that, from a leadership perspective, if needs are not being met in balance this may be affecting thinking and behavior. Awareness of such impact is vital for leaders. It is also important to note that scores need not be at the lowest number for them to warrant attention. Rather, an exploratory conversation can help ascertain whether there is cause for any question to be looked at more closely. Also, as with any coaching session, the quality of the coach–client relationship is likely to be a significant factor in the success of this exercise. Rapport is especially important since an open conversation is unlikely if rapport has not been well established, and particularly if the boundaries of confidentiality have not been defined.

What is also important to take into account is that if an emotional need is not being met, then this may diminish a leader's ability to be coached effectively through the rest of the model. The same effect may also exist if the leader is overly focused on an emotional need being met in an exaggerated, unrealistic and obsessive way. This is not meant to imply that every score must be at its maximum and that perfection is required before moving forward. Rather, it is for the coach and leader to make a common-sense appraisal of what may cause too high a drag on progress that they need to deal with it before they can move on effectively. It is also worth reiterating that if there is an underlying issue, but the decision has been made to move forwards anyway, it is good that this is recognized and discussed at other points in the process.

We now discuss the ten core emotional and physical needs defined by the ENA in relation to the issues that John faces in his leadership role.

i) The need for security

If John, one of the leaders we met earlier, scores low on security in the ENA this would suggest an area that needs to be discussed. It would be useful as a coach to explore with John the nature of this feeling of a lack of security. It could be, for example, as a direct result of a business challenge, or perhaps there is an issue with "power play" in the company. Discussion with John will reveal the source of the concern. The security issue may not be immediately solvable, but the key thing here is to raise awareness, so that John can see how it may be affecting his thinking, his judgment and his behavior. We would suggest that an exploration of the emotional needs areas may well uncover some imbalance, and that if the imbalance in that emotional need (there may be more than one) appears to be holding the leader back, it is likely that it will need to be explored before the coach and leader can move on. The basic tenet is that the leader will need a balanced emotional base before s/he can begin to consider the brave action. A balanced emotional base arises from having our emotional needs met, and so if one or more emotional needs are not being met in balance, the coach and client may wish to consider how they can have these needs met.

ii) The need to give and receive attention

The need to give and receive attention is interesting in relation to leadership. If John is feeling isolated, this may become apparent here. He may feel he is not receiving enough attention. Or it may be that he is paying too much attention to others—e.g. micro-managing and/or using his focus on others as an excuse to remain in his comfort zone. It is important to remember that the needs should be met in balance. A need to give too much attention can be as detrimental as having a feeling of not being given enough attention. In the case of John, he was well balanced in this area, being considered an integral part of the team, his position was visible (but not vulnerable), and communication between him and others was regular and mostly friendly.

iii) The need to have a sense of autonomy and control

The need for autonomy and control is particularly relevant for leaders. It could be argued that by the very nature of their role, they have a high propensity to seek a much higher level of control than others. We would suggest that this emotional need in particular should be discussed irrespective of the score on the ENA, since as the coaching unfolds there will be points where a leader will be asked to consider certain decisions/actions/routes forward.

John was working for an organization that had changed from a more traditional structure to that of a matrix. This transition had generated a real sense of a loss of autonomy and control for him, despite his senior position. It is therefore very important for him to consider any perceived lack of control. A potentially "blinkered" attitude may hamper John's ability to consider other options. It is possible that he may be seeking too much autonomy and control, and so he will need help in becoming more realistic in his expectations, and to understand more fully the ramifications of this approach.

During coaching with John, this lack of control was noted and linked with his recognition of fairness as an important value. There was nothing that could be done at that point to change the structure of the organization, and a feeling of control is simply that: a feeling. So John was encouraged to frame things differently, to enjoy that which he could control. However, it was important to take this information forward, as it would almost certainly have an impact on how John wanted to act. In particular, John and his coach would need to be vigilant that when a situation is being viewed or a decision is being considered, that there is not an underlying drive to take a particular action simply to gain control; that an inherent emotional need is not skewing the decision. On the other hand, it could be that the leader and coach become very aware that the action being taken is necessary to gain the feeling of control that has been missing from the leader. Awareness here is key, and with that awareness any lack of balance can be either compensated for, or used knowingly to help inform the best action to take.

iv) The need to feel emotionally connected to others

The sense of a feeling of being emotionally connected to others is likely to vary considerably from person to person. John feels fairly emotionally connected to others in his work environment and in general terms this is likely to be a good thing. However, if a leader is not feeling a sense of connection, then this may be due to organizational changes, or some other reason that needs discussion. It may also be that the leader is content with a level of disconnect if this connection need is met outside the work environment.

v) The need to be part of a wider community

The need to be part of a wider community is often met outside work. It could be met in a local interest group, through sport or a hobby, for instance. We suggest that it would be healthier if at least part of this need were met in the business environment. This may be through a professional body and/or through a sense of community within the organization. John has this need met through online networking groups, but irrespective of how this need is met, it would seem that leaders who are isolated both in terms of emotional connection and sense of community are likely not to be functioning as well as they could.

vi) The need for friendship and intimacy

Like the other needs, the need for friendship can be met outside work. The "intimacy" referred to here is not necessarily the intimacy that may be found in a romantic relationship (although it can be), but it can also be the type of relationship where individuals are accepted for who they are: they do not have to put on a façade. This type of relationship is often difficult for leaders to find in the business environment as many other factors can come into play which may make this untenable. For John this role is partly fulfilled by his longstanding mentor within his organization, and to a certain degree by his coach, although this is a shorter-term relationship.

vii) The need to have a sense of status within social groupings

A sense of status does not necessarily mean that an individual needs to be at the very top of the social "tree" but more that individuals have a sense of where they fit in. If leaders are not comfortable with where they fit within the organization or alongside their peers, it may be that this is impacting their ability to be effective within their role. The coach cannot directly influence the social status of a leader. However, it is more the *feeling* of status that is important here rather than the actual status, and so a coach may be able to help the leader in gaining perspective on his/her contribution and standing. Fortunately, John scored fairly high in this area and did not feel the need to discuss status, provided his perceived needs for control and autonomy can be met. If they are not then this may become an issue and revisiting the ENA could then be useful.

viii) The need to feel a sense of competence and achievement

A feeling of achievement is a good feeling for all of us to have. However, we can see immediately here that there are two big stressors for John. There is one particular project where he feels less than competent and he thinks that he is not achieving what he believes he should be achieving, especially as the matrix structure evolves. The coach may be able to help with this, but it is important to note that just as with the emotional need for control, any emotional need that scores low on the ENA could well skew the decision-making process if not recognized and addressed.

ix) The need for meaning and purpose

Confucian theories of leadership suggest that people should recognize the true meaning of life before becoming a great leader. Senge reinforced that suggestion, stating "you must understand yourself first" (Senge et al., 2004, p.180). John gave himself a middling score for meaning and purpose. At the current time, despite organizational change, he is very clear about his role in the organization and his home life is stable. He understands the importance of meaning and purpose in his life and works with his mentor and his coach to strengthen his understanding further. However, John did feel that something was not quite right, that he needed to recalibrate things in some way, but he could not quite articulate what that might be. It is interesting to consider the impact that a lack of purpose might have on the ability to be brave.

x) The need for privacy

The final emotional need suggests that we all have a requirement for privacy to, amongst other things, consolidate learning. We would also suggest that for a leader like John to function at his optimum level, there is a need for time to reflect and consider, and not consistently rush from one meeting to another. Also, as several recent studies indicate, there is a great myth surrounding the idea of multi-tasking. The research of Ophir et al. (2009), for example, suggests that there is a high propensity for multi-taskers to become distracted and ultimately much less efficient. This suggests that privacy should be uninterrupted, with no email or mobile phone.

For initiating discussions around the ENA scores we suggest some general questions. These questions are not meant to be prescriptive; they are simply examples that may prompt other, more situationally relevant questions:

- Are there any scores that you would like to discuss?
- Are there any scores that surprise you?
- In relation to [*a particular emotional need*] are you comfortable with that score?
- So would you like to share the story behind the number?
- What number would you like that to be?
- What might the effect of that new number be?

We would suggest that just like any coaching intervention, the coach and leader work together on what is considered to be a suitable area for exploration; importantly, the coach can use whatever appropriate approaches, strategies or tools s/he is familiar with and that have been successful in the past. Additionally, identifying and discussing personal needs is only part of the solution to finding balance. Further work must be done in order to align the leader with his/her environment, hence our next suggestion that leaders consciously make time to pause and reflect.

2 Reflective Pause

In educational settings, reflection is advocated as a form of personal learning. It also forms a key part of how coaching creates conditions for learning. Reflection is also where professionals come to terms with their feelings: "learning from their mistakes, explore their successes, and develop empathy and understanding" (Cox, 2006, p.199). It is a creative process that enables leaders to make meaning by making connections between experience and the potential consequences of that experience in the future.

We would also suggest that reflection is best done by pausing and "creating a psychological space that allows clients to withdraw from the workplace in order to stand back and think, thus enabling them to gain some perspective on their experiences and on their tasks" (Cox, 2013, p.73). Sekerka et al. (2011, p.9) also promote the use of this "reflective pause" as part of the decision-making strategy, arguing that it represents the ability, "regardless of time constraints, to purposively self-impose a time-out for reflection." Through this silent break, they suggest that individuals examine avenues for right action:

> often weighing the pros and cons of the situation, or thinking about different periods of time and potential implications (i.e. past and present). This display of prudential judgment appears to be an important component of [moral courage] that manifests during reflection periods. It is as though the time-out helps people discern options and garner informed momentum toward moral action.
> *(Sekerka et al., 2011, p.9)*

Reflection also generates options, as Sekerka earlier confirmed. She explained how:

> Professional moral courage is bolstered through reflection as options are generated for moral action in the early stages of a decision-making process. Taking time to reflect often alters, overrides, or postpones some initial reactions while also targeting responses for appropriate use. When applied as a daily habit, this reflection may actually serve as a portal for personal governance practices that lead to self-regulation.
> *(Sekerka, 2010, p.6)*

Like many other advocates of reflective practice, Nancy Adler (2010) champions the use of a journal or log where, she says, the blank pages are an "invitation to spend time quietly recollecting (literally re-collecting) one's personal perspective" (p.93). Adler suggests that "all true leadership starts with coming home to oneself" (ibid., p.93). Not only that, but she reminds us that a journal can act as an "antidote to society's pervasive collusion" (ibid., p.93). Externalizing thoughts in this way is powerful, and we would always support the use of some kind of record where thoughts, ideas and perceptions can be marshaled: "True leaders, whether in the arts, business, government, science, or the military, view the world through their own eyes, their own values, and their own dreams" (Adler, 2010, p.93).

Whereas reflection is often regarded as being concerned with what has happened in the past, recent research has suggested that becoming aware of what is happening in the present can also be effective as a decision-making strategy (Ruedy & Schweitzer, 2010). One of the ways in which this can be supported is through the development of mindfulness. The idea of mindfulness in business has become more and more prevalent, in part we believe as an antidote to constant psychological and emotional demands. The practice of mindfulness is explored next as a central adjunct to emotional awareness and reflective pause.

Mindfulness

In Eastern meditative traditions thoughts are focused on just one idea or experience, like the breath, and through this the capacity for focused attention in the "now" is built. In the West such mindfulness has been described as "the awareness that arises through intentionally attending to one's moment to moment experience in a nonjudgmental and accepting way" (Shapiro et al., 2008, p.841). The moment is allowed to pass without cognitive interventions such as evaluation or analysis.

Brown, Ryan and Creswell (2007, p.272) refer to mindfulness as being "essentially about waking up to what the present moment offers." In leadership coaching, mindfulness can be introduced within the session. The coach may ask the client to give attention then and there to what is happening in the moment. Mindfulness is an opportunity to make contact with aspects of experience that are otherwise missing or missed, and if it can be introduced and practiced within a coaching session, then it may become a habit that can be continued into every day.

In relation to finding balance, Ryan and Deci's (2000) research confirmed how mindfulness is important in separating people from their automatic thoughts, habits and unwanted behavior patterns, and thus plays a fundamental part in the development of informed self-regulation. Here open awareness is seen as crucial in facilitating the choice of behaviors that are consistent with needs, values and interests (Brown & Ryan, 2003). The claim is that automatic processing can *prevent* consideration of options that might be more compatible with current needs and values, but that awareness *facilitates* our attention to the "prompts arising from basic needs" (ibid., p.824), thus making us more likely to regulate our behavior in a way that fulfills those needs. Thus mindfulness would seem to have a big part to play in balancing the needs and demands of the organization with the needs and values of the individual leader:

> The more fully an individual is apprised of what is occurring internally and in the environment, the more healthy, adaptive, and value-consistent his or her behaviour is likely to be.
> *(Brown & Ryan, 2004, p.114)*

The benefits of mindfulness are encompassed in various definitions. Collard and Walsh (2008, pp.33–34) for example, suggest that mindfulness is about "being fully awake, about being in the here and now, about being connected to the flow of every experience and enjoying a sense of oneness between mind and body." They argue that the opposite of mindfulness is "feeling obsessed with the past, or fearing the future or maybe functioning in an 'automatic pilot' mode" (ibid., pp.33–34). From this we can see that mindfulness is a practice that could be useful to an effective and brave leader, since nothing ought to be left to chance: limited awareness or habitual responses might have devastating consequences for organizations and countries. Also, as Weinstein, Brown and Ryan (2009, p.375) report, mindfulness may promote a less defensive approach to challenges and experiences, which in turn reduces sensitivity to stress and encourages a capacity to cope with situations perceived as "challenging, threatening or harmful."

Diaz (2010, p.97) similarly points out that mindfulness modifies and enhances attention span, reducing reactive modes of thinking through the "inhibition of rumination, improved self-regulation, improved ability to choose and switch between competing tasks, and improved vigilance."

Marianetti and Passmore (2010, p.190) have discussed the health benefits of being mindful, proposing that it is by engaging in such moments of stillness that opportunities are created to "step out of this overwhelming flow, regain composure, strength and clarity of thought." In addition, mindfulness practice in the coaching session can demonstrate to clients that emotions are normal. Bachkirova and Cox (2007) noted how traditional suppressive workplace attitudes towards emotions cause anxiety, whereas being in the present moment and being allowed to accept our feelings without judgment allows clients to accept themselves and their situation. In coaching to develop braver leaders, encouraging clients to understand their emotions, as well as their other needs, thoughts and anxieties, helps them to accept themselves and to accept others too. As

Cox (2013, p.124) points out, "it would seem that mindfulness has a grounding role for both coach and client, ensuring that each is fully aware of what is happening cognitively, somatically and environmentally in the moment."

In addition to its benefits for individuals, Ruedy and Schweitzer (2010) report on research that links mindfulness with ethical decision making, suggesting, for example, that mindfulness can actually help overcome "ethical fading," where people use "various forms of self-deception, such as justifications and euphemistic language, to shield themselves from their own ethical infractions" (p.74). These authors also highlight that situational factors and ambiguities, such as those found in complex leadership contexts, can make acknowledgment of ethical issues more difficult. Mindfulness with its emphasis on present-centered and engaged thinking, can, it is argued, promote ethical decision making: "Because of its accepting, non-judging quality, mindfulness encourages a consideration of all the relevant information for a given decision" (ibid., p.77).

Closely related to the form of self-awareness stimulated by mindfulness is the idea of self-regulation where awareness is seen as a vital part of facilitating a choice of behaviors consistent with needs and values. In the next section we look at self-regulation and its role in finding balance.

3 Self-Regulation

Sekerka (2010) confirms how the personal governance that self-regulation offers in support of professional moral courage is driven from within. She describes how it serves as an "inner strength and compass that provides motivation and direction" (p.7). Self-regulation also involves self-control and Sekerka describes how this control can support moral courage: "Learning to quiet one's impulse to react or ignore the problem, then reflecting upon and managing immediate thoughts and feelings can begin a course of personal development marked by habits of moral strength" (ibid., p.7). Indeed, Sekerka (2010, p.6) has argued that in order to "habitually pursue right action and to manage and address tough moral decisions, individuals must balance their reactions, knowing how to manage responsibilities with desires for various goals and the possible means for achieving them, as they decide whether to postpone action or to engage in it." She goes on to explain how this requires "restraint coupled with an ability to move forward despite the perception of negative impacts to self" (ibid., p.6), especially when peers or other leaders are engaged in dubious activities or if they are asking others to engage in action that they believe to be morally questionable.

Self-regulation, as the name implies, is self-monitored process of direction and control: it is a skill that can be "managed and enhanced by the individual" (Baumeister & Vohs, 2007, p.28). According to Neal, Wood and Quinn (2006, p.200), it involves "monitoring and adjusting responses in the service of the self […] by comparing current states with goals, and engaging control process when the two are discrepant." However, as Sekerka et al. suggested, only rarely do some people apply self-regulation automatically. They confirm that for most there is great potential for developing this ability: "Quieting one's impulse to react, then reflecting upon and managing immediate thoughts and feelings, can begin a course of personal development marked by habits of moral strength" (Sekerka et al., 2011, p.12).

Ives and Cox (2012) reported how self-regulation acts as a mediator at the intersection between the internal influencers of future actions, such as past experience, values and expectations, and the actual choices the person needs to make to direct those actions: "past experiences lead a person to develop perceptions or attributions about his or her abilities and circumstances. These in turn lead to judgements or expectancies about what is likely to occur in the future" (p.29). Ives and Cox point out that our choice of actions is mostly guided by these expectancies, and "unless consciously countervailed will exert overwhelming influence of what goals a person will choose, and thus the consequential actions and outcomes" (ibid., p.29). They argue that self-regulation is for that reason a "crucial mediating pivot that, if activated, can critique and assess those internal and external influencers, and allow the person to make reasoned decisions about future actions without being imprisoned by the past" (ibid., p.30). Self-regulation can therefore be seen as a key mediator between individual and environmental characteristics, and actual behavior or performance.

According to Carver and Scheier (2011), behavior is governed by processes of feedback and control. These (semi)automatic methods of self-regulation are about managing our feelings and desires and demonstrating the ability to apply restraint in our actions. Feedback is seen as vital in self-regulation theory (Carver & Scheier, 2011), being used primarily to inform future decisions and motivate future actions. However, it is intended to "assess past performance and compare to goals set, rather than facilitate long-term learning and development" (Ives & Cox, 2012, p.3).

Sekerka (2010, p.7) also suggests that self-regulation has an important role to play in doing the right thing at the right time. Managers, she suggests, must decide "whether to postpone a response or engage in immediate action." This ability to regulate reactions, as mentioned in

Chapter 4, is an important part of self-governance, involving "withholding the impulse to act immediately as well as knowing when to proceed" (ibid., p.7). Sekerka's research reports that managers interviewed, "expressed that they should have acted sooner, but their respect, appreciation, or care for someone, as well as a sense of loyalty to their command, served to inhibit action and/or their self-regulation (at least initially). Many who waited however, say in hindsight that this just exacerbated the problem" (ibid., p.7). This suggests that timing can be crucial.

Ives and Cox present coaching, particularly goal-focused coaching, as a self-regulation tool that works at the intersection between antecedent influences, such as values and expectations, and the subsequent goal choices that eventually lead to action. Thus self-regulation operates as a monitoring mechanism, facilitating the achievement of goals, raising performance towards those goals, and subsequently enhancing self-efficacy: "interventions that seek to boost self-regulation are perceived as highly effective in bringing about positive outcomes by raising performance levels and by influencing future self-efficacy judgements" (Ives & Cox, 2012, p.3). Effective self-regulatory activity also enhances self-control, task focus and feelings of competence (Schunk, 1991, p.29).

Just as monitoring progress is also a key part of self-regulation, so it is also at the heart of coaching since, as Carver and Scheier (1998, p.34) claim, "increases in *self-focus* can promote increases in *task-focus*," facilitating appropriate adjustments to the goal (Carver, 2007). The primary function of coaching as a tool for developing self-regulation for leaders, therefore, can be seen as helping them progress towards their self-set tasks. It can play a vital role in enhancing self-regulation by fostering optimal choices and actions, helping leaders to focus on those things over which they feel they do have control and can change (i.e. effort and skills rather than aptitudes) in order to foster performance-enhancing choices. Some clients can tend to blame their environment for their problems, but the self-regulatory emphasis in coaching could help them to assume responsibility for their own outcomes (Ives & Cox, 2012).

4 Moral Preparation

Throughout this book we are concerned with how brave leadership requires moral preparation. We began by suggesting that identifying a brave exemplar from history or their own experience enables leaders to hold a subconscious role model of someone they see as outstandingly moral and brave. This is an appropriate beginning, for as Sekerka (2010) stresses, moral preparation stems from understanding ourselves and having predetermined that we are moral agents: that is, the leader has already declared that s/he plans to act with moral courage, even before an ethical event occurs.

Sekerka et al. (2011) have further suggested that commitment to right action can be developed through preparatory thought processes concerning how we may and may not act when faced with an ethical challenge in the future. These authors also argue that people who operate with professional moral courage seem to think through the consequences to other people and themselves before the event:

> Their ongoing preparatory efforts, including a review of situations in which they have acted or failed to act and a consideration of their emotions and evaluations, enable them to do the right thing when they encounter a moral situation.
>
> *(Sekerka et al., 2011, p.136)*

In addition, they argue that those who are aware of how emotions and situational factors influence their reactions are then able to "choose to respond in similar or different ways as familiar scenarios play out and new ones emerge. Their heightened level of moral preparedness for ethical challenges, often expressed by continued vigilance of "the moral line," helps them to deal with ethical issues while they are still manageable" (Sekerka et al., 2011, p.136). These authors also proposed that moral preparation involves "sustained self-awareness, personal introspecting and the willingness to remain open to learning" (ibid., p.137). Rehearsal processes can help prepare leaders to respond mindfully and effectively when problems crop up by helping them plan to prevent such issues from recurring. In addition, "they also maintain a continuous improvement mindset, always considering how they will deal with similar or nuanced situations they may encounter in future" (ibid., p.137).

Sekerka et al. (2011, p.136) also note that:

> moral preparation is likely intertwined with and potentially dependent upon the use of the other personal governance competences. For example, emotional signalling, taking a reflective pause and exercising self-regulation are typically precursors for the ability to proceed with right action.

In the coaching conversation that follows, we join one of our leaders, Ron, preparing for a brave encounter with a member of his board as a first step to reasserting his moral stance. Until now, Ron seems to have lost his way; his energy, his optimism and even his sense of "right" have all been eroded.

COACH: As you know, Ron, we are preparing for the first step in terms of you "turning up the heat," as you described it, on those who have been turning up the heat on you—a bit like Superman, your brave role model. There is one individual in particular who I think you wanted to tackle first?

RON: Yes, that's right, and even just thinking about it at the moment makes me feel slightly nervous if I'm honest.

COACH: That is entirely understandable. What are you nervous about specifically?

RON: Well, I'm not sure if it is specific or general, but what I'm just not looking forward to is the conflict.

COACH: Will there be conflict?

RON: Well, I suppose that's a good point, I don't know of course, but that is what I'm worried about.

COACH: What is it about the conflict that you aren't looking forward to?

RON: The disagreement, the fact that there are conflicting views.

COACH: Isn't that normal?

RON: Yes, but I just hate to disagree in a forceful way.

COACH: Describe forceful.

RON: Well, shouting, anger, that type of thing.

COACH: Are you worried about you being angry or them being angry?

RON: Well, I suppose both.

COACH: Well, maybe there is a way to reduce that worry by 50 percent.

RON: Ah! You mean only one person might get angry—and it needn't be me. But if that is the case, and it would be my preference, where would I hide in the conflict?

COACH: Hide?

RON: I mean that if you are in a conflict, then at least if you are angry you can focus on that, you don't feel so vulnerable.

COACH: But you don't want to get angry.

RON: No.

COACH: So what could you hang on to?

RON: I'm not following.

COACH: Well, it sounds like you could use anger as a sort of "anchor" during conflict, and so if you don't want to get angry, I was wondering what else you could use?

RON: I'm not sure, but I think I see what you are getting at. I need some way of staying resolute, not necessarily being totally calm, but somehow unmoved. But how do I do that? What would I use?

COACH: Let me ask you this Ron. Why are you doing this? Why are you making this stand?

RON: Because it is the right thing to do, I have reached the point where I can't stand what I'm seeing, it is the right thing to do; it really is for me a moral imperative.
COACH: So this is a moral issue?
RON: Absolutely. I suppose that is what is ultimately driving this. It is just morally wrong. I need to stand up and be counted; otherwise I will not be able to live with myself.
COACH: I see. So what might you be able to hold onto during any conflict which might help you avoid anger?
RON: My moral sense: my sense that once this situation is viewed from a moral perspective, I am right. The other person might not think so, but to me this is not about moral high ground, this is the whole landscape. I can now see that my stance is rooted in that soil. I can't guarantee I won't get angry, but I am far less likely to want to hide there. In fact, come to think of it, I want to be seen, I'm happy to be visible on that particular field. I can be the change that I want to see around me—to misquote Gandhi. Thank you. That has helped me tremendously. I think I have made a little breakthrough here.

Summary

In this chapter we talked about the need for the leader to find a balance using gravitational factors to ensure that equilibrium is achieved. We highlighted how the factors are frequently in tension resulting in stress or loss of wellbeing. Pulling factors create disturbances that challenge values and pull leaders away from ethical or morally sustainable courses of action.

We suggested that in order to maintain a balance it is necessary to take stock in four key areas that can support a strong "core": emotional awareness, reflective pause, self-regulation and moral preparation.

All four of these areas involve raising attentiveness to internal processes. Our discussion of emotional awareness included suggesting to leaders that they undertake an emotional needs analysis as a way of opening up a discussion with the coach that could lead to a greater understanding of self and others and therefore more effective interactions. The reflective pause idea is not new. Leaders will be familiar with the need to reflect, but we would emphasize the importance of even the shortest pause to allow time for discernment and therefore a more prudent, informed approach not only to tensions for self-preservation, but also for decision making. We also included a discussion of mindfulness, which has its emphasis more in the moment. A number of benefits were highlighted, including the feeling of acceptance and oneness that can be achieved through increased attention to the present.

In introducing self-regulation our key concern was to stress the role of monitoring and feedback (key parts of self-regulation) for deciding how to act or react in situations. Coaching was highlighted as a tool for developing self-regulation, since it helps move the client towards self-set tasks and includes monitoring and feedback elements. The two are synergistic and we could even say that self-coaching is a form of self-regulation.

Our final section focused on moral preparation and we suggested returning to leaders' brave stories as a way of reminding them that they are moral agents. We saw Ron shift from being fearful about his encounter with one board member to feeling more powerful as he remembered his Gandhi quote.

Our exploration of finding balance illustrated the evolutionary aspect of the brave coaching model. The journey through the model could be thought of perhaps as peeling away layers of an onion to get to the heart of what is important to the leader, or using a different metaphor perhaps equipping the leader with different patinas, one on top of the other, and seasoning them to allow them to act more effectively and ultimately bravely in a challenging environment.

Moving away from the central core image that we have discussed in some detail in this chapter, in Chapter 6 we are going to explore the next part of the coaching model, a mechanism by which the coach can help the leader move conceptually around the organizational "solar system" and take a high-level view of the pulling factors or forces, both positive and negative, that are apparent there.

6
THE BRAVE SPHERE

Introduction

In previous chapters we explored gravitational factors and pulling factors as elements of a leader's role that can create tension and imbalance. In fact, linking together the gravitational process and the pulling factors suggests a dynamic "planetary system," where components move around with varying degrees of resistance or tension between them which required balancing skills, such as reflection and self-regulation, in order to maintain stability.

In this chapter, taking the notion of the reflective pause, introduced in Chapter 5, a stage further we introduce an active reflection framework where we focus on how the coach can help leaders create a metaphorical "observation center": a center for observing and analyzing the various tensions created in the organizational system in order to understand the problematic dynamics they frequently create. We suggest that the coach needs to support the leader in observing the detail of the different tensions, but without getting drawn in by the force fields that might accompany that detail.

Continuing the space metaphor, the "brave sphere" is used as a craft or satellite that can facilitate "space travel" from one location of organizational interest, attraction or concern (such as one of the pulling factors) to another in order to enable clear observation of those factors. The sphere enables exploration of the organizational system and can move swiftly and gently to hover over problem areas, giving attention to any latent negative issues or potential solutions as well as providing a worldview not otherwise achieved. This craft can therefore allow the leader to travel through both time and space as various thought exercises are performed and questions asked. Being able to determine how to work with the restrictions of the organization is, according to Mumford et al. (2000, p.15), "the most common manifestation of leader innovation." We would also add that being able to consider when and how those restrictions should be challenged is also an essential skill for the brave leader.

In this chapter we look at how the metaphorical sphere involves three different but interdependent stages of reflection for the leader by:

- providing a place of calm to reflect on problems (the sphere of sanctuary);
- enabling the exploration of different perspectives and needs within the organizational landscape (the sphere of observation); and
- providing the opportunity to analyze feelings in relation to the observations and holding whatever is found as a resource for sustainable decision making (the sphere of influence).

We propose that using the framework of the sphere, and with some astute cognitive and emotional guidance from the coach, leaders can be helped to navigate through some wicked environments and problems, i.e. those where they have to ask questions and make decisions in the wake of increasing uncertainty and the requirement for collaborative resolution (Grint, 2008). The sphere provides leaders with the opportunity to engage or disengage mentally with issues, problems and environments which might otherwise be so emotive or blinding that either the issue is not considered in enough detail or a high-level overview of the interconnectedness of seemingly separate issues is never achieved.

As explained, the brave sphere performs three interrelated functions that encourage development of a place of calm, a space for non-judgmental observation and a space for critical reflection in which the fundamental nature of problems can be considered. Thus the leader is able to navigate the entire organizational system and to examine feelings that help with identification of and, most importantly, the ability ultimately to hold the brave position. The three functions are shown in Figure 6.1 and described in more detail below.

1 Sphere Of Sanctuary

Keywords: place of sanctuary, silence, calm, mindfulness, safety

We have hinted already at the dangers of leaders being too emotionally attached to a problem or situation, or feeling too pressured and opting for

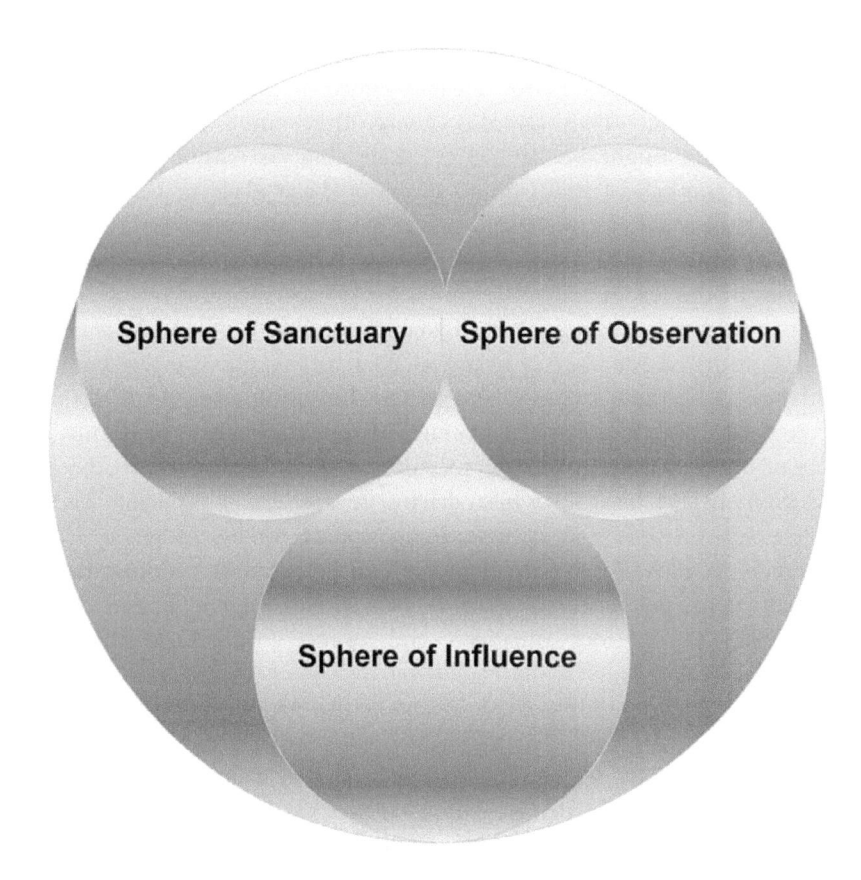

FIGURE 6.1 The three functions of the brave sphere

a habitual or culturally acceptable solution, which may be inappropriate. However, we have not yet described the process by which the leader, potentially assisted by the coach, can begin to generate the tranquility required for reflecting on significant organizational issues. This is the initial function of the sphere: what we call the "sphere of sanctuary."

The function of the sphere as a sanctuary is to provide the opportunity for the leader to withdraw momentarily from the hurly burly of organizational life in preparation for focusing on observing and analyzing the best course of action. The sanctuary provides a space for the leader to consider situations calmly and make choices from the balanced emotional state accomplished by the "finding balance" explorations described in Chapter 5. A calm, safe space is created by mentally bracketing what is called the "natural attitude" (Bitbol & Petitmengin, 2011) and the cultivation of mindfulness as described in Chapter 5. From within this space, leaders can learn first to let go, then to give attention to the present moment. They do this in the created safety of the sphere and from a position of balance. They can also observe their emotional state and any effect that this might be having on their ability to think clearly. The interior of the sphere itself should therefore be a place of calmness and contemplation, a reflective space where leaders can purposefully retreat, with or without their coach, in times of indecision or other extreme demands of the leader role.

What follows is a transcript from a coaching session where the sphere is being introduced as a place of calmness. Matt's challenge was that he had a tendency to be quite reactive, and to see the world solely from his perspective. His slightly volatile temperament was causing him to dismiss the ideas of others before genuinely considering them. His focus on the tactical elements of his role whilst driving for results also meant that his communication style was at times inappropriate for his audience. It was important to allow Matt to experience and get used to working from a position of lower emotional arousal. This in turn, it was hoped, would allow him to consider situations and events from more than one perspective.

First, a guided breathing exercise was used to promote mindfulness:

COACH: Okay Matt, let's ensure that we have all cellular devices turned off, and that your PA is fielding all your calls. It would be really useful if nothing were to beep or whistle whilst we are beginning this next part of the journey and that there are no distractions.

MATT: Fine, sounds great.

COACH: Firstly, I'd like you to consider that the process we are about to practice is to allow you some genuinely reflective thinking space. And in order to really reflect, it is going to be important for you to relax as deeply as possible. I want you to imagine that we are pushing back on these four walls and generating a space, a kind of Tardis or oasis for you to relax in, to think and be safe. What I'd like you to do is to sit so that you are nice and comfortable. It's probably best to place both feet flat on the ground and allow your hands to rest in the area of your lap.

MATT: [Nods and leans back in chair.]

COACH: What I'm going to ask you to do, but only if you are comfortable doing so, is to close your eyes and take a really deep breath in, filling your lungs up as much as you possibly can, and then as you exhale control your out-breath—it's often easier to do that by breathing out through your mouth. So empty your lungs of all the air and now breathe in again, filling your lungs to their maximum capacity. Then, and only then, breathe out again, controlling the out-breath until every last bit of air is gone, and then breathe in again, filling your lungs up and up and up—then, very slowly breathing out, really elongating the out-breath.

And now as you are hopefully feeling a little more relaxed, what I'd like you to do is to put your attention on your breathing, and nothing else. Firstly, notice how your chest rises and falls with each breath. Just put your focus on that for a few moments, noticing every subtlety and nuance of the movements involved.

And now, shift your attention to your nose. Notice how the air feels as you breathe in through your nose, and follow that air as it flows further down. Focus on how that air feels as it flows from outside of the body to inside the body … and as you do this, notice that some thoughts may well appear. Please do not judge those thoughts, just simply let them come … and let them go. Notice how they can drift in, and drift out. These thoughts are not there to be judged, they simply are. So simply observe them as they drift in, and drift out, continuing to focus on being aware only of your breathing.

And now as you become more relaxed, notice how your abdomen rises and falls as you breathe. And if any thoughts appear as you are doing this, let them appear, without judgment, and let them disappear, without judgment. Simply focus on noticing how your abdomen rises and falls. And if you find yourself chasing one of those thoughts, then simply allow yourself to return to focusing on your breathing, with no judgment.

And now begin to notice the full cycle of your breathing, from the feeling as you breathe in through your nose, where the breath flows to, any sensations in your chest and abdomen, and notice how your abdomen expands on the in-breath and contracts on the out-breath. Remember not to judge the experience, or any thoughts, just let the thoughts come and go, without judgment.

During the coaching sessions emphasis needs to be placed on the need to be relaxed and as calm as possible during the imagined journey to the various parts of the organizational landscape. This need to remain calm and not overly emotionally aroused is important to ensure the leader can manage his/her own emotional state effectively. Although not quite strictly neurologically correct, we find that for simplicity and to illustrate how our thinking can be influenced by emotions and the environment, the brain can be thought of as comprising three evolutionary elements—the reptilian brain, which controls bodily functions; the limbic brain, which monitors emotional states; and the neocortex, which directs rational thinking (Maiocchi, 2015). If the limbic brain guides the leader's responses, decisions will be governed by feelings instead of logic and this is often not effective. Consequently, measures to self-regulate responses and reflect on alternative solutions are important. Practicing how to breathe, especially in difficult situations can be learned like any other skill, and the leadership coach can help with this. The benefit of the sphere of sanctuary is that it gives the leader a metaphorical place to focus and become more self-aware.

In leadership situations, decision making is subject to many kinds of biases, and behaviors can be heavily influenced by individual emotional needs—not only those of the leader, but those of stakeholders in various parts of the organization. If we remember how quickly leaders have to think and make decisions every day it is easy to see that certain patterns of behavior become habitual. However, although some fast, immediate responses can be extremely useful—they can be dangerous when an issue or a problem becomes more complex or wicked than normal. Then it is potentially dangerous to presume that those same habitual responses will serve well in that situation, particularly if they are being reinforced by cultural and historical influences within the organization. Additional attention is therefore needed when leaders are:

- facing problems that have more complexity than normal;
- connected emotionally in some way to the problem; or
- generally more emotionally fraught or stressed than normal.

Leaders thus need support to develop ways of knowing how and when to step away from habitual responses and access the sphere of sanctuary. They may do this by feeling and recognizing when they experience any kind of disorienting dilemma (Mezirow, 1991). Disorienting dilemmas occur when people experience something that is not in line with their expectations. An event occurs that requires a non-habitual response and acknowledging this and reflecting on it enables the recognition of the new situation and the consequent revision of meaning perspectives. Mezirow (1991) describes this change as "perspective transformation," a process of becoming critically aware of how and why our particular assumption has come to "constrain the way we perceive, understand, and feel about our world" (p.167). He also suggests that for perspective transformation to occur, people go through ten stages: stage one begins with the disorienting dilemma, then there are various stages of reflection including self-examination of feelings, values and judgments, and the process concludes when the transformed perspective is integrated into who we are and how we approach our next experiences. For leaders, a disorienting dilemma can occur when they encounter tensions in the workplace and the subsequent learning occurs when they reflect critically on that tension. We would suggest that once a dilemma has been identified it is important that the leader accesses his or her reflective space as soon as possible in order to observe the tension inherent in it.

2 Sphere Of Observation

Keywords: detached, non-judgmental, observation of physical, emotional and cognitive signs of tension or need

Building on the mindfulness and acceptance created by accessing the safety and calm of the sphere of sanctuary, another function of the brave sphere is to facilitate leaders' observation and examination of different viewpoints and needs from around the organization. The tranquil and yet extremely maneuverable sphere of observation allows leaders to visit various elements of their corporate environment and consider what is important. It enables leaders to consider all aspects of the problem at hand, including reflecting on what further information or data they may need to inform decision making. Cox (2013) divides the reflective experience into two distinct parts for discussion purposes, suggesting that this allows coaching clients the opportunity to "see their personal experience from a distance, free from value judgements and emotional entanglement" (p.87). This "objectivity" allows the coach and client ultimately to talk about the issue without prematurely discriminating or evaluating before all perspectives have been considered. It is this neutrality that characterizes the sphere of observation.

The movement and focus of the sphere of observation is similar to the "helicopter view" advocated by Simmons and Sower (2012). These authors suggest that a high-level perspective is vital for managers and leaders and confers the ability to "see beyond the specifics of a particular situation to see it in its overall context and environment" (p.300). They explain how the concept focuses on facilitating strategic thinking and assessing tactical issues in order to inform decision making, but does not involve making judgments: "The strategic thinking detailed by this concept could be considered to be a function or subset of acumen, but it does not include the aspects of judgment and discernment required to maximize effective action" (ibid., p.300).

However, the helicopter analogy has some negative implications, as sometimes employees are concerned that management only ever look at the high-level picture and don't understand complexity, detail or connectivity. The same negative connotations could also be generated where a consultant is "parachuted in" to solve problems—although in this instance, the negativity can be about a perceived lack of emotional connection and/or historical attachment to the team or organization.

The sphere, on the other hand, although enabling the leader to consider organizational situations and perspectives calmly and from a "safe distance," actually promotes the ability to reflect on and understand specific areas in detail, and enables the tensions to be experienced and understood prior to making a decision. It allows leaders to travel around their current system with a level of emotional impunity and distance, and potentially allows them to observe areas within this system where often complex forces and counter-forces exist.

Bogardus (1927) was probably the first to suggest that leadership involves a degree of social distance between a leader and followers. He described it as a vertical social distance. Grint also supported this need for distance, saying that it is "a device for facilitating the execution of distasteful but necessary tasks by leaders and of generating the space to see the patterns that are all but invisible when very close to followers or the action" (Grint, 2010, p.94). Grint cites Heifetz and Linsky's (2002, pp.65–67) metaphor of "getting on the balcony to see the patterns created by the (organization's) dancers."

We prefer to extend our space metaphor to describe how the leader uses the physical distance created by the sphere to orbit the organizational landscape and observe vital constellations and conjunctions. The leader also needs to be aware that, "while physical distance may be critical, symbolic distance must be much narrower to ensure identification between follower and leader" (Grint, 2010, p.94). We would, however, suggest that whilst the leader does indeed require an element of distance to "see the patterns," the idea of social distance should be approached with caution. Yes, the leader needs to be able to rise above the emotional quagmire that might surround an issue, and make decisions from a calm and balanced perspective, but s/he must not be so socially removed that there is immunity from any sense of "social pain." There should be some space for empathy.

Zaccaro et al. (2000, p.38) have described organizational leadership as a "skilled performance grounded in the leader's capability to solve complex and ill defined organizational problems." Emphasis during coaching needs to be on helping the leader understand the nature of those problems. This includes examination of what we have called pulling factors and whatever else must be considered whilst orbiting those areas. Similarly, the gravitational factors must be revisited and considered carefully. It is easy to overlook or dismiss certain areas, depending on the values of the leader. So leaders are asked to move the sphere in such a way as to observe the pulling factors, to become aware of the tensions within the protection of the sphere, to reflect on the strength of the drag and the different directions of the pulls, and also to notice the gravitational factors: what happens when they move towards these, or away from them?

In this part of the thought exercise the sphere must be directed to a focal point (pulling factor) and held there long enough for tensions and reactions to be felt, observed and processed.

Mumford et al. (2000, p.17) note that "capabilities such as wisdom and perspective-taking enable leaders to 'go outside themselves' to assess how others react to a solution, identify restrictions, develop plans, and build support for implementation." We believe also that constructive problem solving begins in the sphere since the new information acquired allows existing perspectives to be restructured, thus affording new understandings that will become the basis for solution generation and implementation.

In the following extract from our coaching with Matt it can be noted how we move towards observing the organization from a range of different perspectives:

COACH: And from that relaxed, non-judgmental space I would now like you to imagine that you are inside a sphere. This sphere allows the easy transfer of clean air but keeps out any unwanted energies. And you can perhaps imagine yourself sitting on a comfy chair in the middle of this sphere. The sphere is going to allow you to observe things in your environment. It will allow you to observe in the same way as you have been observing and focusing on your breathing, without judgment, from a space of quiet contemplation. You can observe situations and events in the organizational environment with complete calmness, just being aware of any thoughts, as they come and go.

This sphere of observation is also safe and secure, but it can move anywhere and at any speed. The sphere is the calmest place in the universe, but it is where brave leadership begins. Imagine allowing the sphere to be buffeted and moved by the various factors which are acting upon your current situation. Notice where the tension and torsion is on the sphere. Remember, the sphere is indestructible and will take all of the load. You can simply observe, and think in complete freedom and safety.

I would now like you to recall the pulling factors that you identified earlier. These are the situations, events or people in the organization that have a tendency to affect, distort and change your thinking. Also, keeping you "grounded" to a lesser or greater degree are the gravitational forces of your values and needs. As we talked about earlier, these keep you grounded. However, there is a tension between these pulling factors and the gravitational factors that you may have noticed and these forces must be considered before a balanced and brave decision can be made.

From the distance created by the sphere and with the protection it provides, it is safe to observe what is happening within the organization. You might want to move closer to some of the pulling factors, perhaps starting, as you have suggested, with the company culture. Zoom in close and notice what issues there are that need to be considered, that are seeking your attention, and that in their way are demanding that you take them into account. Which ones are able to pull you more in their direction? Take a mental note for the moment, or if you prefer, open your eyes briefly, write down any key points. We can consider each of your pulling factors in exactly the same way.

[Pause for leader to consider and make notes if necessary.]

COACH: And now let's move to the gravitational factors. Think of some of those factors that you identified previously and relate them to the current pulling situation. Does this situation, for example, demand truth, or fairness, or openness, or honesty, or justice (whichever of your gravitational factors is most appropriate)? Once you have located both the pulling factor and the gravitational factor or factors, just be aware of the subtle interplay between them.

During the coaching, the leader is encouraged to travel around each of the pulling factors and then examine the gravitational factors, all the time sharing or recording the feelings and tensions that arise. At certain points the sphere may move to a position where all factors are being felt but the sphere is being held by a tension between the different gravitational forces. It is at this point that contemplation requires deliberate effort and energy to hold the tension for enough time to ask what feels right and to enable the germ of the brave decision to emerge. Taylor (2014) talks about a need to hold the tension between efficiency and quality in organizations and this is one example of the twin pressures leaders may identify. When such tensions are identified, they enable leaders to observe their feelings and biases, balance them against the different pulls on their energy and begin to test different preferences.

The observation function of the sphere, as initiated with Matt in the visualization above, is also important in supporting data-informed leadership decisions. Often the information used to inform decision making is incomplete or, as Knapp, Copland and Swinnerton (2007, p.74) point out, "insufficiently nuanced to carry the weight of important decisions." Weiss (1995) also reminds us that despite our best efforts at systematic data gathering, other factors will always influence our decision making: stakeholder interests, ideologies and the organizational context all play a part. Making the space for the leader to observe tensions and then consider what information is necessary is therefore vital. It should be stressed that, as Weiss identified, there are many factors to be considered during such data identification exercises, including different aspects of the organizational context, interests of different departments or teams, different ideologies and stakeholder interests.

Knapp et al. (2007) also confirm how leaders are in a position to define the focus for the information or data that need to be collected or generated and that this focus will reflect their own leadership priorities. Leaders need the ability to extract, share and then use the useful meaning gleaned from their organizational experience. These data might ultimately be used for:

- diagnosing or clarifying organizational problems;
- weighing alternative courses of action;
- justifying chosen courses of action;
- complying with external requests for information (government, shareholder, policymakers);
- informing daily practice; or
- managing meaning, culture and motivation.

Knapp et al. (2007) also suggest that data are not the same as evidence: "data by themselves are not evidence of anything until users of the data bring concepts, criteria, theories of action, and interpretive frames of reference to the task of making sense of the data" (p.80). They point out that there are several factors that have an influence on a leader's capacity to work with data or information: "what they are focused on, their core values and theories of action, their 'data literacy,' and their access to available data sources" (ibid., p.81). They also emphasize that lack of a focus makes data gathering a waste of time, "an empty exercise, consuming time and yielding little of consequence" (ibid., p.81), making the sphere exercise even more important.

As discussed in Chapter 4, values are closely associated with the "theories of action" that the leader holds. These theories of action are assumptions about how the world works and provide a justification for how to improve it (Argyris & Schön, 1974). Consequently, wherever a leader directs his/her focus, it will be driven by values, as Knapp et al. (2007, p.82) have pointed out: "data-informed leadership rests on a foundation of values and strategic thinking that guides the leaders' reach for data, engagement in inquiry, meaning-making, and subsequent actions."

The benefits of the detached position of the sphere of observation are the ability to observe values as "theories in action" as they relate to and interact with real-time situations. Such observation opens up the possibility of gaining new perspectives and a corresponding deepening of knowledge and understanding. The data and information-gathering aspects of the sphere of observation would also appear to accentuate an expert rather than a hierarchical authority. This connects well with brave leadership thinking, which is based on a distributed, relational and post-heroic leadership philosophy, where it is recognized that information can reside within different communities of practice.

3 Sphere Of Influence

Keywords: exploring energy, feelings and biases, critically analyzing perspectives and needs of stakeholders in relation to gravitational factors

The third element in our guided reflection is the sphere of influence—a conceptual division which helps leaders determine not only what further information is needed, but also what it is possible to change. The sphere of influence therefore considers the reach of the leader in a given situation; it considers whether it is an issue at all, whether the issue is likely to resolve itself, if it is necessary for the leader to get involved, and to what extent it is even possible to intervene at all. Equally, leaders may need to look at what might need to be downplayed or overlooked. Like John's ex-boss, Alison, in Chapter 2, it is important to be prepared and to know all the potential moves in advance. Alison was described as unbiased and fair, but equally didn't shy away from conflict if it was necessary. She appeared to be operating from a position of balance.

The concept of balanced processing has been identified as an important aspect of leadership and involves solicitation by leaders of the different needs, perspectives and viewpoints within the organization and the subsequent impartial consideration of those viewpoints. So leaders need to gather and analyze all relevant viewpoints before making decisions (Walumbwa et al., 2008). Simmons and Sower (2012, p.300) also considered such rationality or sagacity to be vital for leaders, to enable them to recognize creative ideas and provide leadership for innovative work, two attributes that are often in short supply. With the discernment that comes by observing what is happening within the organization and then considering how much influence or reach the leader might have in any situation, such leadership can be enhanced.

In order to reflect critically on issues of influence and reach, the coach asks the leader to float the sphere around the pulling or gravitational factors previously identified as problematic, and then asks questions about each area. The questions may in turn "drive" the sphere to places where there is potential for dynamic tension and ultimately create the opportunity for the leader to recognize the "brave point." For example:

COACH: Now, as you imagine moving away from your gravitational factors, be aware that distance is weakening their effect, and as you move towards the pulling factors, you may notice their pull becoming stronger. Now pause in the sphere for a moment, and consider the subtle and yet powerful interplay between the pulling and gravitational factors. For example, we discussed the need to move forward in the reorganization in a way which gives more control to your teams, but we also noted that one of your pulling factors insists that decision making of that nature should exist only at board level. Is that the area you want to focus on now?

Okay, consider that area in more detail. Is this something you can influence? Is it something you should influence? What do you think your brave role model might do?

Are there any other areas that will be affected, either positively or negatively, by devolving power to the teams? Does that feel right?

The questioning in the sphere of influence encourages the preservation of the dialectical relationship between pulling factors and gravitational factors by holding the tensions between them in continual interplay. Using a dialectic lens, it allows a dynamic overview of the issue, highlighting the nature of the relationship, but also suggesting a point of entry and management strategy for these tensions. This more critical reflection enables an external exploration of organizational constraints, cultures, conflicts. The sphere must eventually be driven to a "point" and held there. It is unlikely that there would be a point of natural equilibrium in any part of the process; rather, by its very nature it will require an act of will, an intention to swim against contradictory currents and possibly hold a position despite the flows and eddies of conflicting forces.

Holding the tension is an important stage in the reflection on problems and some leaders may find it difficult to reflect enough to make tough decisions. One reason may be that they fail to consider all perspectives fully enough to feel confident enough subsequently to act upon what is the right thing to do. Perhaps from a financial perspective they feel comfortable, but they feel uncomfortable that this may be ultimately beneficial to some elements of the workforce whilst being detrimental to others.

Leaders also need to be aware of the temptations and failings that may hinder this fair-minded process and so sabotage their best efforts, causing weakness that can sidetrack them from the real work of brave leadership. Barnard (2008) identified five pathologies that are often evident in the everyday lives of leaders: narcissism, over-optimism, fear, anger and depression. She argues that leaders, like most people, "find it hard to question their own prior judgments; they may 'over commit' to earlier decisions [...] They will also often ignore or discount new information" (p.408). Whilst there are many elements that can influence the angle of approach that a leader might take towards a particular situation, the first three pathologies identified by Barnard are, in our experience, the main traps to be consciously aware of in relation to brave coaching. Below, we examine these three "influence traps" in more detail and provide examples of how the coach can work with the leader to explore and perhaps circumvent pathological responses.

Influence trap 1: Narcissism

It is particularly important for leaders to maintain a balance between having a strong sense of self-worth (too little is not healthy for the leader or for anyone), and cultivating an overbearing sense of self-importance and power which can be especially destructive and result in egotistical and self-aggrandizing narcissism, where the leader believes s/he is right and will not listen to feedback or other people's opinions (Barnard, 2008).

Unfortunately, serving the ego seems to be built into our organizational systems. As Scharmer and Kaufer (2013, p.111) pointed out, "the primary leadership challenge today is the fact that our economic reality is shaped by globally interdependent eco-systems, while institutional leaders, by and large, operate with an organizational *ego-system* awareness" (our emphasis). These authors suggest that institutional leaders tend to be driven by individual targets and performance rewards which manipulate and feed the ego rather than taking account of the wellbeing of the organization, or indeed the planet as a whole.

In order to consider the extent to which the ego is driving leadership decisions, a coach can ask a series of questions to promote self-awareness:

COACH: As you hold the sphere above that pulling factor, notice whether any effort is needed to hold it there. Are there any factors which are exerting a force on the sphere and trying to move you closer? What are those factors? Are they situational or are they aspects of your own value system or leadership style? Is it possible that ego may be playing a part here? What influence are you already having on the situation?
   Then think about what influence you would like to have on this particular situation. How far do you want your reach to extend? Are you seeking more control and influence?

The answers to these questions will be subjective. However, in some situations, they might also have the effect of identifying a level of self-worth and just possibly highlight problematic egotistical tendencies. The coach may then explore the answers and attempt to help the leader decide whether this may be affecting his or her judgment.

If we consider how important leaders are in the organizational system, we see how they have the ability to direct energy and resources towards one area, whilst possibly "starving" another. The leader can be in many ways the most important power within that system. Whilst self-worth and a sense of having a locus of control are important to wellbeing, if a leader is motivated by the need to gain an unhelpful level of control and influence, simply for the sake of having control and influence, then this can lead to an unbalanced state within an organization. As Spiderman learned, "with great power there must also come—great responsibility." Therefore, we would suggest that it becomes important for leaders not only to search for a decision, but also to ensure they are in the most responsible space to be able to consider all the options and make that judgment.

Influence trap 2: Over-optimism

Barnard (2008, p.413) suggested that evidence of over-optimism is not as easy to identify as narcissism, mainly because it "often feels good to subordinates and co-workers and rarely fosters resentment or leads to the press." Also, over-optimism can be an effective part of leadership success. However, Barnard also pointed out that there is a difference between well-founded optimism and over-optimism, or what Lovallo and

Kahneman (2003) called "delusional optimism," where the limits of control over a given situation are not readily acknowledged. In fact, Hayward (2007) has suggested that over-optimism arises from the combination of a surfeit of pride, the failure to read the situation or to get the right help, together with a failure to anticipate undesirable consequences. This reality check is an area where the coach, using the framework of the brave sphere, can be of considerable help to the leader. To help clarify the reality of a situation, coaches may use some questions to test the veracity of the apparent situation. Some examples are given below:

COACH: As you move the sphere to the next pulling factor, consider whether there is more information you need in order to understand the situation fully. What are the less obvious influences at play here?
From what you understand as happening, how can you be sure that this is what is actually happening? Did you actually witness this yourself?
How can you be sure that this information can be trusted? Has this ever turned out to be wrong in the past?

The coach may also wish to act as a counter-balance against over-optimism. Some examples of questions that could be asked to help the leader combat any overly optimistic tendencies are shown below.

COACH: Can you describe how that might work? What does the critical path analysis look like?
Has everyone been consulted?
When you say some people think this is dangerous, do they have a point? What do you see as the dangers? What would a cautious friend suggest?
It is important to be realistically optimistic, and so how realistic is that? How can you be certain?
Has this approach always worked? What is your backup plan?

Sometimes the over-optimism of the leader can result in corporate failure, as unmitigated risks are taken. Combined with narcissism, over-optimism can be disastrous in the business world, as evidenced by several high-profile failures (Barnard, 2008).

Influence trap 3: Fear

There is a famous saying which suggests that it is not power that corrupts, but fear (Harris, 2012). Fear is a major behavioral driver which can cause spectacularly bad or untimely decisions or judgments to be made. The main problem with fear, especially the fear of humiliation, is that it creates mental barriers that prevent people from looking inwards and so hinders self-awareness. It is therefore vital that leaders are aware of the potential impact that fear may be currently having on their thinking.

One of our leaders, Ron, was led through a simple emotional awareness-raising exercise, and as a result became much more aware of how fear had crept up on him to become quite a powerful influence in his life and work:

COACH: We have talked about how strong emotions can impact our thinking and decision making. As you know, we wanted to check that there wasn't some false sense of security or invulnerability at work that might have been making you feel overly optimistic. We also talked about anger and control. As you know, anger can radically alter our thought processes, and feeling out of control or feeling the need to overly control can also skew our thinking and behaviors. I wanted to check with you about any other emotions you think may be affecting your thinking and decision making. Is there anything which you need to consider before continuing?

RON: Well, yes, actually. When you mentioned a false sense of security earlier, I was keen to explore that whole area of me perhaps, being overly optimistic, but what I've realized was actually happening below the surface was that I felt kind of the opposite. I didn't want to disrupt the flow of our earlier conversation, but being totally open here, I feel particularly insecure. In fact, I'd go so far as to say that I feel quite fearful. I hadn't really thought about quite how much it has been sitting there in the background, a sort of knot in my stomach. And just exploring that a bit further has made me realize what a predominant emotion fear has actually become in my life. I do actually feel very fearful just now; I'm feeling low as a leader. And so I've got to be aware, as you have suggested, about strong emotions when I make a decision—this feeling may be impacting on my thought processes.

COACH: Thank you for mentioning that, it is very important. I would suggest that before we proceed we should deal with that emotion first. It might not disappear, but we may stop it from becoming debilitating, or at least we can be aware of how it may be impacting things, and so be ready to scrutinize it with an understanding that we might need to look at it from a non-fearful counter-balancing position. First, I'm going to suggest that we get you as relaxed as possible, and then we might want to understand where this fear is coming from.

RON: I do feel more relaxed now and yet I know that there are likely to be situations which trigger me back into feeling fearful again.
COACH: And so …?
RON: And so I need to deal with the issues.
COACH: Yes, and I think that from what you've described, there are two main challenges here. One is a need for you to desensitize yourself, a little bit like overcoming a fear of spiders. I'm not suggesting that tackling some of your colleagues and saying "no, that isn't right, I disagree, we should do this instead" is like approaching a spider, although at the moment it might feel like that to you! And so I was wondering about desensitizing in stages.
RON: You mean, like disagreeing slightly, or perhaps just getting my voice heard, even if it is in agreement?
COACH: Exactly. And for the other challenge, I think that we need to look at what you are telling yourself about you. I think that we need to explore your narrative about yourself and about others. From what I've heard so far, they both seem slightly fantastical! I've heard how great and powerful everyone else is, and how lacking you are. I do think that we must look at the frames you are putting around you and others. As I heard you talking earlier, it reminded me of the movie, *The Wizard of Oz*. There often is just a little man behind a curtain!
RON: Ah! And I'm the cowardly lion?
COACH: Actually, I was thinking more Dorothy.
RON: [Laughs.]
COACH: Yes, probably the lion … but the point being that he wasn't cowardly!
RON: Ah!
COACH: The lion had done some amazingly brave things, but he still told himself he was cowardly. It was only when he reflected on what he had actually achieved that he began to change his internal dialogue—and of course also when he was validated as being brave from, ironically, the little guy from behind the curtain!
RON: So I need to do some reflection on what I have achieved and also probably what my strengths are.

As well as the well-known "imposter syndrome," feelings of impotence can seem to generate genuine fear for leaders. This is the fear that comes when there is a need to make a decision quickly without complete information. Thus, in order to make their decisions, leaders may also need to learn to rely on intuition as well as the evidence available to them. One concern is that without the confidence to trust their intuition, which may only come with experience, leaders may spend too long analyzing or they may change their mind and appear weak or indecisive. In addition, fear might be evident in relationships with stakeholders, particularly shareholders who can be very influential in the decisions a company makes.

The brave point

One extremely important aspect of all three of these traps is that at some point during the process the leader will need to have his or her "feet held against the fire" by the coach. There will need to be some form of challenge to current thinking and the potential power of the sphere lies in the coach's ability to help the client arrive at what we might call the "brave point"—the point or moment at which the leader feels there is a balance between, for example, organizational needs and organizational values. This process may be very uncomfortable, but it will lead to a more effective and, it is hoped, braver decision. For example, it might be that a client, as was the case with John in Chapter 4, perceives a conflict between the gravitational factor of being fair to a group of employees and fulfilling an economic priority (pulling factor). In this example it may be that the brave point is closer to the gravitational factor of "fairness to the individual" rather than to the economic pull of the organization, or if the economic pull was stronger for the right reason, the decision could be different. The "brave point" then highlights the way forward for the brave decision itself.

Summary

In this chapter we have examined how the brave sphere thought exercise uses the idea that it is important for leaders to think about organizational issues calmly and from a "safe distance." In the chapter we explored how using the metaphor of a spherical spacecraft has three benefits for the leader: it provides a place of calm and sanctuary to reflect on problems; it enables a focus on different perspectives and needs within the organizational landscape; and it creates the opportunity for feelings to be analyzed, holding what is found as a resource for brave decision making. The opportunity to reflect in an objective way on real events was preceded by an exercise in focused breath control to increase mindfulness. Following this, the sphere of observation and the sphere of influence enabled tensions to be experienced, held and considered in relation to organizational needs and values as a precursor to finding the brave point—a key element in the decision-making process.

The three-phase reflection model encompassed by the sphere suggested a linear approach to problem solving. However, in real-world settings, these three phases are actually more dynamic than is possible to illustrate using words. They interact in a non-linear, cyclical way, possibly triggering further cycles of problem-focused cognition. The potentially potent mix of enabling leaders to consider what a brave person would do, what they would do if they were brave, and what would be the "right" thing to do, was designed to allow the leader access to as much of what he or she considers being brave as possible.

Guided visualization techniques such as those outlined in this chapter can help leaders to gain confidence. Successful decisions that result from critical reflection on problems can foster necessary self-assurance to be decisive and brave in later decision-making circumstances. Leaders who are committed to using such techniques can thus boost their intuitive thinking in the longer term. They learn to trust their instincts, knowing that these are based on early reflective work, so that when wicked problems demand quick decisions or when complex problems defy straightforward answers, they have the capability to tackle the situation. As suggested earlier, there is a paradox in that as leaders grow comfortable with using reflective techniques and are open to the fact that although initially they can seem time consuming, they actually enable the leader to come to a decision more quickly. The time invested is well worthwhile, resulting in greater confidence and ability to make more assured and quicker decisions as time goes by.

There is a further conundrum, in that whilst the actions of the leader are likely to have wide-ranging implications for the organization, the leader is often under the greatest pressure to be seen to lead, but this "seen to lead" can take the form of an expectation that speed of execution is a measure of success. Of course, there are roles and situations where time is very much of the essence, and fast and accurate decisions are required, but if that is the case consistently then there is little time to generate "concrete experience," and reflect and learn and possibly change the approach for next time. We would suggest that as the sphere may be a mechanism by which such reflection can take place, it could become a valuable asset for both leader and coach.

Bennet and Bennet (2008a, p.7) suggest that the preparation process for decision making includes:

> understanding the domain of interest as well as possible; recognizing the level of uncertainty, surprise potential and nature of the landscape; preparing for the journey in terms of resources, flexibility, partners,

expectations, goal shifting, etc.; making sure that individuals carrying out the decision strategy are ready (i.e., sustainability criteria are met); and ensuring that all relevant alternatives have been considered.

In this chapter we have suggested consolidating understanding of the domain of interest through use of the brave sphere. In the next chapter, after discussing different types of problem, such as wicked and tame, and the implications of these for decision making, we introduce a process for probing options. The decisions that leaders like Ron and John are likely to have to make will probably be multi-layered and the sphere exercise will have allowed them to think through some of the subtleties. Next, their "brave point" resolutions are taken to another level of discussion, away from the sphere, to explore what they actually mean in practical, decision-making terms.

7
THE BRAVE DECISION

Introduction

In the management of any action, there are three processes: "pre-decisional processes (engagement), the cognitive process of determining what action to take, and post-decisional processes (execution), ensuring implementation of the goal" (Ives & Cox, 2012, p.29). So far in this book we have spent some time looking at the pre-decisional processes, which are the main work of the leader and the coach together as the leader prepares to make brave decisions and take action. We saw in Chapter 5, for example, how self-regulation plays an important part in the balancing activities necessary in the pre-decisional phase. In Chapter 6 we then suggested that opposing values, imperatives, pressure points and tensions (the pulling and the gravitational factors) can be observed operating within the organizational system by visiting them using a safe, private "spacecraft" which we called "the sphere." The sphere provides the reflective and critical thinking space needed in the pre-decisional phase to assess complex problems. It is in this space that, as Bennet and Bennet described, the decision maker is:

> learning how to *feel* the system's pulse through close attention, listening, experience and reflection. This feel for the system is essential since analysis and logic produce useful answers only if their assumptions are correct, and if all material causal relationships can be taken into account—an almost impossible task in a complex system.
>
> *(Bennet & Bennet, 2008a, p.4)*

In this chapter, we look at how that assessment can be used for decision making, explore cognitive processes for determining the action to be taken and how options for deciding can be identified. Later, in Chapter 8, we examine the post-decisional or implementation process in more detail. Figure 7.1 summarizes the path we suggest for brave decision making.

In our view coaches need to be aware of the complexity of leaders' tasks and to develop questions to help leaders identify patterns and uncover relationships and networks, as well as helping them develop strategies, anticipate decision outcomes or use their intuition. This chapter therefore begins in section one with an overview of the nature of problems and the difference between the problems tackled by managers and those faced by leaders. In section two we describe a rational approach to decision making proposed by Drucker (1970, 2004), before going on to examine of the role of intuition in decision making in section three. In section four we return to the complexity of the task and introduce two techniques that can be used in coaching—one for recognizing connections and one for identifying options and working both rationally and intuitively towards the brave decision point.

1 The Nature Of Problems

As mentioned in Chapter 1, one of the differences between management and leadership is in the nature of the problem to be solved. According to Grint (2008, p.12), "management is the equivalent of *déjà vu* (seen this

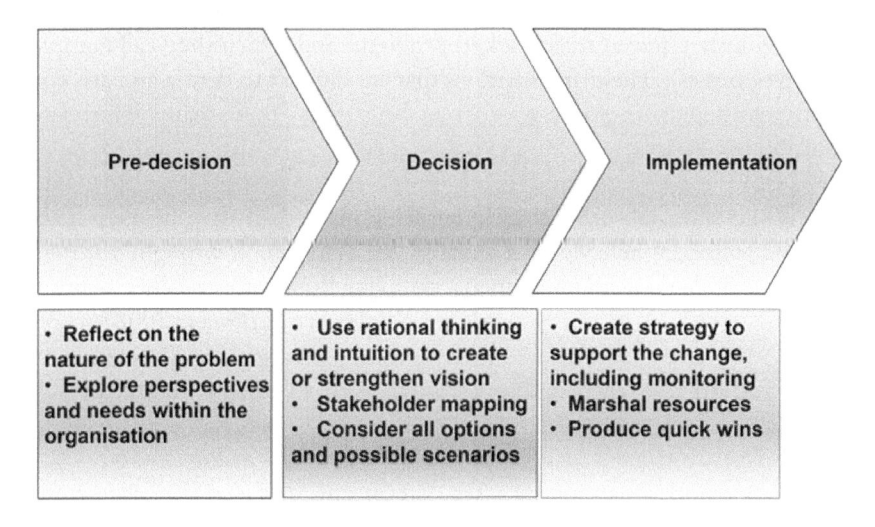

Pre-decision	Decision	Implementation
• Reflect on the nature of the problem • Explore perspectives and needs within the organisation	• Use rational thinking and intuition to create or strengthen vision • Stakeholder mapping • Consider all options and possible scenarios	• Create strategy to support the change, including monitoring • Marshal resources • Produce quick wins

FIGURE 7.1 The brave decision-making process

before), whereas leadership is the equivalent of *vu jàdé* (never seen this before)." This suggests that a manager focuses on solving problems that draw on experiences of similar problems in the past, while a leader is "required to reduce the anxiety of his or her followers [...] by facilitating the construction of an innovative response to the novel problem, rather than rolling out a known process" (ibid., p.12).

These two types of problems have been referred to as either tame or wicked (Churchman, 1967; Rittell & Webber, 1973; Grint, 2005, 2008). Wicked problems are those that are complex and have contextual dependencies that cannot be unraveled in a simple way: there is no one solution to the problem. Churchman (1967, p.141) described wicked problems as a "class of social system problems which are ill formulated, where the information is confusing, where there are many clients and decision makers with conflicting values, and where the ramifications in the whole system are thoroughly confusing." Examples of wicked problems could be: devising an environmental policy that satisfies all stakeholders in a large, fast-moving retail organization; implementing a child protection policy in inner-city areas; or working out a way forward for a country's independence. Tame problems, by contrast, are less uncertain; they may be complicated or divergent, but can generally be resolved by examining what has been successful before and/or applying logic to a solution. Grint (2008) gives examples of timetabling the railways or conducting wage negotiations as examples of tame problems.

Bennet and Bennet (2008a) have also explored the decision-making process as it relates to complex situations in complex environments (what we previously referred to as wicked problems and which they call complex adaptive messes). These are situations that are difficult to define and are constantly shifting in response to change because of their many interrelated contributory factors:

> While sinks (absorbers) and sources (influencers) may be identifiable and aggregate behaviour observable, the landscape is wrought with surprises and emergent phenomena, rumbling from perpetual disequilibrium.
> *(Bennet & Bennet, 2008a, p.2–3)*

These authors also argued that in order even to discuss complexity, we require:

> an appropriate language, a set of concepts and ways to characterize the situation. For example, without an awareness and understanding of concepts such as the tipping point, butterfly effect, emergence,

feedback loops, power laws, nonlinearity, etc., it is difficult to have a frame of reference which would adequately recognize and permit an integrated view of a complex situation. Thus, rather than intelligence or brilliance, it is more likely to be homework, learning and "some experience living with the situation" that guides the decision-maker through the landscape and subtle underlying patterns that facilitate an interpretation of the future of a complex situation.

(Bennet & Bennet, 2008a, p.10)

Bennet and Bennet (2008a, p.1) also suggested that the process for decision making in such circumstances includes: "laying the groundwork for decision making, understanding and exploring complex situations, discussing human additive factors, preparing for the decision process and mechanisms for influencing complex situations." In laying this groundwork several phenomena are important to bear in mind:

- emergence, where organizational learning needs to be factored in as well as individual contributions;
- butterfly effect, where a small change in part of the system can result in a larger, harder to predict event; and
- tipping points, where previously quite stable systems hit a threshold and large-scale change occurs.

Bennet and Bennet identified further mechanisms for manipulating complex situations which included boundary management (changing funding, people, information flows, etc.), simplification (by keeping a clear sense of purpose), and seeding (encouraging emergence), as well as systems modeling and scenario development. They proposed that decision makers could construct strategies to guide problem resolution through sequencing decisions and actions, thus leading eventually to acceptable solutions. In addition, both cognitive and emotional resources are considered vital, together with experience, education, knowledge of the environment, networks, individual preferences, frames of reference and emotional intelligence, all of which have a part to play in an informed decision-making process.

The difference between tame and wicked problems is summarized in Figure 7.2. This model draws on Grint's classification of tame, wicked and critical problems, but includes a further problem type, inspired by Pidd and Woolley's (1980) work on problem structuring. It also takes into account Bennet and Bennet's (2008a) discussions of complex adaptive messes. It can be seen how critical decisions have an imminent timeline

130 The Brave Decision

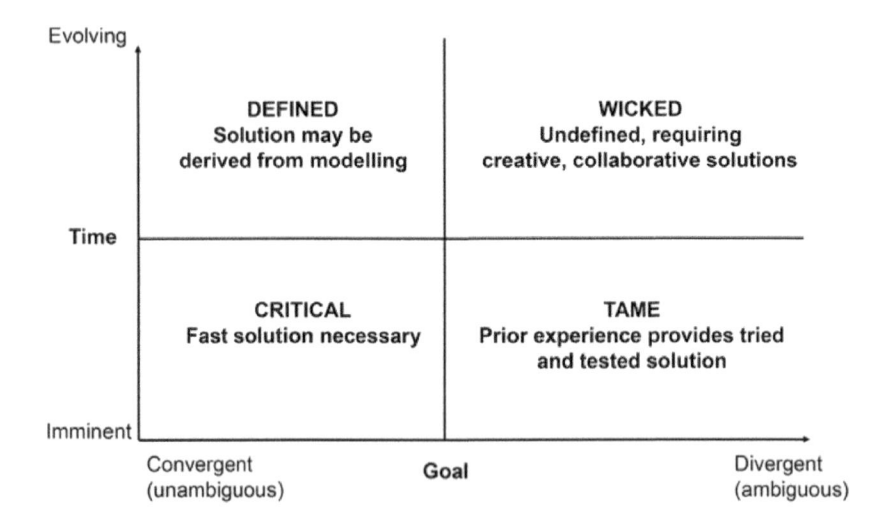

	Convergent (unambiguous) — Goal — Divergent (ambiguous)
Evolving (Time)	**DEFINED**: Solution may be derived from modelling / **WICKED**: Undefined, requiring creative, collaborative solutions
Imminent	**CRITICAL**: Fast solution necessary / **TAME**: Prior experience provides tried and tested solution

FIGURE 7.2 Classification of problems facing leaders

while (well-)defined decisions have a more emergent trajectory, but both have convergent goals (Ives & Cox, 2012). Tame and wicked goals, on the other hand, have more divergent or ambiguous goals, tame being the more imminent in relation to time, and wicked being characterized by an evolving timeframe.

For coaches of leaders facing wicked problems it is useful to understand the differences in authority in relation to the problems being faced so that they may help the leader identify the nature of the problem. Grint explains how "the social construction of the problem legitimizes the deployment of a particular form of authority" (Grint, 2008, p.14). His typology suggests there are three forms of authority: command, management and leadership, which in turn deal with problems in different ways: answers, processes, questions. Some "critical" problems, such as those that confront military leaders on active service, have to be responded to quickly: answers have to be forthcoming. By contrast, "tame" problems that face managers in the everyday running of an organization can usually be solved through implementation of appropriate processes. Wicked problems, such as those tackled most frequently by leaders, however, can only be dealt with by asking the right questions and gathering enough information to set up a series of improvisations, taskforces or other multi-pronged strategies that might help provide a solution. Leadership is often perceived by others as the ability to act decisively and resolve problems, but as Grint points out, "we cannot know how to solve Wicked Problems, and therefore we need to be very wary of acting decisively precisely because we cannot know what will happen. If we knew what to do it would be a Tame Problem not a Wicked Problem" (ibid., p.4).

Following a similar unambiguous/ambiguous trajectory, the outcome of Fulop and Mark's (2013) work is to introduce a further quadrant model. This model suggests that problems are both knowable and ordered (simple or complicated), or they have patterns and interactions that are unordered (complex and chaotic). However, an important difference in this construction is the inclusion of an element of disorder that these authors suggest infiltrates all quadrants, applying when there is lack of clarity about which of the other four contexts predominates. Disorder suggests that "multiple perspectives jostle for prominence, factional leaders argue with one another, and cacophony rules" (ibid., p.260).

2 A Rational Approach To Decision Making

There is a wide range of advice on decision making in the management and leadership literature and the majority of it is presented as a rational process, involving normative or prescriptive models for choosing alternative courses of action (Vroom & Jago, 1974). Vroom and Jago present a decision tree model where problem attributes are considered in turn using a series of closed questions, such as: "Do I have sufficient info to make a high-quality decision?" or "Is acceptance of the decision by subordinates critical to effective implementation?" (ibid., p.323). This model is quite complicated to use for most decision making and is probably only useful as a process to help with very complex or novel decisions, when the leader has time to contemplate in some detail.

Another influential management thinker is Drucker (1970, 2004), who also proposes a prescriptive model of five logical steps for effective organizational decision making:

i) Determine if the issue is a generic problem or a true exception

Leaders are usually faced with the exceptions; it is their managers who face the repeating problems. This means that the coach's role is to help the leader to pause, to reflect and to consider whether this problem could be dealt with more effectively by someone else in the organization. Within a high-pressure environment where leaders feel the need to be seen to act quickly and decisively on the exceptional problems, particularly whilst trying to prove themselves early in their careers, it is very possible that they will fall back on successful tactics from their previous role. Whilst these may initially work, it is likely that the nature of the wicked problem/

environment will quickly trip them up. So the sanctuary of the coaching session and the sanity check which that provides could prove an essential component in the leader's "survival kit."

It should also be remembered that leaders focus mainly on high-level, strategic or generic decisions, rather than problem solving (Drucker, 1970, p.115). When they are assessing need, therefore, they aim to identify constants in the situation: "They want to know what the decision is all about and what the underlying realities are which it has to satisfy" (ibid., p.115).

Drucker (1970, p.124) advises that it is best to assume that the issue in question is a symptom of some generic problem. He suggests that for most of the time this assumption will be accurate. Therefore leaders need to create policies and principles that address generic problems, but at the same time be aware of any true exceptions and to respond logically with an adaptation of a rule. Often what is required is more than a superficial examination in order to see the relationship between symptoms of the issue and the exact cause. This is one of the reasons why the exploration of pulling and gravitational factors is so important, together with the reflective space provided by the sphere.

ii) Clearly specify what the decision is expected to accomplish (the desired results) as well as all existing boundary conditions

Drucker's next advice is to state the minimum goals that will be acceptable as a solution and to identify any boundary conditions or pre-existing circumstances that, if they change, will have an impact on the results. He argues that clearly setting out the boundary conditions is as vital as clearly stating specific goals because any changes in those conditions make it easier to identify if a particular decision or strategy needs to be abandoned.

However, we believe that Drucker's advice should be augmented here. Any organization, team and/or individual will bring their own habits, preferences, biases, groupthink, earlier solutions, blind spots, etc. to the problem. It is essential therefore to consider how to broaden the thinking to counter the potential "tramlines" of thought that can exist, but also because especially when emotional thinking is involved (which may well be the case when facing highly charged wicked problems), the brain tends to trip into much cruder thinking. Then, if this emotional thinking is shared by several people, the problem may seem insurmountable and/or only able to be solved by a limited number of options. So it would seem that getting different perspectives or "borrowing someone else's brain," particularly to gain a more rational or creative perspective, would be a wise option to choose. We would suggest that a good coach could be invaluable in such a situation. Mentors, advisors, consultants and members of different organizations could all also play a valuable role here. Coaching in particular will provide the leader with the space to become calmer, to consider other options, to consider habits and blind spots, and to consider boundary conditions and alternative solutions. It should be borne in mind, however, that even with these other elements in the "mix" the leader may not ever be able to know all the boundary conditions of the wicked problem that are likely to occur. On the other hand, these additional considerations may help to diminish radically the scope of the unknown.

iii) Base decisions on the outcome being "right" vs. just being "acceptable"

Aiming for a potential "right" outcome is what we would refer to as a "brave" decision. It is about striving for what is the best and right decision at that time. Drucker (2004, p.17) explains how it is important for effective executives to ask: "Is this the right thing for the enterprise?" We agree, but would caution that simply asking if it is right for the executives on the board, even though they have ultimately to support the decision, is the wrong focus. If the vision for the organization and the vision-linked strategy is in place, the brave leader can judge what is best for the organization, for that particular enterprise. The brave leader realizes that the share price is important, but he or she also realizes that if a decision is not right for the enterprise it will not be right for any of the other stakeholders. Coaches may need to ask leaders a number of questions to test the rightness of the decision for the organization: "Is this course of action ethical? Is it acceptable within the organization? Is it legal? Is it compatible with the mission, values, and policies of the organization?" (ibid., p.18).

Drucker (1970) has emphasized, however, that decisions are rarely choices between right and wrong. More often, he says, they are judgments between seemingly reasonable alternatives: "At best a decision can be a choice between 'almost right' and 'probably wrong,' but more often a decision involves choosing between two courses of action, neither of which is probably a great deal more right than the other" (ibid., p.152).

iv) Converting decisions into action

Drucker also points out how until a decision is actioned, there really has been no decision made at all. Therefore leaders need to ensure that plans are actionable and that they match the resources available; indeed, they need to plan their course of action to include proximal goals (Ives & Cox, 2012). As Drucker (2004, p.18) points out, they need to think about "desired results, probable restraints, future revisions, check-in points, and implications." Questions that need to be asked by the coach might be: What results are acceptable? What deadlines are acceptable? Drucker points out that "affirmative answers don't guarantee that the action will be effective. But violating these restraints is certain to make it both wrong and ineffectual." In addition, the action plan is a statement of intentions rather than a commitment: "It must not become a straitjacket. It should be revised often, because every success creates new opportunities" (Drucker, 2004, p.18).

v) Feedback

Drucker's five steps also include a plan for monitoring the results of the decision against the goals and expectations. This includes observing first hand as much as possible; rather than relying on reports and second-hand information. In addition, the created action plan needs to have systems for checking results against expectations and should include checks against time and feasibility. Drucker notes that Napoleon is attributed with saying that "no successful battle ever followed its plan," and yet it is reported that Napoleon also "planned every one of his battles, far more meticulously than any earlier general had done. Without an action plan, the executive becomes a prisoner of events. And without check-ins to re examine the plan as events unfold, the executive has no way of knowing which events really matter and which are only noise" (Drucker, 2004, p.18).

Finally, Drucker (1970, p.158) suggested that leaders ask themselves whether any decision is really necessary: "One alternative is always the alternative of doing nothing." He proposes the leader should determine whether action or inaction is the best solution by comparing the risks and rewards of each, choosing to act if the benefits greatly outweigh the costs or risks. He warns that "every decision is like surgery. It is an intervention into a system and therefore carries with it the risk of shock. One does not make unnecessary decisions any more than a good surgeon does unnecessary surgery" (ibid., p.158). More recently Steve Jobs is also noted as saying "deciding what not to do is as important as deciding what to do" (Isaacson, 2011, p.336).

We would suggest that Drucker's rational steps could readily be used as a framework by coaches to address the issues inherent in both straightforward and wicked problems, but only provided they are held loosely and flexibly, as described in more detail below.

3 The Role Of Intuition

Up until now we have been talking very much about a rational process of decision making, based on gathering information and considering a range of factors. However, although the rational approach to decision making is useful, wicked problems do not have simple solutions. Therefore leaders also need to take account of how the complexity affects decision-making processes, especially since so many decision-making models are based on the existence of a problem that has an answer—e.g. tame or critical problems. The existence of a wicked problem needs a different approach.

In addition, there are a number of recent criticisms of an emphasis solely on a rational approach to decision making, which result in the view that "the adoption of a deliberative and analytic approach can also disrupt intuitive and automatic functioning" (Zhong, 2011, p.7). Zhong questions reliance solely on deliberative decision making on moral grounds, suggesting that a purely rational focus "may actually increase unethical behaviors and reduce altruistic motives when it overshadows, implicit, intuitive influences on moral judgments and decisions" (ibid., p.1). Zhong explains how the majority of organizational researchers base their thinking on Kohlberg's model of moral development and so see ethical decision making as "a conscious, intentional, and deliberative process" (Kohlberg, 1963, p.2).

Bennet and Bennet (2008a, p.5) also suggested that complex situations need to be studied using a combination of reductionist and holistic thinking, thus fully engaging the decision maker's experience, intuition and judgment in order to solve problems. They suggest that the "competency to use intuition and judgment to solve problems without being able to explain how they know is a common characteristic of experts. These individuals actively learn through deliberate, investigative and knowledge-seeking experience, developing intuition and building judgment through play and intensive interaction with the system and its environment" (ibid., p.5). They explain how experts use "long-term working memory, pattern recognition and chunking rather than logic as a means of understanding and analyzing" (ibid., p.5), and suggest that by "exerting mental effort and emotion while exploring complex situations knowledge becomes embedded in the unconscious." In addition, it could be that by manipulating, modifying and "generally playing with information," understanding patterns and their relationships to other patterns in complex situations, leaders can proactively develop intuition, insight and judgment (Bennet & Bennet, 2008a).

It appears, therefore, that as advances in psychology are beginning to suggest, factors other than rational deliberation are important in how people make choices. Intuition also has an important role to play in how people resolve ethical dilemmas. Some are even suggesting that deliberative decision making can impair the ability to make ethical decisions in some settings in that it interferes with "doing the right thing." For this reason, Zhong (2011) argued, we need to challenge the "worship of reason" and embrace intuition. According to Haidt (2006), as well, many of us determine whether an action is right or wrong automatically, making a snap judgment, rather than checking for the often more subtle feeling of intuition. Comparing moral intuitions to aesthetic judgments, Haidt suggests that we instantly know whether we think something is beautiful, for instance, even though we do not necessarily know why. He further accuses the rational mind of being like a press secretary who advances our own interests and merely "spins" a rationale for our intuitive moral decisions. However, Haidt does not advocate going with gut instincts when contemplating a moral decision. His advice is to check the perceptions of others to see what they think. Zhong, on the other hand, unequivocally champions the use of intuition rather than a rational approach to moral judgment, stressing that "recent research on moral intuition and embodied morality proposes a messier picture in which morality is grounded in our flesh and bones and intertwined with emotions, tactile sensory input, and other concrete somatic experiences" (Zhong, 2011, p.6). These components, he suggests, are integral to our moral experience and contribute significantly to our sense of right and wrong. Importantly, he says: "the effects of these somatic factors are not always conscious." Crucially, Zhong argues, "a deliberative decision-making approach may overshadow the influences of intuitive factors and, instead, lead people to focus on other salient and plausible factors, such as monetary payoffs, as the basis for their choices" (ibid., p.7).

Dane and Pratt (2007, p.40) define intuitions as "affectively-charged judgments that arise through rapid, non-conscious and holistic associations." The process, they say, is "driven by intention, of trusting and acting upon one's knowledge, at a particular moment in time, and without conscious evidence of the logic of doing so in that moment in time" (ibid., p.40).

In addition, Cox (2013) explains how intuition is conceptualized in two distinct ways, either as holistic hunch, as suggested by Dane and Pratt's definition, or as automated expertise. Intuition as hunch is where judgments or choices are made through the subconscious synthesis of information drawn from previous experience, whereas intuition as automated expertise corresponds to an identification of recognizable situations and a subconscious application of previous understanding to that situation. Miller and Ireland (2005) have pointed out that this type of intuition develops over time as more experience is accrued in specific domains. We would argue that both definitions are useful in decision making. Francisco and Burnett (2008, p.239) even suggest that intuition is a key part of the problem-solving process and that it is "the product of directed thought."

These arguments and suggestions arise from a better understanding in recent years of the dual processing by the brain that distinguishes conscious, deliberative and rational thinking from the more automatic processing involved in intuition. One of the most influential theories of dual processing is the system described by Evans (2003). Evans proposed that in the dual-process system, two equally important systems of the brain are interlinked. Effectively, he argues, there are "two minds in one brain" (Evans, 2003, p.454), with each having a different, but important function. System 1 is considered rapid, parallel and automatic, while System 2 allows "abstract hypothetical thinking that cannot be achieved by System 1" (ibid., p.454), but is somewhat slower and more ordered in nature. Cox (2013, p.143) reports how theories of thinking have traditionally been associated with these two distinct modes or systems of thought, the first incorporating "the seemingly more irrational forms of thought, such as intuition," and the second "the cognitive rational activity that aspires towards pure reason." The two principal modes, automatic and controlled, could therefore be referred to as "intuitive" and "analytic," respectively. The latter has usually attracted more credence than the former, as discussed by Croskerry (2013).

Croskerry (2013, p.2445), whilst examining medical decision making, explained how the two brain systems involve "different cortical mechanisms with associated neurophysiologic and neuroanatomical substrates." He points out that "although the two processes are often construed as two different ways of reasoning, in fact very little (if any) reasoning occurs in Type 1 processing—it is largely reflexive and autonomous." Such intuitive processes, he argues, "are generally either hardwired or acquired through repeated experience. They are subconscious and fast and mostly serve us well, enabling us to conduct much of our daily business in all fields of human activity" (p.2446). This type of intuitive process, we would suggest, is more aligned to Dane and Pratt's suggested "automated expertise" than their "holistic hunch."

By way of contrast, Croskerry explains how analytic processes of Type 2 (or System 2 in Evans terminology), are: "conscious, deliberate, slower, and generally reliable. They follow the laws of science and logic and therefore are more likely to be rational." Croskerry suggests that the major drawback of this analytic reasoning is that it is time and resource intensive: "Although analytic reasoning can often be done quickly and effectively, in most fields [...] it would be impractical to deal with each decision analytically" (Croskerry, 2013, p.2446).

Bennet and Bennet (2007, p.406) have also explained how decision making requires "not only facts and information but also experience, intuition and judgment." The capacity to make a good decision often lies, they say, "in the unconscious mind as relevant patterns of knowledge that may come forth when needed." Their argument is that an individual experiences from tacit knowledge, which is critical to judgment and decision making: "As situations become more complex and decision time compresses, leaders must create, nurture and rely on their tacit knowledge and its mouthpiece, intuition" (ibid., p.406).

Later, Bennet and Bennet (2008a, p.5) pointed out that the ability to use intuition and judgment for problem solving is a common characteristic of experts. They give the example of master chess players who rely on "effortful practice" to set them apart from people who play chess for many years but still maintain average skill. They suggest that "by exerting mental effort and emotion while exploring complex situations knowledge becomes embedded in the unconscious." Thus by manipulating, modifying and generally playing around with information, and starting to understand patterns, leaders could proactively enhance their insight and judgment. Exploring wicked problems with a coach can enable a leader to recognize patterns in the flow of complex situations, thus enhancing intuition. Certainly it could be argued that coaching dialogue and the enhancement of critical thinking can significantly improve a leader's understanding of complexity within the organization and help them get a feel for the complex situation and consequently improve decision-making potential: "Sharing ideas and dialogue can surface and clarify confusion, paradoxes and uncertainties to an extent far greater than any one individual mind can do" (Bennet & Bennet, 2008a, p.6).

Research has not yet suggested how we can use both intuition and rationality to good effect in decision making, but our own intuition and logic would suggest that the two need to work in tandem. Thus we propose that the role of the coach is to encourage a combination of rational and intuitive thinking. Indeed, Sadler-Smith and Shefy (2004, p.77) strongly suggested that intuition is "as important as rational analysis in many decision processes," and suggest that there are a number of ways in which leaders and executives can improve their intuitive understanding and skill. For instance, they might pay attention to what Claxton has identified as the "voices of intuition," which include physical feelings, insights, images and dreams, guesses, inklings, hunches and the aesthetic sense. Intuition, Claxton argued, is based on "deep intellectual knowledge of the subject [that] makes use of expert knowledge and manifests as intuitive, elegant and beautiful responses" (Claxton, 1999, p.159).

So what is the role of intuition?

Sadler-Smith and Shefy (2004) have argued that both individuals and organizations are frequently involved in new opportunities that take them into unfamiliar territory where there may be little information and knowledge and there is a need for fast decision making. This puts limits on the time available for rational information processing and makes big demands upon leaders' cognitive abilities to deal with necessary information at speed. This information overload, they suggest, may limit in-depth evaluation and balancing of different courses of action. This is where intuition can be useful: "Intuition is a capacity for attaining direct knowledge or understanding without the apparent intrusion of rational thought or logical inference. Our fundamental precept in the context of executive decision making is twofold: first, intuition is as important as rational analysis in many decision processes; second, there are ways in which executives can improve their intuitive knowledge, understanding, and skill" (ibid., p.77).

Cox (2013, pp.17–18) has described intuition as a "bubbling over of experience into consciousness." Atkinson and Claxton (2000, p.34) described it as an "immediate apprehension, without the intervention of any reasoning process." These authors also consider intuition as coming with a "built-in confidence rating, a subjective feeling of 'rightness,' that may vary in its strength from 'complete guess' to absolute certainty" (ibid., p.40). However, Cox (2013) explains that this observation about rightness could be seen to arise from a direct link between the emotions that are linked to our values, the feeling generated in the body as a result, and the accompanying brain signal that we subsequently call intuition.

It would seem to us that in order to be a brave leader, intuition has to be encouraged, as a combination of knowing and feeling. In the workplace, however, a reliance on intuition, with what can seem like emotionally generated hunches, has been criticized. The feeling is that "strategic thinking should not be debased by feelings; efficient thought and behavior must be called upon to subjugate emotion; and good organizations manage employees' feelings or design them out of the process" (Sadler-Smith & Shefy, 2004, p.77). Sadler-Smith and Shefy have highlighted that there is an inherent assumption within organizations that knowledge is "recognizable and valuable only when it is explicit, untainted by feelings, and open to conscious thought and introspection" (ibid., p.77). However, they also caution that against this rational backdrop, "the significance of unconscious mental processes and feelings should not be underestimated or overlooked since they can be a source of intuitively based judgments that may provide an alternative to consciously derived rational choices" (ibid., p.77):

> When deliberative rational thought is not achievable or desirable (for example, where unambiguous or sufficient "hard" data is not immediately at hand, might never be available at all, or where creative solutions to problems are needed), one way of managing and coping with uncertainty and complexity and of "thinking outside of the box" is by relying upon intuition.
>
> *(Sadler-Smith & Shefy, 2004, p.78)*

As a process, Sadler-Smith and Shefy (2004) have suggested that intuition is automatic and involuntary. However, they point out that "the working environment of executives can support or suppress this automatic and involuntary process through socio-cultural factors which may lead, for example, to general conformance to a rational paradigm (for example, by "groupthink") and collective forms of cognitive inertia (such as "grooved thinking") (ibid., p.80). They caution that if intuition is suppressed persistently it ceases to operate, suggesting that if we invite and practice intuition it will become easier and more frequent. They offer several questions to help judge whether intuition is evident in decision making and some of these could be helpful for coaches to use with their leader clients:

- Do you trust your hunches when confronted by an important decision?
- Do you feel in your body if a decision is right or wrong?
- Do you put a lot of faith in your initial feelings about people and situations?
- Do you put more emphasis on feelings than data when you make a decision?
- Do you rely on your gut feelings when dealing with people?
- Do you trust your experience when arriving at the reasons for making a decision even if you cannot explain why?
- Does your intuition often turn out to have been right all along?
- What is (or would be) the reaction in your organization to decisions made on the basis that they felt right?
- Do you keep your intuition close to your chest? If so, why?

In view of the arguments put forward in support of intuition we suggest that coaches can help leaders not to ignore their intuition but to use it to support other data. Leaders might be encouraged to be comfortable with their intuition and to leverage the potential it offers.

However, Sadler-Smith and Shefy (2004) also warn us not to confuse insight with intuition or instinct. Insight, they say, means being able to see a solution to the problem and being able to explain its elements and its logic: "Hence insight ultimately is conscious and explicable (sometimes after a process of incubation)" (ibid., p.81). Instinct, on the other hand, involves the "in-built fast biological reactions with which evolution has equipped us in order that we can respond to stimuli in ways that maximize our chances of survival in the face of a physical threat" (ibid., p.81). These authors suggest that often intuitions may become insights. However, this is not inevitable, "they may remain for a time as unvalidated hazy felt senses or hunches which may eventually reveal their accuracy or otherwise" (ibid., p.81).

In such complex settings, then, leaders need to make sense of situations that may initially make no sense. It is therefore important for coaches to understand the nature of complexity in order to help their clients observe and reflect, as described in Chapter 6, but also to "use intuition to develop a 'feeling'; for the key relationships and patterns of behaviour within the system" (Bennet & Bennet, 2008a, p.4). The kinds of questions the coach may need to ask include: Is this a problem or is it a symptom of some deeper issue? What can be controlled? What can be influenced? What can be nurtured to emerge?

4 Techniques For Decision Making In Complex Settings

In this section we discuss three techniques that can inform help with understanding the nature of specific complexities and aid decision making in complex environments. The first uses rich pictures to map the organizational setting, the second is the scenario development mentioned earlier, and the third is a brainstorming technique that holds options tentatively in "light boxes" whilst the alternatives are identified and discussed.

i) Rich pictures

Day and Schoemaker (2005) remind us that changes in one industry or sector often affect companies in other areas and give the example of how the Internet affected the music industry, even though this was not anticipated. Thus we can see how complex systems will inevitably have built-in

142 The Brave Decision

unpredictability. Coaches need to understand this in order to ask the right questions and support leaders with mapping such intricacies.

Figure 7.3 shows an example of a rich picture of organizational complexity and the relationships between internal and external stakeholders. Rich pictures have their origin in the theory of soft systems analysis (Checkland & Poulter, 2006), and can be a useful tool in coaching to map out the contingencies in the environment, especially the wider pulling factors. In the example in Figure 7.3, we can see how a railway authority is influenced by many different factors including government policy, trade union decision, customer feedback, media, etc. The relationship between each factor is also identified.

Checkland and Poulter (2006, p.210) suggest that the aim of the rich picture is to "capture, informally, the main entities, structures and viewpoints in the situation, the processes going on, the current recognized issues and any potential ones." With encouragement from the coach, a leader can create such pictures to help thinking and understanding. They can become, as Checkland and Poulter advocate, a trusted way of representing intuitions, insights and perceptions about the organizational system. This rich picture method is distinct from the pulling factors process because it maps external factors that impact one another and can connect

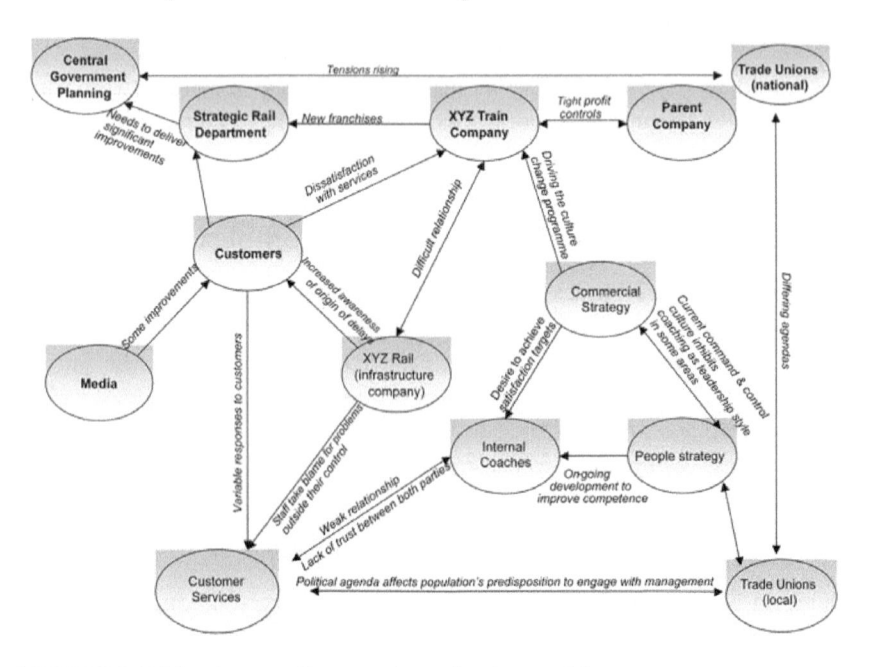

FIGURE 7.3 Rich picture of a complex adaptive problem

to situations and forces far removed from the organization itself. The pulling factors are those that pull specifically on the leader, causing tension and often arousing emotion.

Camillus (2008, p.99) has also explained how companies are increasingly unable to develop models of the complex environments in which they operate: "they are confronted with issues that cannot be resolved merely by gathering additional data, defining issues more clearly, or breaking them down into small problems." Thus traditional processes are unable to resolve wicked problems. They cannot be tackled in a limited time by using standard techniques. In fact, trying to do so might aggravate the problem by generating unwelcome consequences. Camillus further points out that "confusion, discord, and lack of progress are telltale signs that an issue might be wicked," and suggests four ways of addressing the issues:

- *Involve stakeholders*, document their opinions and communicate. The aim here is to develop understanding and promote shared commitment to possible ways of resolving the problem: "Documenting stakeholders' assumptions, ideas, and concerns on an ongoing basis is important. It helps enterprises understand stakeholders' hidden assumptions and gauge the effectiveness of the actions they have taken" (Camillus, 2008, pp.98–101). Bennet and Bennet (2008a, p.4) actually describe how talking with people in the system about "how the work really gets done and who influences what goes on, asking questions and dialoguing to discover their insights, can provide an invaluable sensing capability."
- *Define the corporate identity*. In order to tackle wicked problems it is vital to keep a sense of organizational purpose in order to provide a touchstone against which to evaluate choices.
- *Focus on action*. In situations where there is a clear link between cause and effect, leaders can for the most part judge the strategies they want to follow; however, wicked problems involve complex and shadowy possibilities and so leaders are less likely to know if particular strategies are suitable or how they might evolve. In these circumstances they may want to discard the possibility of thinking through every option before choosing a single one as the options may be too numerous or unknowable. In such cases leaders may become indecisive when they realize that any response to a wicked issue will alter the problem the company faces and necessitate another change in strategy (Camillus, 2008). Rather than keep trying to analyze the issues, leaders in such circumstances would perhaps be better off experimenting with a range of strategies that seem feasible: "the consequences will give

them a better handle on the real problem they face" (ibid., p.100). Thus experiments, pilot programs or test prototypes are recommended.
- *Adopt a "feed-forward" orientation.* According to Camillus, traditional feedback does not work in wicked situations: "Feedback helps people learn from the past; wicked problems arise from unanticipated, uncertain, and unclear futures" (Camillus, 2008, p.100), and comprehending the challenge is part of the problem. Leaders need to check constantly their environment for signals as well as examining the organizational landscape.

ii) Scenario development

To develop a feed-forward orientation as well as using feedback, coaches could ask clients to envision the future. In this kind of scenario planning, leaders would describe the set of external and internal circumstances that they would like to see, for example, in the next five or ten years. This will open their minds to the range and unpredictability of possibilities that the future may bring.

In the extract below, one of our leaders, Ron, has been considering his various pulling factors, which in his case have been mainly other individuals with their own agendas and requirements. He has also been looking at the gravitational factors and thinking about how to make an important decision balancing cost efficiency and recruitment needs:

COACH: All right, Ron, we have now looked at two possible ways forward. From the sphere we considered how it felt to tackle the issue by simply following Keith's wishes—essentially capitulating to his proposed plan.
RON: Yes, and from the sphere I did feel that that was not necessarily entirely wrong, and didn't think that it was unjust or unfair …
COACH: I sense a "but."
RON: Yes, there is a but, and that is that I'm not sure that if I go down that route it will entirely hit the mark.
COACH: In what way?
RON: Well, if I run things forward a bit in time, I can see that whilst we will gain an initial victory, and some things will improve immediately, there may be some unrest a little bit further down the line.
COACH: Unrest in what way?
RON: If we follow Keith's, in my opinion, slightly blinkered agenda, and issue this particular edict on restricting recruitment, we will certainly

save money. However, that slight sense of relief will be mixed with a little apprehension that we are going backward rather than forward.
COACH: And this is what you picked up in the sphere.
RON: Yes, as I said at the time, I felt a slight unease as we traveled in that direction, although I didn't feel that that route would have an impact on the gravitational factors, at least at first glance.
COACH: Why don't we think about taking you further out in time then? What will things be like two years from now, or from Keith's plan going ahead? We could do this as a closed-eyes exercise …

[Ron closes his eyes and imagines the scenario in two years' time.]

RON: Well, that was quite vivid. I imagine that if we stick with it and do what else he suggests, in my opinion there would be an element of perceived financial stability, presuming nothing odd happens in the market, but I just can't see where the energy, the drive, the excitement would come from. As I imagine taking that decision, the one to support and implement Keith's grand plan, I can't for the life of me help but think that that future is actually going to cause us to be impacted on the creativity front, and also that we will have retention issues.
COACH: Retention issues?
RON: We need sharp minds, and they need to be challenged. Part of Keith's plan would mean that we would be unable to provide internships, get the best graduates, or in fact any graduates, and that as a result we cannot have a viable research and development unit.
COACH: What about the other main scenario?
RON: Ah, Paula's passion, as I call it: the approach where we attempt to make efficiency savings elsewhere, like having cheaper coffee, and everyone traveling economy and so on; but, that we actively recruit, and recruit the best, and also that we ensure that we have a viable, long-term, robust research and development department. When we thought about that in the sphere using Paula's plan as the pulling factor, I was initially enthused, but then wondered how fair it was on people to cut back on so many things. I wondered how the environment would actually be.
COACH: Well, what if we try the same idea of imagining going forward in time having adopted Paula's plan. We can do a similar closed-eyes exercise?
RON: Yes, I think that would be very useful.
COACH: Okay, please get yourself into a comfortable seated position.

[Ron closes his eyes and imagines the second scenario in two years' time.]

RON: That was very interesting. After an initial period of pain, I imagined the business picking up, and even eventually being quite transformed from what it is today. And of course, this is my project, and I have the casting vote. It is quite a lot of responsibility. The good news is that even though there are distinct financial ramifications for whatever way we go forward, because so much of it is people related, an HR person has got the final word.
COACH: Do you want to then revisit all the factors later? Perhaps to consider the brave action?
RON: No need, I now know what to do, what is the right thing to do. It may be useful, however, to go through exactly the best approach about how to inform the main parties involved; particularly Keith. Maybe should look at some options for implementation.

It should also be noted that the level of ambiguity caused by complex environments can cause stress and anxiety for the leader, particularly if the leader is just moving from a more managerial role to that of a leader. Some leaders have been promoted more because of their skill set rather than their ability to lead, and because they have been successful managers. The need to understand that the usual linear solutions may not work is essential. The coach has an important role to play here. Leaders who are confused, uncertain and fearful are not likely to be doing themselves or the organization any good and they may find that they do not have a confidante or mentor within the organization, so a coach will be vital. The authors have coached managers who have been promoted from roles that were relatively straightforward to roles that were much more complex. The initial mindset can appear to be that of the "construction worker," meaning that the job has a beginning, a middle and an end, and that goals can be set and achieved in a straightforward managerial manner. This type of mindset can be extremely useful for a managerial and/or project-type role, promoting a sense of achievement at various steps along the way, and following a "critical path" approach, where one thing must happen to unlock others. There is a logic, a flow, a sense of progression. The individuals whom we have coached who have made the leap from management to leadership, where cultural currents, stakeholder dynamics and unpredicted changes can lead to a requirement for continuous reassessment and serious critical thinking, can find it very difficult to adjust.

The coach may be able to help the newly promoted leader with this adjustment. For some, it is a question of identifying and changing habits;

for others, it may require a rethink about the nature of work—task versus people, for instance. For still others, it may simply be stepping out of the comfort zone one degree at a time and becoming familiar with the unfamiliar.

Grint (2008, p.11) also confirms that "to get some purchase on wicked problems we need to start by accepting that imperfection and making do with what is available is not just the best way forward but the only way forward." He argues that progress:

> does not depend upon consensus—that would be too elegant and would take too long! We need to start by asking "what do we all (or at least most of us) agree on?" We also need to assume that no-one has the solution in isolation and that the problem is a system not an individual problem and not a problem caused by or solved by a single aspect of the system.
>
> *(Grint, 2008, p.11)*

The process in wicked environments should also involve considering all alternatives and looking at all opposing viewpoints. Drucker (1970, pp.152–153) suggested that "disagreements are safeguards against becoming a prisoner of the organization ('we've always done it that way') or, more simply, being stuck in a rut. Disagreements not only provide viable alternatives, but can stimulate the imagination as well. Organize disagreements and make a special effort to understand the thinking behind the different ideas."

iii) "Light boxes"

There appears to be no magic formula for getting decisions right but the consideration of the pros and cons of each option's choices is one of the most popular methods that leaders use. Coaches can, for example, encourage their clients to make use of tools such as the decisional balance sheet (Janis & Mann, 1977), which is widely used, although it can become quite elaborate or prescriptive in use. The process is based on the anticipated consequences of alternative courses of action, using four groupings: useful gains and losses for self; useful gains and losses for others; self-approval or self-disapproval; and approval or disapproval from others. The first groups consider the practical aspects when making a decision, but the second two groups are concerned more with self-esteem, social approval, ethical and moral principles.

One of the important parts of decision making, therefore, once the problem is understood and different stakeholder perspectives identified and evaluated, is to examine options. In our coaching practice we like to use various tools for this: for example, coaches could use scenario planning which could offer leaders the chance to rehearse options or the outcomes of their decision making (Cox, 2013). We also suggest the use of "light boxes" as a tool.

In the making of the film *Gravity*, light boxes were used to aid perspective and enable different types of lighting effect for the film. In the brave coaching approach we introduce the notion of "light boxes," and use them to similar effect. They order and record all decision-making options, whether rational or intuitive, and enable them to be held "lightly." They thus hold different perspectives in suspension and in the spotlight until they can be considered more thoroughly as viable or flexible enough to provide some kind of right solution. Indeed, Drucker also proposed that it is vital to evaluate all "quick-fix" solutions by asking, "If I had to live with this for a long time, would I be willing to do so? If the answer is no, pass up the quick fix and keep seeking a more general, conceptual, comprehensive solution or principle" (Drucker, 1970, p.125).

Once awareness of the nature of the problem has been built by focusing the sphere, the leader can see options they may not have seen without the focus provided by the sphere activity, or may not have noticed in quite the same way before. Once this starts to happen then the light boxes can start to be populated (see example in Figure 7.4). The light boxes can be seen as a recording device, marshaling all the potential options suggested by the sphere and holding them for individual attention. Each light box provides a physical space for the leader to identify a particular option and hold that option "to the light" for discussion and eventual consideration or dismissal in a calm, tentative and "light" way, whilst s/he considers the variety of other options that may be available. As in other brainstorming activities, it is important that no options in any of the boxes are given analytic attention until all options have been sought and identified. The process follows seven steps:

1. The leader generates a number of potential solutions to the problem or challenge.
2. Then s/he populates each of the eight boxes (we find eight is the optimum number of potential solutions to work with; fewer than this means there may be options that have not yet been thought of and so more thought is needed; more usually means options are being forced and so are not real options).
3. The coach asks the leader to consider questions in relation to each option:

    - Is this the right thing to do?

- Is this the brave thing to do?
- What will it cost the organization if you do not take this action?
- What will the organization gain if you do take this action?

4. At this point it may be possible to identify some "front runners" for decision options. These may also be the ones that intuitively feel right. A coach could ask the leader: "What is your gut telling you to do?"
5. Other, more ethical questions, such as those proposed by Velasquez et al. (1996), can also be asked:

    - What benefits and what harms will each course of action produce, and which alternative will lead to the best overall consequences?
    - What moral rights do the affected parties have, and which course of action best respects those rights?
    - Which course of action treats everyone the same, except where there is a morally justifiable reason not to, and does not show favoritism or discrimination?
    - Which course of action advances the common good?
    - Which course of action develops moral virtues?

6. If two or more options are still in the frame, then the leader could consider if it is possible to combine these solutions. Often the light box solutions overlap.
7. The final step to consider is: "What is the right thing to do, right now, to address the problem?"

It is useful to note that the questions are not concerned with what impact this might have on particular groups of stakeholders or functions. They are only concerned with whether the organizational vision and strategy are being served and whether the solution has moral credibility. As long as this is the focus and as long as the vision and strategy are right in the first place, then the brave decision will emerge. Implementation of the brave decision is discussed in Chapter 8, and the line of questioning used by the coach will then shift to focus on areas such as resourcing, to ensure that the brave decision can be implemented. At this stage, however, it is vital that the brave decision is not hindered by questions of practicality or expediency, but only by those concerned with relevance and integrity. An example of one leader's light boxes is shown in Figure 7.4.

In the following dialogue, Christine is summarizing the content of her light boxes, and discussing each with the coach:

150 The Brave Decision

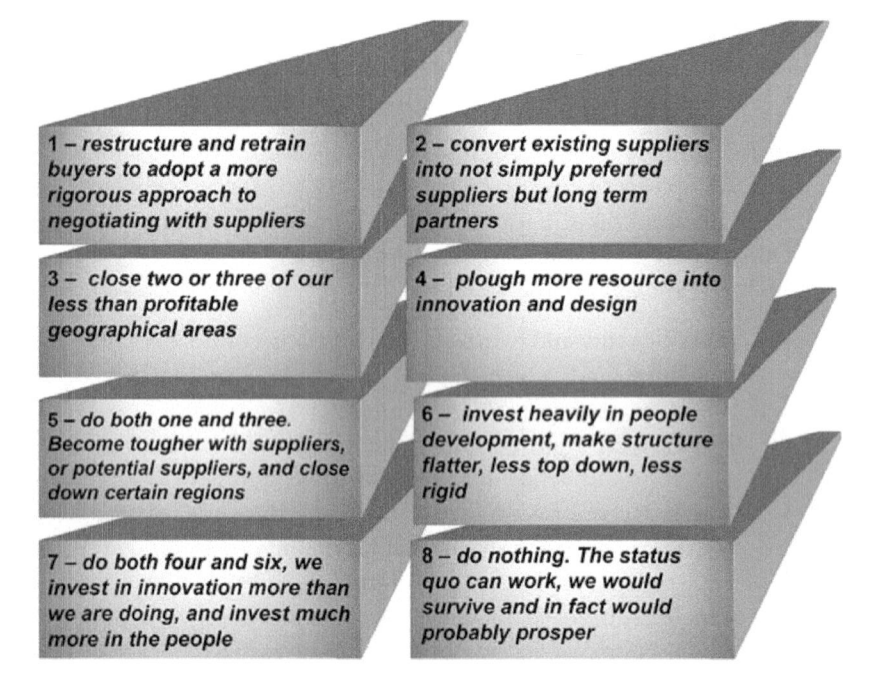

1 – *restructure and retrain buyers to adopt a more rigorous approach to negotiating with suppliers*	2 – *convert existing suppliers into not simply preferred suppliers but long term partners*
3 – *close two or three of our less than profitable geographical areas*	4 – *plough more resource into innovation and design*
5 – *do both one and three. Become tougher with suppliers, or potential suppliers, and close down certain regions*	6 – *invest heavily in people development, make structure flatter, less top down, less rigid*
7 – *do both four and six, we invest in innovation more than we are doing, and invest much more in the people*	8 – *do nothing. The status quo can work, we would survive and in fact would probably prosper*

FIGURE 7.4 Light boxes: Collating options and holding them lightly for discussion and selection

COACH: So now you've identified the possibilities shall we begin to look at each of the options in turn, and see how best you'd like to move forward?

CHRISTINE: I'll just go with the order that we have right in front of us. All right, firstly the overarching issue is the direction we should take as an organization. We have just gained the go ahead from our investors and they have entrusted us to make the right decisions. And based on our conversations I believe that we have eight possible options. But I can really feel some of the tensions here, between our lean culture, which is heavily bonus driven, and the need to really genuinely begin to think longer term, which was one of the reasons that our investors invested in us.

Firstly, I'm going to rule out option one right away. That does not sit well with me at all. I believe in getting value for money, and being lean, but I can see exactly where that initiative would head. We would end up driving businesses to the wall, particularly smaller businesses. Our buyers are well trained; we have a pretty rigorous ethical framework and ensure that we keep things fair and unbiased.

Screwing more out of people sounds macho and attractive, but it is a short-term strategy. I'm certain that we are pretty robust in our negotiations.

And that leads me on to option two, which is where I think that we should be heading, in this area at least. I think that we want to build relationships with suppliers, whilst still being aware of not putting all our eggs in one basket. And I think that we should let some of our potential suppliers go. That means that we don't waste time on negotiations where although we might gain an extra 1 percent, we start to run into supply issues because the supplier is then struggling, and frankly they probably have no sense by that point of coming on the journey with us at all. Option three is where things begin to get a little tricky.

COACH: In what way?

CHRISTINE: Well, as I mentioned before, our investors trust us to come up with some return on their investment. Now we do have the go ahead on one level, but on another, they do keep an eye on us, of course, and I would strongly suspect that they would be expecting us to sever our ties with those weaker geographical regions.

COACH: Doesn't that make sense?

CHRISTINE: Well, yes and no. We could make immediate savings, that is for certain, pretty much in the same way that we could hammer all of our suppliers. Now I know that you might think this odd coming from someone with my financial background, but I have to wonder, is that why we are here?

COACH: In what sense?

CHRISTINE: In the sense that this organization is about connection. We value connecting people and businesses, we wax lyrical about the little guy in the middle of the back of beyond who can rely on us, not simply to deliver the right thing at the right time, but also to enhance that sense of connection, to encourage the spirit of a global community. And so with one swipe of the pen, I can stop that.

COACH: Wouldn't your competitors just step in in your place?

CHRISTINE: Yes, I'm sure that they would, but how would they do that? They would do it by hammering their suppliers, by using whatever cheap, unethically sourced packaging and transport methods they could get their hands on. And they would charge a premium rate, and try and monopolize whole swaths of land.

COACH: Isn't that what companies do?

CHRISTINE: Not this one, not if I can help it. I like the fact that consumers can have a choice—that they can buy not just on cost but on quality and not just on quality but on fairness, and ethics and sustainability.

COACH: So, what do you think is best here?

CHRISTINE: If you don't mind, can we come back to that? I'd like to look at option five.

COACH: Not four?

CHRISTINE: No, five, because I just can't do that. It just feels entirely wrong. I can't, as I've mentioned, stand this short-term bullying for profit, savings and so-called efficiencies, and it just seems inconceivable to me that a company whose message is about the global village and connecting should actively close down some parts of that community.

COACH: Will those potential lost savings not be difficult to argue against?

CHRISTINE: Perhaps. But for the moment, I am dismissing option five. And I'm dismissing option eight. This is not a time for inaction. Yes, certainly, a leader has sometimes got to keep their hand on the tiller guiding a steady course, remaining still and calm and resolute, but in this instance, action is required, and that leads me on to options six and seven. I think that this company has been stagnating, and the reason that it has been stagnating is because we think that we have things figured out, that if we are making enough money, and are happy enough, that all is well. We have talked about the phrase corporate social responsibility in the past, but what does it really mean? Is it for us to give a talk at the local school, or to provide some IT equipment, or to make sure that we don't pollute the countryside? And yes, of course, it is those things, but I think that it is more. We have a moral and ethical duty you make this organization the best place that we can for everyone who works here. And I think that one of the ways that we do that is by getting everyone involved.

At the moment, we have a pretty hierarchical structure which has served us well enough, and yet that structure I am pretty certain stifles innovation and creativity. You have been around here long enough to have noticed how edicts are passed down from "on high" and followed blindly even although they are often quite patently pretty silly, if used across the board, and you have also probably seen how any email tends to be copied to at least 30 people, even if it is about changing a light bulb. And I think that we actually have created a culture of fear.

COACH: I can't say I have noticed fear.

CHRISTINE: Have you noticed any gregarious behavior? Any laughter? Anything in fact remotely spontaneous?

COACH: Well, now that you come to mention it, no, not really, but there are lots of companies like that.
CHRISTINE: Well, not this one. Time for change, I think. You see, I have been mulling this over, and I think that what looks like our biggest opportunity is actually our biggest trap, and that what looks like being set in stone needs [to be] demolished.
COACH: Please go on.
CHRISTINE: It looks like the easiest thing to do and the biggest opportunity is for us to squeeze suppliers and consolidate into more profitable areas. However, if I think about what is actually the essence of a business, I see this entirely differently. You have said to me in the past that one way to view a business is as a faceless, soulless, legal framework, which takes people in one end and, if we're not careful, chews them up and spits them out at the other end, used up, squeezed dry.
COACH: Yes, and I meant it as a warning about what could happen, if people aren't careful.
CHRISTINE: Well, it struck a chord. Suppose we turn that on its head, suppose we say that a business is there to nourish employees and others who come in contact with it. Suppose we say that its purpose is to help people gain purpose in their lives if at all possible. And at the moment, I think that we have to a degree reduced our workforce to a bunch of automatons. I want to unlock that. I'm not sure of the steps at the moment, but I want to spend much more on staff development, and I want a different leadership approach. We may or may not have to change the structure, but for me it is essential that we have a different mindset towards leadership.

And I want ideas, lots of them. This would come from a general "power shift" in the organization, and a focus also on pure innovation, from communication to transport to packaging to marketing, to whatever, right across the board. Nothing sacred, nothing barred, there would just be one simple message; how can we further serve the people in this organization to be the best that they can be, and how can we best serve the communities and people that we touch?
COACH: Wow. That is pretty powerful stuff.
CHRISTINE: I told you that I had been thinking.
COACH: So how do you begin?
CHRISTINE: I'm glad that you asked that. Well, as I have mentioned, I think that it is objectionable to simply reduce our connectedness to certain geographic areas on the basis of cost alone. Now, I am also a business person, and I don't think that the PR around doing that will

make us look very good either, and that may be where I can gain some traction.

COACH: In what way?

CHRISTINE: By suggesting to the board that we may well garner some pretty bad publicity by doing that, which our competitors would leap upon, and by then suggesting that with a new focus on investment in our staff, and innovation, that our first task will be to find ways to support those regions in a way which is as ethical and cost effective as possible. I think that I may let that embed for a little while, and hopefully come to fruition before tackling the issue of leadership.

It can be seen how the light boxes exercise is a useful way of initiating discussion about potential options and how it leads to an in-depth exploration of a range of issues, including the pulling factors, and draws on existing values and brave ideals in the process.

Summary

In this chapter we explored a range of theories and strategies concerned with making brave decisions in the organization. We began necessarily by exploring the nature of problems and introduced a classification of four types of decision, based on convergent or divergent goals and whether they are imminent or evolving in relation to time. We concluded that because of the nature of the leadership role with its focus on novel and strategic issues, the type of decisions faced most often by leaders are related to the wicked problems identified by Grint (2008). In order to make decisions and solve wicked problems we suggested it is necessary to heed the rational decision-making processes suggested by Drucker and others, but also to incorporate the flexibility and dexterity that intuition provides.

In our exploration of intuition, a number of questions were proposed to help the coach guide clients. These questions revolved around what feels right and what to do with those feelings, rather than operational and contingency concerns. Considering the mundane, too, soon can result in the right decision for some stakeholders, but this may be the wrong decision for the organization as a whole. In particular, it may not be the right decision from a brave perspective and so the moral or ethical component that often reveals itself through intuition is vital to consider as well.

In the chapter we also introduced three techniques for assisting the brave decision-making process. The first suggested the use of rich pictures to map stakeholder relationships and identify tensions; the second demonstrated scenario development as a way of rehearsing decision outcomes; and the third, the "light boxes," captured various options for solutions to wicked problems. The coaching conversation with Christine went on to illustrate how the light boxes allow a leader to identify a good number of potential decision options, but to hold these lightly whilst further discussion and exploration into their efficacy is made.

In the next chapter we begin to focus on how the decision can be operationalized once the right decision has been made. As Vroom and Jago (1974) identified, decision making is a social process involving people, rather than being an individual process. They suggest that one of the outcomes of successful decision making is acceptance or commitment on the part of others in the organization. We explore this and other issues in further detail in Chapter 8.

8
THE BRAVE ACTION

Introduction

According to Pury et al. (2007) and Pury and Kowalski (2007), courageous actions rely on individual readiness to: i) initiate the process, ii) show vulnerability and confront fears, iii) reflect on personal values and goals, and iv) understand potential consequences of actions based on those values and goals. In previous chapters we have tackled i), ii) and iii). We have shown how the decision-making process develops out of a recognition of pulling factors that prompt a need for decision making and the identification of gravitational factors that ground us throughout the decision-making journey. The acknowledgment of emotions and fears, and the need for reflection on values, goals and organizational tensions was described in Chapters 4 and 5.

In this chapter we build on our discussion of decision making begun in Chapter 7, taking the process a step further by exploring decision implementation—the point at which planning ends and brave action begins. Often coaching assignments are ended once an action plan has been set, or a decision point has been reached (Cox, 2013), but we would argue that there is significant work still to do, including understanding the consequences as suggested by Pury et al. above. Thus, in this chapter we examine how coaches can help leaders implement decisions taking account of the tensions and challenges that arise during that process. The barriers to implementation could be seen as mimicking the internal and external barriers to transfer of learning highlighted by Cox (2013, p.153):

"Internal barriers can be related to energy and motivation, difficulty in changing entrenched habits, in changing priorities and in persistence of distractive thoughts or emotions," while "[e]xternal barriers are the organisational climate stressors that disrupt implementation intentions through unpredicted problems and tasks and reactions in the environment."

We begin by looking at some of the restrictions leaders may encounter during decision implementation and then identify the need for a support strategy to sustain a complex responsive approach to decision implementation in the wake of external pressures. Importantly, we identify the need for communication of plans and support for structures. The chapter is divided into three main sections. First, we discuss some psychological challenges for the leader as an individual and include a brief discussion of attachments and biases that can hinder progress towards brave action. We also consider the role of both intuition and critical thinking at the implementation stage. In the second section we then identify challenges arising as a result of external factors. These include stakeholder concerns and tensions such as those between the commercial and financial needs of the organization and conflicting quality or service needs, many of which are exacerbated if the leader tries to "go it alone" when implementing decisions. In section three we examine a "complex responsive" approach (Stacey, 2007) to implementation, which takes account of social and relational aspects of the organizational structure, examining the skills and strategies that can help deliver smooth implementation and considering the role of the coach in this situation. Such accountability leads, we would argue, to the ability to build social capital and sustainability, important aspects of leadership that we discuss in the last part of this chapter.

1 Implementation Challenges For The Leader As Individual—Psychological Challenges

In this section we consider the role of the leader as an individual in implementing decisions and examine the shift from deliberating about and planning the brave decision to becoming confident in implementing the decision. We look at the historical notion of "crossing the Rubicon," a river in northern Italy that Julius Caesar decided to cross in 49BC (Johnson & Tierney, 2011a), and highlight the attachment and cognitive bias that is frequently bound up with decision implementation. Included in this discussion is a further examination of intuition and the impact this can have on execution. Towards the end of the section we examine the role of the coach and some coaching strategies and questions to help the leader think about the challenges of implementation in more detail and in particular how the coach can help the leader increase awareness of such biases.

Crossing the Rubicon and other biases

Johnson and Tierney (2011a, p.7) explain how people cross a psychological "Rubicon" when they perceive a decision point to be imminent: "they switch from what psychologists call a 'deliberative' to an 'implemental' mind set." However, Johnson and Tierney also point out how this triggers a range of psychological biases, most especially the bias of overconfidence. They argue that it is vital for decision makers to understand that the very act of making a decision, rather than deliberating over it, can trigger overconfidence and closed-mindedness, thus limiting rational judgments and the ability to find compromise (Johnson & Tierney, 2011b). There is, they say, a fine line between boldness and excessive risk taking since the implemental mindset can create a dangerous overconfidence, drawing leaders into promoting overly optimistic plans. The Rubicon theory suggests leaders should guard against developing an implemental mind-set as it can mask a "dangerous delusion" and prevent accurate assessment of a situation. It may also encourage risky behavior. Johnson and Tierney (2011b) warn that leaders must understand that things might look quite different when they eventually reach the other side of the Rubicon and that what might look like a short crossing to success now, could turn out to be a costly illusion.

Psychological biases, such as overconfidence may be difficult for leaders to recognize on their own and this is where a coach can be useful. The coach can help bring a skeptical voice to question the leader's thinking and any potential biases that may be lurking beneath it. The role of the coach here is to play devil's advocate and ask a range of uncomfortable questions.

In the extract from a coaching session with John, below, the coach is playing devil's advocate in relation to the speedy implementation of a recently made decision:

COACH: Okay, just to clarify, John, you have suggested that the course of action you have decided upon is in line with your values. You have also said that your core value is that of fairness. And so I just wanted to double check if this is the primary driver in you making this decision?

JOHN: Yes, it absolutely is. And the second that I realized how unfair the alternative was, it was like everything just clicked into place. The picture became very clear, and I am certain about exactly how to proceed.

COACH: That is good to hear, and yet I am now wondering about the implementation and the sense of the timescales involved—and the need for buy-in.
JOHN: I think that the timescales involved make sense, and I probably have enough of the key individuals on board, or I can get them on board pretty soon.
COACH: Okay, good, but there are a couple of things that I would like to come back to, if you don't mind.
JOHN: Please do.
COACH: Well, firstly, are you saying that the picture has become very clear, and that you are certain about how to proceed, and that the timescales involved make sense?
JOHN: Yes.
COACH: The slight niggle that I'm feeling here is that because you are certain, and because this action aligns exactly with your value of fairness, that when you say the timescales make sense, do they simply make sense to you? I'm not suggesting that this isn't doable in that timescale, but I am suggesting that others may not agree with you.
JOHN: I'm not sure I follow.
COACH: Well, let me try and explain it this way. Because this decision has been taken, things have clicked into place for you; it is as if you were riding the crest of a wave, maybe even feeling a sense of euphoria. Fairness is such a big issue for you that now that you can implement a decision which you see as being incredibly fair, I wonder if there is just the possibility that you may be overestimating the speed of actual implementation.
JOHN: I've run what I think is a fairly conservative calculation.
COACH: And how much of that calculation is based on everyone engaging with this with the same enthusiasm as you?
JOHN: Hmm. Okay, yes, I take your point, but I am thinking more about the guys who have already "bought in": I'm basing my assumptions on having them on side, and presuming that others will take longer to get on board. But I will still have the main people on board.
COACH: That sounds very wise. And I'm wondering as well if those people who've already bought in are going to be getting out of the starting blocks quite as quickly as you are. They may share your sense of fairness, but we know that this implementation is going to shift the balance of power in some ways, and whilst fairness may be one of their values, is it as fundamental a core value to them as it is to you? And do they perhaps have other conflicts going on which may be

pulling them in different directions? And lastly, might there be some people who could actively drag their heels?

JOHN: Well firstly, yes, there are people who might drag their heels, but as long as they don't actively sabotage things that shouldn't affect the timings.

COACH: Good.

JOHN: But ... I have to say I do think that everyone who is on board is enthused and will come out of the starting blocks as quickly as I will. However, that could just be my assumption. This is going to take a lot of focused energy and work, and probably lots of late nights, and that is something which I may not have made clear enough, and even when I make it clear, I suppose if I'm really honest with myself, there are probably one or two who may work hard but perhaps not hard enough, at least hard enough to meet the deadlines that I have set.

In another example of a coaching session, the coach helps Ron to identify how another emotional bias may be getting in the way of implementation:

RON: Mentally for me this is a spring clean. I do feel like a weight has been lifted off my shoulders now that I'm going to tackle this issue.

COACH: Have you thought about how you are going to structure your argument?

RON: There is no structure beyond telling it like it is. The two individuals involved have been a thorn in my side for years now, and I think that this is payback time.

COACH: That sounds a little bit like revenge?

RON: Ha! Well they say that revenge is a dish best served cold, don't they? And so I'm not sure if I would classify it as revenge as I'm feeling far from cool about it.

COACH: Isn't that a bit of a red flag then?

RON: The fact that I'm slightly annoyed?

COACH: From where I'm sitting, this looks way higher up the scale than annoyance. We have worked together for quite some time now and I'd say that you seem angry.

RON: Perhaps.

COACH: You know, Ron, we have talked a lot about emotions and how that can skew our thinking, and we have also talked about your love of the Gandhi idea of being the change that you want to see around you. I'd have to say that the way that these two individuals have behaved has been less than exemplary, in my opinion, but I'd like you to consider the possibility that now you have made the decision to confront these behaviors, that the emotional floodgates have been released, and that this may now be affecting your clarity of thought and your approach.

RON: Maybe.

COACH: I'd like to throw in a challenge to you here, and to paraphrase your paraphrase of Gandhi. As I mentioned just now, you have suggested that Gandhi said that we should be the change that we would like to see around us—but I don't think that he was saying that we should become that which we despise the most in order to tackle that which we despise the most.

RON: Hmm. I hadn't seen it that way. Maybe I need to give that some consideration.

Framing effect

De Martino et al. (2006) have also argued that the "framing effect" is an important process that can impact a leader's choices. The framing effect is where decisions are biased by the way in which different information or options are presented, often through the use of affect, sentiment, passion, etc. Logic would imply that rational decision making cannot be transformed by such framing, yet research seems to suggest that when information is incomplete or overly complex we tend, when we need to make a decision, to depend upon a range of "simplifying heuristics, or efficient rules of thumb, rather than extensive algorithmic processing" (De Martino et al., 2006, p.1). The message from De Martino et al. is that "the framing bias reflects an affect heuristic by which individuals incorporate a potentially broad range of additional emotional information into the decision process" (ibid., p.1). In evolutionary terms, they suggest that this mechanism could confer a strong advantage because contextual cues can carry vital information: "Neglecting such information may ignore the subtle social cues that communicate elements of (possibly unconscious) knowledge that allow optimal decisions to be made in a variety of environments." So although framing can cause bias, it can also provide useful information.

Croskerry (2013, p.2446) points out that in life we mostly move from "one of the intuitive mode's associations to the next in a succession of largely mindless, fixed-action patterns." He suggests that these patterns are indispensable but they are "also the primary source of cognitive failure," and argues that "most biases, fallacies, and thinking failures arise from the intuitive mode" (ibid., p.2446). We would suggest that this may be due to the "automated response" approach rather than the more nuanced holistic hunch.

The following extract from a coaching meeting with Matt shows how a discussion of intuition can be helpful for the leader and enhance understanding:

MATT: Well, the way forward is obviously to challenge the status quo, reduce the length of meetings and devolve some of the decision making to a wider group of individuals.

COACH: Given the current situation, that is a pretty big change. I'm interested in the word "obviously."

MATT: Well, it's obvious to me! It just feels like the right thing to do, and I have a strong sense that this will give us the result that I think we need.

COACH: Where does that strong sense come from?

MATT: I'd call it intuition. And I always trust my intuition.

COACH: Yes, we have talked about some of this stuff before, Matt. Remember we discussed the book *Blink*, by Malcolm Gladwell, and there were various examples of what I think we called "thin slicing" where some individuals were able to make uncannily accurate predictions and gain seemingly supernatural insights.

MATT: Yes, I remember.

COACH: I really like that book, and what struck me was that the ability to "thin slice" was a form of pattern matching to something in the environment. If memory serves, I think that there was an example of a fire chief who sensed that a situation was really dangerous. The fire chief seemed to be drawing on years of experience which caused him to spot things that he may not have been consciously aware of, but were pattern matching nonetheless, and this manifested in a feeling of just "knowing" something was wrong, or no doubt in some cases, right.

MATT: Yes, I read the book and really enjoyed it. But wasn't there also an example of where some poor youngster was accidentally shot because the police thought that he had been carrying a gun and had shot a police officer?

COACH: Interestingly, that was exactly what I was just going to mention. What do you think was going on there?

MATT: I would say that it was that pattern matching thing going on that you talked about, I think that there was some confusion about whether this young guy had a gun, which as it turned out, he didn't, and to add to the chaos, a police officer slipped or something, and the other officers presumed that he had been shot. I think that there was more to it than that, but I remember reading it and thinking that it was pretty horrific.

COACH: Yes, it certainly was. And that story stays with me, mainly because of the horrendous outcome. It also stays with me because I believe that we have to guard against what we think might be intuition, but in actual fact might be more like instinct. I tend to think of it as "crude intuition" as being likely to have been heavily influenced by strong emotion. We are picking up some of the subtle and often subconscious clues as we pattern match, but we are also being flooded by emotion. And that can cause us to paint the picture with much cruder brush strokes. We can miss out the more subtle patterns and nuances that are available when we are emotionally balanced, and able to access what I call "enhanced intuition." I don't think that enhanced intuition is always accurate, but I do think that following "crude" emotionally charged intuition is sometimes very likely to lead us into some pretty big traps. If our sense of "knowing" is being influenced by, say, fear or anger, then we would have to question its veracity.

MATT: Do you think that I should be questioning whether I might be basing my thinking less on a subtle sense of knowing, and more on some other cruder driver?

COACH: I think that it might be useful to check for any emotional biases.

Croskerry also asks why, if cognitive biases are so profuse and potentially troublesome, they cannot be identified and "debiased" using strategy to avoid them. He answers his own question:

> Unfortunately, that's not as easy as it sounds. First, many decision makers are unaware of their biases, in part because our psychological defense mechanisms prevent us from examining our thinking, motivation, and desires too closely. Second, many [leaders] are unaware of, or simply don't appreciate the effect of, such influences on their decision making. Becoming alert to the influence of bias requires maintaining keen vigilance and mindfulness of one's own thinking.
> *(Croskerry, 2013, p.2447)*

It has been suggested that when a bias is detected, there should then be a deliberate "decoupling" from the intuitive mode, so that "corrective 'mindware' can be engaged from the analytic mode" (Croskerry, 2013, p.2447). Croskerry defines mindware as the "rules, knowledge, procedures, and strategies that a person can retrieve from memory in order to aid decision making and problem solving." We might also refer to it as "critical thinking." It includes an understanding of the nature of the particular bias and the strategies that could eliminate or reduce it. Croskerry identifies a range of debiasing strategies but suggests it is not an easy process: "no one strategy will work for all biases, some customization of strategies will be necessary, and debiasing will probably require multiple interventions and lifelong maintenance" (Croskerry, 2013, p.2447), but he suggests that the habit of conducting regular and frequent "surveillance of their intuitive behaviour" is vital.

The term "intuition" may not sit well with every leader, of course, and so perhaps the role of the coach here is to challenge habits, in this case habitual thinking.

Intuition, Claxton (1999, p.159) claims, is based on "deep intellectual knowledge of the subject [that] makes use of expert knowledge and manifests as intuitive, elegant and beautiful responses." As mentioned earlier, this often comes with a feeling of "rightness," which although viewed as bias by some, could be seen to arise from a direct link between an emotion (as defined by Damasio, 2000), which is linked to our values, the feeling generated in the body as a result, and the accompanying brain signal that we subsequently call intuition. The key thing for the leader and coach is not to be seduced by the power or attractiveness of biases and intuitions and to ensure they are examined critically and used consciously and effectively.

Deliberate intuition

Just as Croskerry suggests deliberate decoupling of the intuitive mode from a more analytic thinking approach, so Francisco and Burnett (2008, p.237) have described the idea of deliberate intuition where the intentional engagement of intuitive skills is organized in service of "uncovering hidden relationships, ideas and insights to harmonize intuitive and logical information processing while generating creative change." Francisco and Burnett therefore suggest that it is possible to make the tacit role of intuition more explicit and propose that there are two areas the coach can encourage in relation to deliberative intuition. First, *sensing gaps* (i.e. being purposefully aware of gut feelings and choosing to act on them). This, they suggest, draws on an innate ability "to recognize that something 'is missing' or 'not adding up' without being able to explain how this conclusion was reached" (ibid., p.243). They suggest that the capacity to identify gaps is reinforced by experience—i.e. experts are more able to perform this function—and this suggests that unconscious processing of tacit knowledge is an essential element. Thus deliberative intuition is a process that develops over time.

The second area the coach can promote is *focused convergence*. This, Francisco and Burnett (2008) suggest, requires balancing intuition with critical analysis in order to achieve convergent thinking. Critical analysis is needed to counterbalance the ambiguity associated with intuitive decision making and is required also to overcome a tendency towards "analysis-paralysis" (ibid., p.243) that can arise from objective decision making where there might be information overload.

The role of System 1 and System 2 in implementation

As discussed in Chapter 7, research into how our brains manage and process information has provided various conceptualizations of the reasoning process, including System 1 and System 2 thinking. In decision making, and particularly at the implementation stage, the speed of thinking is important. With this in mind, the deliberations of System 2 thinking may be acceptable when brainstorming a potential plan of action, but at the action stage itself, it is often System 1, our intuitive side, that comes to the fore. Cox (2013) has also explained how intuition belongs in System 1, while critical thinking belongs in System 2.

Coaching with System 1

Sadler-Smith and Shefy (2004) suggest it is important to promote intuition by encouraging the leader to be open and talk about issues, and gradually to become clear about what intuition is. They say that insight is related to information but that instinct is a gut reaction (a crude intuition) whereas intuition is a deep-felt sense which usually has a feeling of rightness about it because it is linked to values. Questions the coach might use with leaders to challenge them to acknowledge their intuition are shown in Figure 8.1.

Coaching with System 2

Questions the coach might use with leaders to challenge them and promote their rational, critical-thinking side are designed to allow the coach to play devil's advocate. As we saw in our earlier examples, the coach needs to oppose, to test the level of conviction, the robustness of thinking through critical thinking and encouragement of metacognition.

We would suggest that the coach needs to balance questions to get the best from both System 1 and System 2 thinking, and in Figure 8.1 we provide a list of potential questions to promote these two different types of cognitive activity.

Coaching with System 1 Questions to promote intuition	Coaching with System 2 Questions to promote critical thinking
• Where do you feel that in your body? • Do you feel that it is right or wrong to do that? • Do you believe that the project will be successful? Where does that belief come from? • Which one of those options makes you more excited? • How often have your intuitions been correct? • How could you make your environment more nurturing for your intuitive skills?	• Is the information you have on this unbiased? Is it sound? Can you trust it? • Have you thought about this from another perspective? • If this decision isn't accepted by the Board, what will be your next step? • If the Financial Director is opposed to this expenditure, how can you modify the plan? • Why do you think this project will be successful?

FIGURE 8.1 Coaching with System 1 and System 2

Critical thinking

Cognitive failures, as we have seen above in our discussion of Croskerry's argument, can be addressed by strategies that embrace critical thinking: self-regulating through critical thinking may need training or support from a coach, but it can lead to well-judged interventions by System 2 thinking when needed, especially since it can intervene and override the intuitive mode. Croskerry explains how this critical step has been referred to variously as "decoupling, metacognition, mindfulness, and self-reflection" (Croskerry, 2013, p.2447). He also cautions that most of us never reach our ceilings for critical thinking, and many people go through life unaware of their thinking limitations, which suggests that we all need some support to develop our critical thinking abilities.

Cox (2013, p.102) examines the importance of such critical awareness for coaches and their clients, explaining how different lenses and perspectives are used to examine options and so transform their thinking. The role of critical thinking in coaching is seen as achieving three main outcomes:

- a more rational understanding of intuitions, dilemmas and goals;
- rational thinking to aid decision making; and

- the evaluation of incidents to create conditions for rapid decision based on experience.

Most important, Cox suggests, is the shift in emphasis that critical thinking provides: "from validation to transformation" (Cox, 2013, p.102), achieved through an iterative process which helps clients read beyond their individual aims and vision: "If coaching fails to help them bracket and then accept their views as contingent, to see their experience differently and then challenge their original perceptions, then it isn't coaching!" (ibid., p.103).

Metacognitive processes

Flavell (1979) has explained how metacognitive experience involves using previous experience to make sense of present situations, suggesting that such experiences are recognized as feelings or thoughts. This definition is close to one of our definitions of intuition, but it is suggested that metacognitive experience is accompanied by more self-awareness and control (Mitchell et al., 2011, p.686); indeed, Flavell (1979, p.908) argued that metacognitive experiences were more likely to occur in circumstances where conscious consideration was required. This process in our view has synergies with the notion of deliberate intuition described by Francisco and Burnett (2008). According to Mitchell et al. (2011), metacognitive processes can allow individuals to exert cognitive control by enabling them to "generate multiple alternative decision frameworks focused on interpreting, planning, and implementing goals" (p.686).

Sadler-Smith and Shefy (2004) suggest that one way of using intuition is to develop the kind of intuitive awareness that can validate our gut feelings. Such benchmarking, they say, can help identify misleading inferences and counteract the tendency to "over-rely on intuition in situations when a rational approach may be more appropriate." Sadler-Smith and Shefy also suggest that it can help to try and "distinguish intuition from fears and other emotions." For example, they suggest that "the emotional reward and euphoric feelings that an executive may get by intuitively 'calling it right'" needs to be weighed against times when less perfect intuitions have been made. Critical reflection on our use of intuition can be very helpful. The following questions have been suggested for promoting a more systematic approach to analyzing specific incidents where gut feelings have played a role:

- Think of an instance where you relied on your gut feel that resulted in a positive outcome.

- What was the context?
- What happened and what were the consequences?
- Can you identify the assumptions and inferences that led you to follow the gut feel?
- What were they?
- Think of an instance where you relied on gut feel that resulted in a negative outcome. What was the context?
- What happened and what were the consequences?
- Can you identify the assumptions and inferences that led you to follow the gut feel?
- What were they?

(Sadler-Smith & Shefy, 2004, p.80–81)

In this section we looked at some individual challenges to implementation and examined whether the attachment bias that comes with "crossing the Rubicon" can be useful or not. Cognitive biases are usually thought of as negative, and since intuition introduces all kinds of bias, it is therefore also frequently considered negatively. The important point for coaches to bear in mind is that awareness of bias is vital. We do not have to eliminate bias or intuition. The coach can help leaders become aware of both and use them to advantage in decision making as well as implementation. In the next section we look at some of the tensions that arise as a result of interactions between stakeholders and other functions in the organization.

2 Stakeholder Tensions

In attempting to implement a decision within organizations, leaders will have to cope not only with individual limitations, but with a range of tensions and potential oppositions from different stakeholders within the organization. This section examines some of those tensions and looks at ways in which a coach can support the leader to tackle them effectively in readiness for implementation.

Operating polarities

Within organizations there are a number of fundamental operating polarities. The first is one we have already mentioned earlier in this book—i.e. the almost constant tension between the need to make a profit or surplus (the bottom line) and the needs of employees and other stakeholders who may have more service- or quality-oriented needs within the organization. Previously we mentioned the maxim "profit by all means, but not by any means," which we suggest could be adopted by most organizations in order to work through or ameliorate such tensions. More recently the profit–quality polarity has been overtaken by a profit–sustainability division, as discussed by Hoover and Harder (2014).

A second tension is between the need for change, which enables the organization to remain viable in the market, versus the need for stability. Individuals, teams and departments within the organization will most likely have different needs, habits and coping strategies, some of which will be historic and embedded. For example, Mumford et al. (2000, p.13) have highlighted how organizational leaders need to "search for goals and paths to goal attainment that will maintain the organisation and ensure that the work gets done." Tensions, they say, can be generated by collectives within the organization—teams, departments, groups of individuals—and these manifest during decision-implementation phases. The tensions might be a "lack of commitment, lack of understanding, resistance or possibly malicious compliance, and long-term damage to relationships between decision makers and stakeholders and among stakeholders—can be eliminated" (Musselwhite, 2009, p.7). Thus a leader's performance is a function of whether s/he can identify goals, construct viable goal paths, but more importantly it is about whether s/he can direct others along these paths despite a volatile, changing complex-adaptive or socio-technical environment (Mumford et al., 2000, p.13).

A third tension arises when there are clashes in values, especially between the espoused organizational values and individual values, but also between the values held by different individuals and the teams within which they work. Value clashes are common in organizations, despite a general trend toward homogenization of the culture. Such clashes might be between achieving quality and reducing costs, as mentioned above, or monitoring outcomes and allowing freedom from control. More recently, sustainability and environmental issues have been identified as causing tensions in various sections of the organization once those ideas become "politically popular." Then "inherent tensions between the nature of sustainability initiatives versus structures, assumptions and practices already in place, can lead to conflict or territoriality" (Hoover & Harder, 2014, p.8).

In a conversation with our leader, Christine, the coach helps her to come to terms with tensions between her values and operational imperatives: The coach helps with external polarity issues, such as corporate social responsibility by helping the leader look consistently at the bigger picture:

CHRISTINE: We now know more or less where we need to head to, but it does throw up a fundamentally difficult issue.

COACH: Which is?

CHRISTINE: Which is that we are at a basic level a distribution organization—one which moves things around our planet—and in doing so, is quite obviously burning up resources.

COACH: Is that not what many organizations do?

CHRISTINE: Well, yes, I suppose it is. Actually that's a good point. Do you know that I hadn't actually considered it that way before. I'm not sure if this is what you meant by that comment, but what it has suddenly highlighted to me is that I am presuming and feeling a greater guilt because we do the really obvious environmentally unfriendly things. We use airplanes to transport things, and trucks and sometimes cars.

COACH: Hmm. Do you pollute rivers, destroy parts of the rainforest, gouge deep holes in the earth?

CHRISTINE: Not that I am aware of. And we have been investigating our suppliers and their suppliers to attempt to make ourselves as green as possible. I take your point that in many ways we are not even close to being the worst offenders.

COACH: I can think of quite a few who are a lot worse.

CHRISTINE: But that doesn't make it right.

COACH: No it doesn't. What then can you do?

CHRISTINE: Well, we could close the whole business down, I suppose, or diversify into something else.

COACH: What would happen then?

CHRISTINE: Well, we had this discussion before in a slightly different way when we talked about shutting down some difficult geographical regions. Basically, someone else would take our place.

COACH: And would they tend to be more or less ethical in terms of the environment?

CHRISTINE: Being really very aware of our competition, and actually making it one of my primary focuses, I think that I can say unequivocally that there is no one out there who would be more environmentally ethical, let's put it that way.

COACH: Does that mean that there are those who simply don't care?

CHRISTINE: That is certainly what I have observed.

COACH: Let's then go back to your company and the possibility of it stopping doing what it is doing.

CHRISTINE: There would be a bun fight. Some less than desirable practices would be employed, and I suppose that, and I'm guessing this is where your thinking was heading, in some ways the environment would be worse off.

COACH: That was kind of what I was thinking, yes, but it is very interesting that you agree. How does it make you feel when you say that out loud?

CHRISTINE: It makes me bloody well determined to hang in there. To get this right. I have always maintained that we improve people's lives by allowing businesses to build and create, and improve the lot of their customers. But I have also always maintained that we can't do this at the expense of the planet. We must continue to invest in ways to undo any damage that we do, and also to find new and innovative ways to reduce pollution to zero. To do that, we not only have to be the best that we can be, we have to ensure that our whole culture is aligned passionately to sustainability. I could never forgive myself if we did anything less.

When there are evident divergences within the organization, such as in Christine's example above, leaders then have to decide which value to uphold and this can only be done when one value is deemed to be more worthy than the other. This is why a value or mission statement is so important within the organization, since it can become the touchstone, especially in time of uncertainty or change. The mission statement needs to be one that the leaders of the organization have created or co-created, and one that individual leaders feel they can uphold. We would suggest that a mission statement must be more than a "poster on the wall" that people simply see as bland "corporate speak," or a box that has to be ticked.

Communication

Also related to the third tension described above is the need to understand the communication needs and values of people in the organization. To illustrate this we want to extend our earlier space metaphor even further in this section. Just as re-entry into the Earth's atmosphere can cause the destruction of a craft and crew, the angle of approach of the implementation of decisions has to be judged correctly to avoid damage. A simple example that illustrates this point concerns a colleague of ours who knew that giving and receiving "feedback" was an important part of any change process. He had recently been promoted to head up a larger team in a more complex learning and development environment. Despite being very well read and understanding the structure of some feedback models, his blind spot was that he presumed that everyone was like him. Whilst he had many good traits such as being a hard worker, and being open and honest, it was perhaps surprisingly his tendency to be quite forthright that caused difficulties during the implementation stage of the change strategy. Whilst he followed certain feedback templates it was, according to those who were aghast at his behavior, his attitude that appeared to be the issue.

Our colleague was considered blunt to the point of being rude. When he received this comment via a 360° feedback exercise as part of the change program, he was astonished. He was happy that the feedback had been so candid, but he was someone who wanted to do a good job, who valued performance above politics, and who did not want to cause others any distress. Whilst talking to us, he discussed his dismay and shock at being told his attitude was "blunt and sometimes abrasive," particularly whilst giving feedback himself. When we asked him what his overarching thoughts were on the feedback process, he replied:

> for me it is about enhancing performance and getting better. It is about getting better as quickly as possible, and so we don't have time to muck about. And so my broad approach to feedback is that I give it the way I like to receive it, right bang on the nose!

It is interesting to note here that the term "attitude" is also an aeronautical term; it means "the angle of approach," and it is apparent that our colleague would simply not have flourished in his role if he had continued with that particular attitude. So the angle of approach of the leader is something that leader and coach could discuss, especially in relation to the alignment of values during implementation.

Gregory, Beck and Carr (2011) have pointed out that if a client is not comfortable with feedback or works in a feedback "vacuum" where he or she receives very little feedback, then the coach might help the client to seek out feedback to promote development. The safe coaching environment can support clients while they elicit such feedback and take more responsibility for their own development through adopting, for example, a mastery goal orientation (Gregory et al., 2011).

Resourcing

Another tension concerns resourcing for the decision. In addition to tensions concerning values, resourcing tensions can inadvertently be created through inappropriate or outdated systems. For example, without appropriate reward or administrative systems that are in line with the values of the organization, a decision may be blocked at or near the point of implementation, despite support from the leadership team. Administrators may feel they need permission to change processes to facilitate implementation, for example. A command and control environment would probably hinder this flexibility, so the leader may need to shift to some kind of relational or distributive leadership philosophy to allow mission-based decisions to be implemented elegantly and efficiently.

Resources can include finance, training and development, logistical planning, stakeholder commitment, etc. Harvey (2014) suggests that the leader may need to consider the balance between the desired strategy and available or potential resources. For example, the strategy could be too ambitious. Again, the role of the coach could be crucial here. Some organizations, for example, appear to reward attendance at meetings or long hours working, but by the same token they hope for innovative research and an impactful contribution to society, which might entail more flexibility, such as working at home or working out in the community. Thus processes, communication channels and appraisal methods must also match the desired outcome. Harvey confirms that "If the match between strategy and resources is good enough, the results will follow" (ibid., p.15). This inevitably requires monitoring and not falling prey to the belief that results will deliver themselves. The coach can remind the leader to think about resourcing and the needs of each particular decision.

Along with many others in organizations, we hold that the most important and valuable resource is people: so valuable, in fact, that calling employees a "resource" is seen by some as demeaning. Crucially, as Graber and Kilpatrick (2008) describe, the failure to reward employees or other stakeholders for working towards desired values can lead to the failure of leaders to overcome a "crystallized bureaucracy" (p.190), where the organization continues to reward "non-optimal behaviours" and suppresses creativity. In this case, staff might need to work through layers and layers of bureaucracy to try to implement new programs or ideas. As Graber and Kilpatrick comment, it is not enough to "profess important values only at the top of the organization" (ibid., p.191). They argue that "those at the top must establish mechanisms that reward those who enact these values" (ibid., p.191). This has a number of clear benefits for all concerned in the organization, not least because there is a lower risk of burnout for all concerned.

Harvey points out how the completion phase of leadership is the delivery of results: "the 'what' stage which provides the substance of achievement, as an idea is finally transformed into a concrete reality" (Harvey, 2014, p.15). He also argues that "crossing the finishing line requires inspirational communication or even a bold declaration of the consequences of repeated failure. It usually means understanding the real motivations of the personnel involved in executing a strategy" (ibid., p.15). Harvey also suggests that expertise in delivery is crucial to the leader as when it is combined with other skills, it can help the leader to move from the possible to the actual. Harvey is adamant, however, that "an unrelenting insistence on the implementation of a policy" is vital for success (ibid., p. 55) and that monitoring and feedback are a key part of that. Diagnosing, for instance, what might be going wrong with implementation is something leader and coach need to be "on top of." The leader will need to find ways of keeping abreast of what is happening in the process (maybe using the skills developed in the sphere—see Chapter 6), and so build awareness of what is necessary to create results.

In this section we looked at how the coach can support the leader in thinking through some of the challenges and tensions arising from external factors, such as stakeholder resistance, as well as conflicting commercial and operational needs of the organization. In the next section we look at the role of the coach in relation to the complexity of decision implementation, particularly as it relates to communication with others in the organization.

3 Complex Responsive Approaches To Decision Implementation: The Role Of The Coach

Stacey (2007, p.300) defines complexity as "a particular dynamic or movement in time that is paradoxically stable and unstable, predictable and unpredictable, known and unknown, certain and uncertain, all at the same time." Words such as complexity and uncertainty are frequently used in relation to the organizational problems that leaders face, as encompassed in our discussion of wicked and tame problems in Chapter 7. Stacey's argument is that remedies for effective action are not only influenced by the type of environment—whether complex or simple, wicked or tame—but, from a complex-responsive perspective, human relating itself introduces another level of complexity and uncertainty.

Stacey (2007) proposes, therefore, that organizations should be considered as patterns of interactions between people. He suggests that it is in the "simultaneously cooperative-consensual and conflictual-competitive relating between people that they perpetually construct their future together in the present" (ibid., p.298), adding that these complex responsive processes of relating "can be understood as acts of communication, relations of power, and the interplay between peoples' choices arising in acts of evaluation." Thus, when we consider how to resolve the tensions in the workplace, some of which we have identified above, it could be that a more complex responsive process is needed. Stacey reminds us that "[i]t is because human agents are conscious and self-conscious that they are able to cooperate and reach consensus, while at the same time conflict and compete with each other, in the highly sophisticated ways in which they do" (ibid., p.298).

Echoing this argument, Bennet and Bennet (2008, p.6) have further suggested that tackling complex problems during any decision-making process presupposes a "commitment to embark on a journey toward an uncertain future, creating a set of iterative actions whose consequences will cause a move from the current situation (A) toward a desired future situation (B)." However, because there can be no direct cause-and-effect relationship that is discernible between the decision to the desired future situation, the journey is likely to require considerable preparation: The decision strategy, they say, "must therefore have the capacity and internal support mechanisms needed for an implementation journey that cannot be predetermined. The decision-making journey itself, then, could be thought of in terms of complexity" (ibid., p.6). In fact, Grint (2010, p.4) argues that "the uncertainty involved in wicked problems implies that leadership [...] is not a science but an art—the art of engaging a community in facing up to complex collective problems."

We also support the idea that it is not possible to implement decisions without others' commitment—partly because of the tensions that need to be addressed, but partly because of our own limitations. Grint (2010, p.8) explains how we become "prisoners of our own cultural preferences," becoming addicted to them and having "great difficulty stepping outside our world to see something differently—to act experimentally." He quotes Proust (2006, p.2), who wrote how "the real voyage of discovery consists not in seeking new landscapes but in having new eyes." This is an apt quotation for a book on coaching, since we might argue that the coach becomes the leader's "new eyes." Grint also talks eloquently about what he calls "cultural cataracts," proposing that, notwithstanding Proust's injunction, having new eyes is actually extraordinarily difficult: "our way of perceiving the world is the opposite of Proust's new eyes, we have occluded and tired visions of normality to the point of being addicted to our internally coherent 'elegant' views of the world" (Grint, 2010, p.8).

It has also been suggested that as the roles and responsibilities of leaders change and become more complex, they need to "expand from an internal leadership perspective to a broader world view, from a shareholder mindset to a stakeholder orientation with respect to the leadership mandate" (Maak & Pless, 2006, p.100). These authors further proposed that this cannot be achieved in isolation by the heroic or charismatic leader:

"In a stakeholder society, leadership has to reach beyond traditional leader-follower concepts." It is here that the leader becomes a facilitator of relationships with different stakeholder groups. Thus Maak and Pless (2006), like Stacey, contend that "leadership takes place in relationships"—they are at the core of what leadership is.

However, Maak and Pless (2006, p.101) also highlight how interaction with such stakeholder groups presents a number of challenges for leaders, and indeed we have seen some of these played out in our conversations with leaders:

- Ethics challenges: How to recognize, assess and deal with a multitude of stakeholder interests, based on different world views and values; how to cope with ethical dilemmas, etc.
- Diversity challenges: How to lead diverse people across distance, businesses, countries and cultures or how to create a multicultural and inclusive environment in which people can find meaning, feel valued and respected.
- Business in society challenges: How to earn the license to operate; how to make the business case for responsibility; how to become a good corporate citizen.
- Stakeholder challenges: How to create sustainable and trustful relationships with different stakeholders; how to rebuild trust in a business world that has been shattered by corporate scandals.

Like others since, Mumford et al. (2000) identified how, ultimately, performance within an organization depends on the implementation of a plan, but that implementation depends on "the efforts of others in implementing proposed solutions" (p.17). They recognize how implementation occurs in the social context and how the leader will depend on others and their efforts to implement decisions. They suggest that a vital requirement during the implementation phase is:

> a knowledge of subordinates, peers, and superiors, people the leader is interacting with during solution implementation. The leader must be able to communicate vision, establish goals, monitor progress and motivate subordinates as they attempt to implement a given solution plan. This requires flexibility in dealing with others and in adjusting plans opportunistically, as dictated by the demands of a changing social environment.
>
> *(Mumford et al., 2000, p.17)*

Furthermore, as Densten and Gray (2001) point out, understanding the viewpoints of others is important for building trust, which in turn is vital for developing the kind of creative tension necessary to encourage follower learning: In contrast, they say, "over-emphasis on control strategies and follower compliance, often lead to follower self-denial and loss of self-worth resulting in followers acting as programmed robots" (Densten & Gray, 2001, p.122).

The need to develop and implement solutions with and through others places a premium on the social skills of the leader (Zaccaro et al., 1992), especially skills used in acquiring information, discriminating between types of information, framing actions and promoting coherent actions: "Capabilities such as wisdom and perspective-taking enable leaders to 'go outside themselves' to assess how others react to a solution, identify restrictions, develop plans, and build support for implementation" (Mumford et al., 2000, p.15).

The role of the coach

Bennet and Bennet (2008a, p.5) suggest that the potential of the human mind can "often be more fully engaged when working in teams, communities and networks," and that working with others can make an important difference when tackling complex situations. We suggest that the role of the coach in complex situations is also crucial in order to challenge thinking and develop multiple perspectives. The brave action requires a number of skills on the part of the leader that the coach can facilitate. These include drawing on experience and knowledge of how people react, particularly when their values are challenged, acknowledging differing perspectives, and building relationships using the leader's knowledge of the organization. Often leaders distance themselves and this can lead to a lack of awareness of current organizational concerns that may impact action. The reflective space provided through the sphere will have emphasized the need to examine all areas of the organization in some detail whilst the problem-solving and the decision-making process described in Chapter 7 will have consolidated the leader's thinking around the problem. The task, then, of the implementation phase is to support the decision with resources, and encourage and persuade others to support the action too.

The coach can hold the right kind of environment for the leader at the implementation stage by:

i) Asking the right kind of challenging questions

There are a number of questions that the coach could ask in order to unpack tensions that arise during implementation, including:

- What resources are needed to support this decision?
- Are those resources in place?
- Are the systems in place to support this decision?
- Are any new systems needed?
- Who do you need on your side?
- When and how will you make the announcement?
- Who will need to know?
- Where is there likely to be the most dissention, and why?

It might even be useful to play devil's advocate, as our examples have shown, and to ask questions that champion an alternative case. This has the effect of testing the strength of the leader's convictions and of showing them alternative perspectives. The following further exchange with Ron illustrates this:

COACH: So, taking the Gandhi idea further, Ron, what do you think he would do?
RON: I think that he would talk. He wouldn't shout, he wouldn't scream, he wouldn't stoop to the level of others. I think that he would stand up and say what had to be said in an eloquent and calm manner.
COACH: Would he be calm?
RON: Actually no, not like calm as in not caring, but he probably wouldn't be angry.
COACH: Probably not.
RON: But he would be passionate.
COACH: And how do you feel about the issue?
RON: Ha! I'm pretty passionate about it. And so I suppose what I need to be thinking about is replacing the anger with passion.

ii) Providing opportunities for rehearsal, role play or scenario planning

Brown and Gillespie (1997) have highlighted the value of role playing and other improvisational strategies for skills development. They suggest that feelings, words and gestures that are generated in dramatic exercises provide the opportunity to rehearse responses to the complex interactions that are likely to be encountered in real life. When analyzed, such rehearsals provide a useful opportunity for feedback that can strengthen insight, confidence and ability. Drawing on Aristotle's thinking, Brown and Gillespie (1997) suggest such rehearsal is indispensable for developing courage since it provides opportunities to demonstrate virtuousness. Thus, people become brave by doing brave acts. According to Aristotle, "men become builders by building, harp players by playing the harp. By a similar process we become just by performing just actions, temperate by performing temperate actions, brave by performing *brave actions*" (Aristotle, 1980, p.28 f.1103, our emphasis).

Cox (2013, p.152) explains how there are a number of ways in which actions might get easier through practice and priming. She explains how such rehearsals "begin the building of new neural pathways. In effect they 'blaze a trail' that can then be completed when the client is actually in the new situation." One phrase that is used in neuroscience to capture this process is "cells that fire together, wire together" (Doidge, 2007, p.427). Role play, too, enables the "participation in simulated social situations that are intended to throw light upon the role/rule contexts governing 'real' life social episodes" (Cohen & Manion, 1994, p.252). Scenario planning is also useful and offers the leader an opportunity to test decision-making outcomes: "The hypothetical preparation involved in creating potential scenarios alerts them to critical information that they might other-wise have missed" (Cox, 2013, p.152). Helsdingen, Van Gog and Van Merriënboer (2011) have explained that training for professional decision makers, such as military commanders, often involves scenario exercises. In addition, "the combination of metacognitive understanding and analysis of practical application in scenario planning is powerful and leads to a deeper understanding of how to approach problems and/or identify cues in the environment" (Cox, 2013, p.152).

iii) Supporting the social skills necessary to trial different leadership approaches, such as servant or relational leadership, which require a different mindset from the traditional command-and-control approach

The focus on interaction or interdependence between complex situations, stakeholders in the organization and the leader's behavior has been identified by Stacey (2007, p.297) as vital. In fact, Stacey calls for more focus on "the actual processes of our interdependence" (p.297), rather than a reification of the organization as a set of processes that can be moved around. This emphasis on communication and the interplay between people within the organization can suggest a different leadership paradigm. Such a paradigm would seem to involve an emphasis on social perspective taking that perhaps is not emphasized enough in the leadership development literature at the moment. Social perspective taking involves seven core values of individual, group and societal interaction: consciousness of self, congruence, commitment, collaboration, common purpose, controversy with civility, citizenship (Dugan et al., 2014). Other values could be added, and we would like to see "sustainability" in the list.

Galinsky, Ku and Wang (2005) confirm how social perspective taking involves using the cognitive and affective domains in order to empathize with another person whilst maintaining individuality. It is considered a higher-order cognitive skill, linked with "complex judgment, critical thinking, and problem solving" (Dugan et al., 2014, p.3).

We would reiterate that bravery must be in the very weave of the leader's character. Taking social perspective as an example, the leader may well have to be brave to empathize with others. As incongruous as that may initially sound, many leaders in our experience hide behind the label and the position. This may, of course, be because of an inherent lack of connection to others, but it is as often as not due to a leader being too shy, or not comfortable enough in their own skin, or indeed just simply residing in the comfort zone. So, in addition to perspective taking, leaders also need to communicate with their employees in a relational, conversational way that does not involve command and control (Groysberg & Slind, 2012). This is important because talking with colleagues, rather than issuing orders, enables leaders to generate a culture of employee engagement, and following on from that the kind of operational flexibility that they need to implement brave decisions.

In a real example from our own coaching, one leader we worked with decided to leave his organization. He decided to resign because he had not been enjoying work for a few months. Here is his account:

> I guess that the thing I struggled with most, and a lot of people struggle with it in our organization at the moment, is the leadership. You're not allowed to be brave. So in a middle-management environment, and in a lot of cases senior management positions, you don't have the accountability to be brave. You're not empowered to make those decisions. So even if you think it's the right time, the right way, the right reason, then you still don't have the accountability to make that change, and that's what I've really struggled with the most. There's no space to be brave and if I can't be brave then I'll just shrink and not get that self-actualization I need. I definitely need to

go and do things that I can't do in my current role. And being brave and leading is definitely one of them.

This leader's sense of bravery was partly triggered by considering what was the right thing to do. The story indicates that simply considering bravery and a sense of "rightness" can generate behavioral change. This example also illustrates the importance of delegating to followers who want the challenge of implementing decisions, and the pitfalls of a command and control approach.

Summary

In this chapter we examined the individual, organization and participative processes impacting the implementation of decisions and suggested some ways in which the coach can support a leader.

We began by looking at the psychological challenges that the leader may face when implementing decisions, including exploring attachment and cognitive biases, such as crossing the Rubicon, framing and even intuition. We gave several coaching examples of where leaders were alerted to their biases and how strong emotion might on occasion adversely affect their thinking. In addition, we suggested that intuition might be deliberately encouraged in order to supplement critical thinking and draw on valuable experience.

In the latter part of the chapter we saw how leaders have to deal with stakeholder tensions and particularly with operating polarities that impact communication and resourcing. We thus examined the challenges arising from external factors, such as stakeholder resistance, that the coach can help the leader unpack and address. Throughout the chapter we have focused on how coaches can support leaders at the point of implementation of the brave decision and in the aftermath, when the consequences of their decision begin to emerge.

9

THE TRUST FACTOR

Introduction

In previous chapters we discussed our framework for leadership coaching aimed at promoting courage and bravery for leaders in the face of a range of complex organizational pressures and stakeholder demands. In this chapter we focus on the trust issues that coaches might come up against when using the coaching framework for supporting leaders in this demanding context. These issues might entail building trust with the leader at the start of the coaching assignment so that there is complete openness between leader and coach. In turn, this might involve the need to meet the leader's expectations in relation to understanding the business environment and the dynamics of stakeholder relationships. Perhaps in some cases there is a need for specific industry knowledge to enable the coach to have more of a mentoring role, or there may be boundary issues that have the potential to adversely affect the relationship.

Trust has been defined as "a psychological state comprising the intention to accept vulnerability based upon positive expectations of the intentions or behaviour of another" (Rousseau et al., 1998, p.395). It is recognized as a vital component in most social and professional interactions and relationships, and especially in the leadership context where trust is seen as a psychological state involving positive expectations about a leader's behavior and intentions (Dirks & Skarlicki, 2004). It is also a fundamental aspect of the coaching relationship (Cox, 2012).

A number of authors also argue that trust is the quality most valued by coachees (Ives & Cox, 2012; Jones & Spooner, 2006), and that it is predominantly important for enabling challenge and stretching tasks that contain a risk of failure (Hunt & Weintraub, 2007). Harvey (2014, p.19) points out how "distrustfulness makes it difficult to really listen to others," suggesting that the coaching may really suffer if trust is not established. In coaching, one of the first tasks in the first session is to generate trust, both in the coaching process and in the coach him/herself.

For a coach, then, building trust with the leader at the start of the coaching assignment is seen as a vital first step since it enhances the mutual security that is required for open and honest discussions between the coach and the leader:

> In order for a client to take risks necessary to learn, develop, and change, the coach has to create a safe space and develop trust. Only through trust can a client feel safe enough to reveal vulnerabilities, expose mistakes and deficiencies, and ultimately grow.
> *(Markovic et al., 2014, p.103)*

Cox (2012, pp.427–428) notes that "a trusting, coaching relationship makes it easier to confront issues and take risks within the relationship," resulting in better individual performance, and ultimately development, for both parties. She highlights the two kinds of trust identified by Dibben, Eley-Morris and Lean (2000), "on-trust," which is based on prior knowledge of the coach and produced through the prior reputation of the coach or a recommendation by a third party. This kind of trust may only last the length of the first coaching meeting whereupon it is superseded by calculus-based trust, knowledge-based trust and identification-based trust. Dibben et al. (2000, p.59) have explained how calculus-based trust is trust "formed between individuals in the early stages of a relationship on the basis of what each sees s/he can get out of the relationship in terms of whether or not the outcomes of creating and sustaining the relationship are greater than the costs of severing it." This type of trust suggests that the initial contracting phase of the coaching relationship is vital since it is where the needs of both parties and a way of working together can be established in order to bolster any "on-trust" that already exists.

Drawing on Mayer et al.'s (1995) earlier integration model of organizational trust where individual ability, benevolence and integrity are seen as vital factors in trustworthiness, Heffernan (2004) has argued that there are three important components to trust:

- a credibility component—whether the partner has the capability and expertise to undertake the purpose of the partnership;
- an integrity component—whether the partner will adhere to written or verbal promises; and
- a benevolence component—whether the partner will be accommodating and act with equity when new conditions relating to the relationship arise.

The benevolence and integrity components are concerned with how the partner meets expectations. They appear to be related to the knowledge-based trust stage of the Dibben et al. model, while the credibility component relates to both the on-trust and calculus-based stages.

More recently, Markovic et al. (2014) have proposed a model of trust for coaching aimed at promoting client trust in the coach. They see the ability aspect of the integration model as underpinned by technical expertise and problem-solving skills, whilst benevolence relies on cultural familiarity, restraint from self-serving opportunism, consideration for client welfare and going beyond the explicit contract (i.e. delivering more than was expected). Integrity, they argue, is about demonstrating professional values, which in turn are honed through reflection and daily analysis. It should also be noted that the decision to trust is a multifaceted affective and cognitive process (Chhetri, 2014), where affective trust is based on complex emotional responses to the trustee (the coach) and cognitive trust is more rational and focused on an analysis of credibility ability and competence.

The remainder of this chapter addresses the three elements of credibility, integrity and benevolence, as described by Heffernan (2004). Under each of these three headings we identify and discuss important aspects and practical concerns that coaches may have when working specifically with leaders.

1 Credibility

The credibility element of trust relates to how well coaches demonstrate to their leaders their capability and expertise to undertake the coaching assignment. Reviewing trust in the coaching context, Cox (2012) explains how for external coaches often commissioned by organizations to support leaders, the credibility component of trust can come "as part of the professional package, through the prior reputation of the coach" (p.428). Prior reputations shape our understanding of how others might behave and so grant a degree of cognitive trust (as opposed to affective trust)

(Massey & Kyngdon, 2005; Dibben et al., 2000). This cognitive trust is built on the behaviors we expect leadership coaches to possess and which are embedded in the perceived role of the coach. Such trust is reinforced over time on the basis of shared knowledge which allows coach and client to make predictions about each other's behavior. Bluckert (2005, p.339) has pointed out that if a coach is perceived as incompetent and lacking in skills and understanding, which usually operate as a proper guide and safety net, the client can experience "a real sense of anxiety" and come to doubt the credibility of the coach as a result.

As Markovic et al. (2014) suggested, ability is one of the key aspects of trust in the relationship. It is particularly important to be perceived as able and competent when coaching leaders. Ely et al. (2010, p.587) explain how a leadership coach requires a "vast and adaptive set of skills to effectively meet the diverse and dynamic needs of individuals and their organizations." They suggest that the set of knowledge, skills and abilities appears to focus on a set of core competencies that include:

> communication skills, analytical skills, assessment and feedback skills, planning skills, goal setting skills, organization skills, creativity and resourcefulness, ability to motivate and encourage, ability to challenge and confront others, results-orientation and accountability, integrity, empathy, caring, personable, approachable, flexible, empowering, and trustworthy.
>
> *(Ely et al., 2010, p.587)*

In addition, they suggest coach qualifications could include "graduate behavioral science training, business awareness, and knowledge of or experience in the client's industry in order to have credibility and expertise" (Ely et al., 2010, p.587).

The need for specific industry knowledge or stakeholder awareness in order to meet client expectations and increase credibility is contentious within coach circles, since such a requirement would increasingly suggest that the coach needs to have a mentoring role. However, in recent research, Bozer, Sarros and Santora (2014) examined the relationship between coaches' academic backgrounds in psychology and their credibility in executive coaching. They found that an academic background in psychology was positively related to executive coaching effectiveness as reflected in greater improvement in client self-awareness and in job performance. They also found that the coach's credibility was positively related to executive coaching effectiveness. Boyce, Jackson and Neal (2010) had earlier looked at the impact of the coaching relationship, in terms of rapport, trust, commitment and credibility, on coaching outcomes. Their research examined coach-client relationships in the military in the United States and, like other studies, their findings suggested that credibility and compatibility positively impact outcomes through supporting the development of the coaching relationship.

Building on the need for trust and the points in the relationship where different components of trust might manifest, we now consider the coaching alliance itself and its contribution to credibility. Cox (2013) uses the term "alliance" to ensure that the coaching relationship is seen as a working relationship, rather than a friendship type of relationship, and to indicate that it has a specific formal structure and timeframe during which problems are discussed and goals can be achieved. Ives and Cox (2012) have also highlighted the centrality of the coaching relationship, but argued that relationship requirements differ, depending on the coaching approach. They draw on Stober (2006) to suggest that a purely goal-focused approach to coaching requires a different type of relationship to the more therapeutic styles of coaching. In Bordin's (1979) theory of the working alliance in counseling there are three dimensions: tasks (activities of the alliance), bonds (the personal relationship, which includes trust), and goals (the desired outcomes of the alliance). The strength of the working alliance then depends on the extent to which the parties can work together on these goals and tasks and develop their relational bond. The bond itself has two levels: the affective bond, and a work bond that focuses on supporting goals and tasks. Conceiving of the relationship in this way confers its own credibility since it encompasses both the need for the relationship and the need for formality through contracting, monitoring and evaluation.

Within organizations particularly, as Huffington (2006) has pointed out, there is almost always a need for double, or three-way, contracting: "once with the organization, and again with the client, in the light of the organization's needs" (p.66). In this kind of triangular relationship, she suggests, there is "potential for divergence and splitting," which might occur if the organization has an agenda that is different from that of the leader. When this occurs, Huffington says, "there is a danger of the coach being 'set up' by the organization and failing either the organization or the client" (ibid., p.66). Markovic et al. (2014, p.587) also emphasize how the "explicitly dual responsibility to the organization and client presents a particular requirement and challenge for the coach to establish and maintain trust, explain and exercise confidentiality, remain neutral and objective, and establish appropriate information, accountability, and role boundaries with the client and the organization."

One of the ways in which credibility is conveyed occurs, as Bluckert (2005, p.339) explains, "when the coach clearly knows their own strengths and limitations and acts within them." De Haan (2008, p.106) also suggests that coaches should coach with an "ongoing and deliberately maintained doubt as their only certainty." He argues that coaches who overestimate the effectiveness of the working alliance with their client may begin to feel overconfident about the coaching they are providing, which might in turn make them less aware of what the client is experiencing. They may even fail to verify the client's satisfaction and comfort level in relation to the coaching.

By way of illustration, we give the example of a coach who had been working successfully for a few years, but had just begun engaging with a slightly different client base. As a result he found that, in his own words, "things were tougher." He felt that there just was not the same feeling of engagement and momentum. With the agreement of his client and the organization, and adhering to strict rules of confidentiality, he was able to video record parts of his coaching sessions. When we viewed the recording together, it was immediately apparent that our friend was very humorous and had an expansive collection of anecdotes to relax and entertain his client. He was able to use analogy to great effect, and asked some good questions but with, we observed, a slightly bullish attitude, which did appear to give his client little or no time to reflect. He appeared to be uncomfortable with silence, even for a brief period of time, and he appeared to have no sense of when to change gear. It was almost at times as if the client was being machine-gunned by a hail of anecdote, analogy, humor, questions and advice. It appeared to us that whilst this approach may have worked for some people, the coach's naturally effusive extraversion was probably limiting his success, and that as he began to work with a more diverse group of individuals, the limitations of his style had begun to show up.

The coach was keen for us to offer him advice from our observations, and we felt that a more "ambivert" approach was required. His rapport-building skills were excellent, and he had what some coaches can lack—robustness when faced with some challenging client behaviors.

Our advice was that he should concentrate on timing his sessions and limiting his naturally ebullient style to the beginning of the session. We suggested that he revisit some questioning strategies and in particular that he should practice and enhance his listening skills.

We felt that in this way, the coach might not feel as restricted as if we had suggested that he remain quiet, reflective and reflexive throughout the full session. In essence, we wanted to allow him to play to his strengths.

He had become accustomed to success in his coaching because he was generally good at building relationships and had been achieving good results. The challenge was that this had generated a blind spot for him. He had not realized how reliant on his "cabaret" style he had become. He had lost sight of the subtle and not so subtle clues that his clients were giving him—i.e. that they were not with him on the journey.

When we first met the coach we have just described, he was certain that his coaching relationships were effective. It was only after some setbacks and reviewing the sessions that he was able to take action to ensure that they really were effective. De Haan (2008) suggests coaches who actually underestimate the effectiveness of the alliance may have more doubts and be more humble about their capacity to support the client. Having more doubts, it seems, results in coaches paying more attention to what the client is experiencing and so their coaching becomes more client centered and may be less problem, or even coach, focused.

The seemingly vast array of coaching abilities that is necessary to enhance credibility is generally achieved through coach education programs and experience. It can also be enhanced through coaching supervision, which we discuss later in this chapter.

2 Integrity

The integrity component of trust as identified by Heffernan is partly bound up with the coach's values such as openness, commitment and reliability. Integrity has typically been thought of as "the perceived pattern of alignment between an actor's words and deeds" (Simons, 2002, p.19). It thus focuses on the degree to which stated beliefs and values are seen as matching action.

Markovic et al. (2014, p.107) suggest that integrity comes from "reliable promises, sharing of valid information, and expressions of honesty." Initial contracting sessions are the obvious place for starting to demonstrate integrity in the coaching relationship, but Markovic et al. propose that each of Heffernan's trust issues can be addressed at all phases of the coaching process. Yes, integrity can be strengthened at the outset, for example, by "sharing an established summary of professional values with a client" (Markovic et al., 2014, p.108).

However, even at the evaluation stage the coach can also demonstrate integrity by helping the client to reflect on what has been achieved and perhaps creating "a specific strategy that would allow a client to stay on track maintaining what has been learned throughout the coaching process" (Markovic et al., 2014, p.108). Revisiting the initial contract at the evaluation stage can also be useful: filling in gaps in previous contracting can often be a way of the coach and client exploring how expectations are being met. Reprising the contract in this way also ensures coaches are exercising caution in relation to their perceptions of what is actually happening within the coaching alliance, thus avoiding the tendency to take client satisfaction for granted.

Baron, Morin and Morin's (2011) study of managers and their internal coaches also suggested that regular evaluation of the working alliance is necessary. Baron et al. recommended using either a formal questionnaire or just initiating a regular open discussion on the topic. Such an evaluation will enable the coach and client to ensure they pay attention to how they respond and react within the coaching process, keeping the focus on working alliance perceptions and, as mentioned, addressing any gaps that might lead to loss of integrity and trust. The health of the alliance is of particular importance in brave leadership coaching. De Haan's (2008) advice about the coach not becoming overconfident is of particular relevance. The leader is, after all, potentially "way out on a limb" and the coach will need to be exceptionally sensitive to the experience of the leader and his/her needs at that level.

In her research on peer coaching, Cox (2012) found that integrity was connected to the formation of trust and influenced by three needs:

- a non-cognitive, values-based attachment;
- confidentiality within the relationship; and
- the subsequent capacity of both peers to make themselves vulnerable.

Shared values were seen as important but confidentiality, in particular, was seen as a major contributor to trust development, "interweaving with other factors and leading to the openness necessary for the foundation of trust and ongoing performance in the relationship" (Cox, 2012, p.440). The link between integrity and confidentiality is seen as crucial and it is important in the contracting stage to attempt to set clear rules and boundaries about what can or cannot be discussed outside the coaching room, within the rule of the law, and then stick to them.

Hannafey and Vitulano (2013) have even suggested that executive coaching involves an agency relation "with specific moral duties that go beyond the usual standards of professional ethics." They suggest that the relationship between coach and leader is one that is based on "high levels of trust and also strict confidentiality" (p.600). They further explain how the relationship between the agent (coach) and the principal (client) will involve the *duty* to serve the interests of the other. In this sense they liken the role to that of a physician or attorney, in that they "share important and privileged relationships with their clients" (ibid., p.600).

This idea of agency is interesting since we might ask how far the agency relationship extends. If we think about the idea that the leader is in an agency relationship with his/her stakeholders (and with wider global concerns), then we can see that, by extension, the coach may have responsibilities there too. Where does the buck stop?

As Hannafey and Vitulano (2013, p.600) point out, "understanding the work of executive coaches in the context of agency relationships can serve as an important theoretical grounding for more effective moral thinking about the actual practice of executive coaching." We would also add that it may increase our understanding of moral responsibility in relation to leaders: "As in all agency relations the agent (coach) has important obligations to serve the interest of the principal (client and secondarily the organization) in all matters of his or her agency" (ibid., p.600). The agency relation can, in fact, "positively inform descriptive and normative thinking about executive coaching moral practices and provide specific ways to manage conflicts of interest, confidentiality problems, and also other moral problems that may arise" (ibid., p.602).

Bright, Cameron and Caza (2006) talk about the limitations of ethical codes and their inability to predict all the dilemmas managers may come up against in a turbulent external environment. The issue here is that even the most rigorous moral code cannot anticipate the necessary ethical stance needed for each situation. As Bright et al. point out, "many of the perpetrators in the scandals at Enron made their decisions based on a frame-of-reference that seemed perfectly legitimate and ethical to company insiders. Indeed many of them still claim that they did nothing wrong" (ibid., p.250), so the "absence of unethical behaviour does not guarantee the presence of highly principled behaviour."

Linked to the necessity to maintain integrity is the idea of continuing professional development and supervision. Professional development is, we believe, an essential part of the ongoing improvement process for the coach and in that context supervision is very important. As many coaches work on their own and are really "at the office" when they are face to face with the client, this can lead to some potentially bad habits if regular supervision is not sought. Also the role of the coach can be quite isolating, and leadership coaches might find themselves working in quite a rarefied atmosphere. Furthermore, as leaders may themselves have issues which they can only discuss with the coach, this unique, special and powerful relationship may run into some difficult areas if the coach is not on a regular basis conducting some sort of reflective "sense check," preferably with the help of a supervisor. Similarly, Kemp (2010, p.160) considers that "the continuous surfacing, reflection, and management of [...] intrapersonal and interpersonal insights can be confusing and confronting for coaches if conducted in isolation from professional supervision." He argues, and we would agree, that continuing engagement in a supervisory relationship is an important foundation for professional practice of coaching and provides a good grounding for continuing personal and professional development. According to Luft and Ingham (1955), supervisory relationships may also serve the purpose of surfacing, illuminating and monitoring the blind, hidden or unknown aspects of ourselves, and so deepen coaches' understanding of themselves.

Similar to coaching itself, the purpose of coaching supervision could be seen as using a structured process of sharing coaching practice to identify the coach's strengths, weaknesses and challenges in their practice, and to consider these in a professional, confidential and non-judgmental manner. In turn, this demonstrates professional integrity and accountability to clients. Supervision also provides opportunities for coaches to identify new methods and practices and so enhance client outcomes.

We would recommend that the supervisor selected has been trained in coaching supervision, but we also suspect that a coach having access to another coach for a supervisory-type conversation, even if the other coach has had no formal training as a supervisor, is probably more beneficial than having no conversation at all.

In our opinion, the real danger of the coach–client dynamic, without supervisory input, is that the relationship could descend into a form of *folie a deux*, in the sense that what might seem right or profound, or "magical," within this relationship might bear no connection to convention or even sanity when exposed in the cold light of day. This may be a rather extreme outcome, but in leadership coaching the stakes can be high, with decisions being made which can impact not only leaders themselves but also many other individuals within and around the organization.

We would suggest that due to the nature of brave leadership coaching, the need for coaches to have a balanced and reflective coach supervisor is an essential part of the ultimate integrity and success of the coach–client relationship. In brave leadership coaching, the stakes may potentially be even higher than in normal leader coaching, and as coaches are part of the "brave dynamic," they can avoid the aforementioned potentially dangerous, hermetically sealed *folie a deux* by finding the space and time to step back from the coaching work and consider it critically.

3 Benevolence

The third aspect of Heffernan's classification of trust is benevolence, which he describes as whether the partner will be accommodating and act with equity when new conditions relating to the relationship arise. This is closely related to the emotionally based "affective trust," identified by Massey and Kyngdon (2005), which relies on feelings generated by the concern or level of care that the coach has for the client. Johnson and Grayson (2005, p.501) explain how affective trust is focused on the personal experiences the client has with the coach and is closely related to the perception that actions are intrinsically motivated. This prediction is borne out by Alvey and Barclay's (2007) qualitative work on trust in relationships between executives and their external coaches, which found that although coach credibility was important in the initial phases, it was the coaches' actual behaviors that became more important in building and maintaining trust over time.

Markovic et al. (2014) suggest that in the early phases where contracting occurs, the coach can demonstrate ability by overtly clarifying the coach's role and outlining the coaching process, building in benevolence by asking the client how s/he feels about the process. It also helps to become *au fait* with the client's cultural and educational background. Perceptions of ability and benevolence can further be enhanced by introducing conversations about trust and discussing the confidentiality agreement, which may highlight client concerns. Later in the relationship the coach can show benevolence while giving attention to clients when they report on successes and failures and helping by discussing specific obstacles and difficulties.

Another way in which the coach can show benevolence is through empathy and the use of self. Lee and Frisch explain the use of self as "a coach's use of his or her insight, empathy, and intuition to tune into the experience of *being with* a client and then finding ways to use those perceptions as part of the coaching" (Lee & Frisch, 2011, p.71, our emphasis). Statements that coaches could use with their clients to demonstrate benevolence during brave leadership discussions can pick up on clients' feelings and attitudes during the conversation. For example:

- From where you are now, I can see you are tired of waiting for senior colleagues to make a decision and that you need to progress this urgently.
- You appear to be feeling impatient even now.
- You appear to me to be angry about how slowly things are progressing.

- I sense that you feel that you have wasted your time in those meetings because nothing has been achieved.
- I wonder if you are saying that you are frustrated.

In the example coaching dialogue that follows, we see the coach picking up on Matt's feelings during the session and also demonstrating vulnerability by using self-disclosure:

MATT: But the problem is that I will need to be nice!

COACH: I thought that you were nice!

MATT: Okay, I'm joking, but you know what I mean. I have someone who has screwed up. And that in and of itself is not an issue of course. In fact you know that I have always been keen to build a culture where it is fine to fail ... as long, of course, as there is an element of learning taking place. But this screw-up, this ... error, was due to someone's ego getting in the way, and you know who I am talking about. And you know that I think that the best type of leader is the leader who works without ego, or is as egoless as possible. So this, this ... incident just makes my blood boil. But I really have to be careful how I deal with this situation.

COACH: In what sense?

MATT: In the sense that I do want to create a proper learning environment where it is okay to fail. I must not over-react.

COACH: That sounds wise.

MATT: However, the issue is, how do I use an element of coaching here? My approach with this person isn't going to work, I don't think. I must find a way to help this person avoid this behavior in the future, and somehow not make it into a clash of egos, with me simply telling. I need to help this person generate a shift, even though I am annoyed with them.

COACH: Perhaps if we took this one step at a time. Are you more or less likely to create this shift that you desire if you go into a meeting annoyed?

MATT: I think undoubtedly I need to be calm.

COACH: Okay, and we have worked on various strategies in the past to assist with precisely that. I know that we are not specifically talking about the brave approach here, but what is the right thing to do here? The brave thing?

MATT: Well funnily enough, I was thinking about that this morning, and I think that we have an individual who is actually not okay. I began to get a strong feeling, when I remember incidents with this individual, where the whole ego thing is to do with massive insecurity, and a need not to be vulnerable or show vulnerability. I think that I need to get this person to realize that it is okay to feel vulnerable, that we don't have to be right all the time, that even the best leaders can get confused, afraid, unsure, etc. And that if we want to encourage a true learning environment, we have to be open to showing that we don't always get it right. That we do make mistakes, that we are flawed and human, but that that is okay because that is how we learn.

COACH: So how do you think that you might approach that?

MATT: I think that I have to go there first, that I have to be vulnerable—but the problem is I also have an ego, like it or not, and hate the idea of appearing vulnerable myself.

COACH: Well, that's an interesting conundrum.

MATT: You see, I think for him, ego is involved in some rather challenging behaviors. I really don't think that I would behave that way, but for both of us, for probably different reasons, we find being vulnerable an issue.

COACH: I think a lot of people do. But what do you think is stopping you from showing your vulnerability?

MATT: What is stopping me is that the culture hasn't truly changed yet, it isn't a true learning environment and this stuff, showing vulnerability, can always be used against you, you can appear weak.

COACH: And yet, someone has to lead by example.

MATT: Correct, and that probably has to be me. In fact, it definitely needs to be me.

COACH: How would you show vulnerability?

MATT: How I thought I might approach this is by telling him exactly how I feel and what goes on inside me, when I have to do some of the bigger presentations, both within the organization and externally. The fear, the self-doubt, etc. Except that I'm not sure I can actually do it.

COACH: Isn't presentation anxiety normal?

MATT: Well, maybe the fact that I hesitate to share this shows how stupidly macho the culture has become. But also part of me thinks that at my level and how it makes me feel, that it is a little pathetic and that I should love it—I'm meant to do this as part of my job, after all. By the way, you have to do presentations. How do you do it?

COACH: Well, the very first time I did a business presentation, it was to three people. To this day I still think of them as the three witches of *Macbeth*. They absolutely savaged me. Looking back, it was the antithesis of a coaching culture. It knocked my confidence sideways and it took me a long time to think about talking to groups again. Even now, for days and days and nights and nights before any big talk, I get particularly anxious. And before the talk, I have to go through particular rituals, and if I don't, I can get almost paralyzed with fear. Naturally, I have used several strategies over the years to deal with it, and I'm better than I was, but it still feels like a tightrope walk. And now and again I fall off.

MATT: I find that hard to believe. You hide it well.

COACH: I can assure you that it is all too true. And can I ask you, how do you feel about me now?

MATT: How do I feel about you now? Well, no different than I did five minutes ago … ah, I see, you mean because you have opened up, allowed yourself to be seen as less in command of a situation than I might have thought you were—has that changed how I perceive you and feel about you?

COACH: Exactly.

MATT: Well, funnily enough, actually, it has changed how I perceive you. I think what you just shared has deepened our rapport. And probably the main outcome, which I'm guessing you were hoping for, is I now know what I absolutely must do to address this issue. I must be open about being less than perfect myself. And actually, when I think about it, that is the brave thing to do.

The coaching dialogue with Matt showed how rapport can shift even in the course of one coaching session. Matt also realized what the coach was trying to do during the session: by role modeling his own vulnerability the coach helped the client think about how he would approach his own situation.

Kemp has suggested that:

> as trust, respect and empathy build and shared meaning emerges, shared purpose and commitment subsequently surface, allowing for high levels of mutual engagement to drive new opportunities and new and creative ways to realize these opportunities. With trust and respect comes support for endeavor and a progressive dissipation of fear, resistance and ambiguity.
>
> *(Kemp, 2009, p.102)*

Gallwey (2010, p.xxii) has also pointed out that unless coaches become "comfortable negotiating the fears and doubts that accompany learning, they will no doubt invite resistance to the very learning they are attempting to evoke." Here Gallwey is concerned that if the coach does not understand the pain of learning then the client may detect that and adopt a similar resistance. The client may feel uncomfortable and even judged, thus s/he will shut down and only pay lip service to the coaching. To overcome this latent resistance, Gallwey says there is no skill more important than non-judgmental awareness, but he argues that the challenge of increasing non-judgmental awareness requires a "suspension of judgment not only by the coach but by the client as well. It is fear of judgment in the eyes of others and oneself that creates resistance to natural learning and inhibits truth from emerging. Creating an environment that minimizes judgment is one of the central attributes of successful coaching" (ibid., p.xxii). Because coaching takes place in the domain of the "inner," Gallwey reminds us, benevolence is vital: "the unique human gifts of compassion, kindness, and clarity are required in greater degrees than are normally expected in the fields of management and leadership" (ibid., p.xxii).

In the case study that follows we can seen an example of how a leader's lack of trust was picked up by the coach, but was not addressed. Instead the coach seems to have focused on being benevolent to the leader, rather than showing integrity and courage in the coaching setting.

Case study

Another coach whom we know had an issue in one of his leadership coaching sessions, with forming a working alliance. Jonathan came into the coaching relationship with one fairly bad experience under his belt in terms of confidentiality. Forming a relationship, according to the coach, was an uphill struggle from the outset. As previously mentioned, Ely et al. (2010) suggest that the relationship, the alliance, is a feature of two individuals, not one, and as our colleague noted, the leader was treating every sentence and nuance with the utmost suspicion. The relationship was not toxic; it seemed, in fact, to become quite friendly. It was, however, doomed to be ultimately ineffectual, for as the coach explained to us:

> I felt that rapport and trust was key, and having this individual enter into the relationship with so much mistrust was very difficult. However, I realized after two sessions that I had made a fatal error. In attempting to gain rapport and to lighten the mood, I went down the road of praise. Praise of hard work and of intellect.
>
> The problem was that this individual was really quite damaged by this point and had, I believe, put up so many barriers, that when I made what I thought were relatively innocuous comments meant to

demonstrate some respect on my part, they seemed to light up part of this person's psyche like a small star, and I could see he craved more. And despite myself, but because the normally steely almost obnoxious persona was so difficult to deal with, I fell into the habit of using that strategy to inject a temporary respite from the "permafrost." And it was during session two that I could see that he was almost not going to play along until the necessary message had been delivered. I still kick myself. I should have nipped things in the bud and called him on it, and quite simply walked away if there was no change.

In this example we can sense the tension between the coach's desired integrity and wanting to be benevolent to the leader. However, as the results demonstrate, being too kind compromises integrity of the coaching. The lack of trust in the relationship, instead of being strengthened, was exacerbated by the coach's lack of integrity: the coach had been too accommodating and perhaps had overdone the benevolence.

We would argue that in the braver leader coaching alliance, there can be no room for a less than brave coach. To help the leader be brave, the alliance must be between two brave peers. This does not mean to suggest a lack of vulnerability, or that it must be deadly serious, but it should be challenging. If the leader is to be challenged then the coach must also be willing and able to challenge him/herself.

Summary

In this chapter we explored some of the trust issues that face coaches when undertaking leadership coaching. After defining and delineating trust, we took the three antecedents of trust identified by Heffernan (2004) to examine trust in the leadership coaching context. We examined the notion of credibility and how that contributes to a feeling of trust initially through reputation of the external coach, but also through the establishment of a robust coaching intervention.

The next component we looked at was integrity. The integrity of the coach is perceived by the client as whether or not the coach has the capability and expertise to follow through on the coaching assignment. It involves meeting three needs: shared values; confidentiality in the relationship; and the ability of both parties to make themselves vulnerable. We used a case example to illustrate how this can work within the coaching session.

The third antecedent examined was benevolence, which involves the client's assessment of whether the coach will be accommodating and act with equity as challenges arise in the coaching. A case study demonstrated how if one or other antecedents is present whilst another is missing, this inevitably leads to a lack of trust. It is important to recognize that this kind of trust issue challenges coaches to consider their own boundaries and ethical position, and we highlighted the importance of coach supervision for ongoing personal development to address such concerns.

The need for trust and its integral components cannot be overstated within leadership coaching. Trust overcomes resistance at various stages throughout the coaching process, which even if only slight, can prevent clients from sharing their thoughts openly. In such cases the coaching process can become if not a complete charade, at least a pretence and a mere shadow of the productive relationship that it could be.

10
POSITIONING BRAVER LEADERSHIP COACHING

Introduction

In this chapter we examine the role of leadership theories in braver leadership coaching. We first highlight the way in which leaders have traditionally been developed through management and executive education where the focus is on theory and the development of specific leadership skills and competences. As part of this discussion we evaluate six familiar leadership theories in order to make the link between these theories and the brave leadership concept. The six we have chosen are: transformational leadership, authentic leadership, ethical leadership, situational leadership, servant leadership and relational leadership, although there are many other leadership theories that we could have included. Toward the end of the chapter we provide a synthesis that explains how coaching may be perceived as the best support approach for developing leaders since it utilizes current, real-time experiences for learning, while at the same time supporting leaders during their day-to-day work in complex settings.

1 Traditional Leadership Development

Traditionally leaders have relied on leadership education or executive development programs that tend to focus on the behaviors, core competencies and traits of the individual. However, as Turnbull James and Collins (2008, p.3) have pointed out, this approach could be described as a "deficit model of leadership development that centres on a concern that necessary leadership characteristics are properly developed." These authors highlight Day's argument (Day, 2001; Day et al., 2009) which suggests there is a subtle difference between leadership development and leader development: the former focuses on the skills and attributes needed for the role, while the latter addresses the fundamental adult development needs of the leader. Coaching, we would argue, is a form of leader development that works on both levels: it uses immediate leadership concerns to support skill development if necessary, whilst also developing the leader according to individual needs. So as well as spotlighting specific attribute or competence advancement, there is an inherent focus on the kind of leader development that Day suggests is missing from traditional leader education programs.

The deficit model inherent in traditional leadership development is fueled by what can be seen as distinct groups of leadership theories, or "schools of thought." Western (2013) splits these theories into five groups: individual, collective, contextual, followers and new leadership. We prefer to classify them into two groups of three which form a continuum from an individual to a more social perspective, as illustrated in Figure 10.1. The first group has been categorized as trait (Northouse, 2009) or values based and is concerned with the leader as individual. It includes:

- transformational/heroic leadership (Bass, 1985; Bass & Riggio, 2006);
- authentic leadership (Gardner et al., 2005; Nyberg & Sveningsson, 2014); and
- ethical leadership (Brown et al., 2005).

The second group focuses on processes (Northouse, 2009) or social relationships within the organization, such as:

- situational leadership (Hersey & Blanchard, 1982);
- servant leadership (Luthans & Avolio, 2003); and
- relational leadership (Uhl-Bien, 2006).

There are many other "sub" theories: Western (2013) identifies 44 types of leadership, including charismatic leadership (Conger & Kanungo, 1998), spiritual leadership (Van Praag, 2004), and strategic leadership (Finkelstein et al., 2009), but these can generally be ordered as part of the two groups, either sitting at the trait/value-based end of the spectrum (e.g. transformational, authentic, ethical), or at the process/relational end (e.g. servant, situational, relational).

We now conduct a short evaluation of the key features of each of the six theories we have identified in order to provide an overview of the

Individual perspective					Social perspective
Transformational	Authentic	Ethical	Situational	Servant	Relational

FIGURE 10.1 A continuum of leadership theories

field and to illustrate how, in order to operationalize them morally and effectively, they each require elements of bravery.

i) Transformational leadership

Bass and Avolio's (1989) definition of transformational leadership had four dimensions: charisma, individual consideration, intellectual stimulation and inspiration. Later, Bass and Riggio (2006) defined these four elements as the "4 I's":

- Idealized influence: Provides vision and sense of mission, instills pride, gains respect and trust.
- Inspiration: Communicates high expectations, uses symbols to focus efforts, expresses important purposes in simple ways.
- Intellectual stimulation: Promotes intelligence, rationality, and careful problem solving.
- Individualized consideration: Gives personal attention, treats each employee individually, coaches, advises.

Various other authors have also discussed these separate elements of transformational leadership. Barling, Kelloway and Loughlin (2002), for example, discussed idealized influence, highlighting the modeling aspect: "with its emphasis on managers becoming role models by doing what is moral or right rather than what is expedient, idealized influence encourages managers to shift their focus" (p.489). However, Rafferty and Griffin (2004) viewed idealized influence and vision as the main characteristics, suggesting that transforming leaders can actually empower people to generate hope, optimism and energy.

It is interesting to note that some authors, such as Barling et al. (2002), also discuss a sense of doing the "right" thing. In fact, Bass (1990) had earlier described one aspect of transformational leadership as involving leaders bringing deep change to their organizations by encouraging others to look beyond their own self-interest for the good of others. Later Bass and Riggio (2006, p.227) talked about "transcending" self-interest, which suggests some significant development is necessary for the leader. This development might involve ego development, as discussed in a coaching context by Bachkirova (2011), or other forms of development as highlighted by Day et al. (2009). Widening the scope of transformational leadership even further, Singh and Krishnan (2008) considered the element of self-sacrifice and noted that other-orientedness or altruism enhances transformational leadership, which in turn leads to higher collective identity and perceived performance.

Precisely what constitutes transformational leadership appears to vary. For example, Pawar (2003, p.398) identified distinctly contrasting perspectives between it and transactional leadership, arguing that research into transformational leadership shows that part of what is involved is the conversion of followers into leaders, which can result in the motivational and moral elevation of both followers and leaders.

In Burns's (1978) work, transformational leadership was also viewed as being distinct from transactional leadership, based on the view that transformational leaders raise followers to a higher level of needs and aspirations, whereas transactional leaders merely identify and reward the existing needs and goals of their followers. Bass (1985, p.22), however, noted how he and Burns differed on this point. Bass saw transformational leadership as the opposite end of a single continuum from transactional leadership. Thus in later work, Bass proposed that the four elements of transactional leadership (set out below) be combined with the four aspects of transformational leadership described earlier to form the "Full Range Leadership" (FRL) model (Bass & Riggio, 2006).

Transactional leadership

- Contingent reward: Contracts the exchange of rewards for effort, promises rewards for good performance, recognizes accomplishments.
- Management by exception (active): Watches and searches for deviations from rules and standards, takes corrective action.
- Management by exception (passive): Intervenes only if standards are not met.
- Laissez-faire: Abdicates or delegates responsibilities, avoids making decisions.

However this eight-point FRL model focuses on what the leader needs to do, rather than who the leader is, and so the vital element of leader development—as opposed to leadership development (Day, 2001; Day et al., 2009)—is neglected here. Transformational leadership focuses on what leaders ought to do rather than how they can develop as people and therefore how they cope as individuals. Thus the deficit model of leadership development is inherent in this theory. It is interesting to consider, too, whether bravery is required in order to tackle the transformational aspects of the FRL, and whether the more transactional aspects require only enforcement.

The dark side of transformational leadership has recently been examined by Tourish (2012), who suggests that theories of leadership such as transformational have become "part of the problems we now face, rather than the solution" (p.199). He argues that these theories continue to "legitimise the concentration of power in elite hands" (ibid., p.199) and points out that transformational leadership theories have not been challenged so that "the potential for abuse" as a result of their unreflexive application is immense. In fact Tourish highlights Fryer's (2011, p.1) warning that "our faith in the capacity of leaders to make a difference verges on the cultish." Tourish asks whether models of leadership can be developed that "require us to think for ourselves" (Tourish, 2012, p.201) and challenge people to engage properly with the organizations for which we work. However, he is critical of seemingly liberating theories such as followership, a relational theory where followers are able to influence leaders. This, he argues, continues to reify a leadership hierarchy.

Copeland (2014), too, has also explained how in previous decades transformational leadership was promoted, encouraged and developed as a "strategy for increasing the effectiveness of leaders and organisations," but that more recently the qualities for exemplary leaders have begun to be challenged, in order to "restore, hope, confidence, integrity and honor to leaders and organizations" (p.106). Copeland considers that we need to look "beyond the lure of a charismatic, ostensibly transformational leader, and ensure that leaders also [possess] a strong set of values, morals and ethics" (ibid., p.106). Thus there has been more focus on the concept of values-based leadership, examples of which include spiritual, servant, authentic and ethical leadership. In fact, Copeland argues that values-based leadership is essential for leaders to be "truly successful and effective." These seemingly more values-based theories are discussed in more detail below.

ii) *Authentic leadership*

The concept of authentic leadership is widely discussed within the management and leadership literature where its application is assumed to bring about improved organizational conditions and performance. However, the concept of authenticity, which has its origins in existential philosophy, is ill defined, or not defined at all in many texts, and is just simply assumed as one of the ideals to which leaders should aspire. George (2003, p.11), for example, states that "authenticity is being and acting consistent with who you hold yourself to be for others, and who you hold yourself to be for yourself." George's five characteristics of authentic leaders are listed as: understanding purpose; having strong values; creating trusting relationships; self-discipline; and acting from the heart.

In other articulations of the theory (e.g. Walumbwa et al., 2008) self-awareness, an internalized moral perspective, balanced processing of information and relational transparency are all identified as necessary. Brown and Trevino (2006, p.599) also highlighted the self-awareness aspect of authentic leaders, suggesting that such leaders are "individuals who are deeply aware of how they think and behave and are perceived by others as being aware of their own and others' values/moral perspective, knowledge, and strengths; aware of the context in which they operate; and who are confident, hopeful, optimistic, resilient, and high on moral character."

Similarly, Wong and Cummings (2009, p.525) noted that definitions of authentic behavior involve "acting in accord with one's values and needs rather than to please others, receive rewards, or avoid punishments." To be truly authentic, leaders must align their core and espoused values and actions. In their review of authentic leadership research, Gardner et al. (2011, p.1142) also concluded that a central premise in the literature is that "truly authentic leaders must lead, but they must do so in a way that honours their core values, beliefs, strengths—and weaknesses."

These working definitions, however, suggest that authentic leadership is a state of being, the search for an essential true self and one that is morally good. Underpinning this is an assumption that within us all is "something good and valuable" (Guignon, 2004, p.147). Guignon suggests that in the language of virtues, "we might say that authenticity is assumed to be a virtue more concerned with the individual's personal fulfilment, rather like temperance, than it is a social virtue comparable to fairness and decency" (ibid., p.155).

These ideas appear to center on an idea of authenticity as a manifestation of "the real self," whereas Nyberg and Sveningsson (2014, p.2) have pointed out that "rather than an inward quest of finding a true or essential self, authenticity is a multi-faceted *outward project* of binding or "crystallising" contrasting and fragmented identities into a coherent life story" (our emphasis). Nyberg and Sveningsson have further recommended substituting the implicit essentialism suggested by many authentic leadership authors with a more constructionist approach that recognizes how leaders are active in building who they are and how they lead in their organization. This more socially constituted self is reflected in the relational approach that has been taken up by leadership theorists in recent years (e.g. Uhl-Bien, 2006). It also sits well, we would argue, with a coaching philosophy and distinguishes coaching from therapy (Cox, 2013).

Nyberg and Sveningsson (2014, p.4) have also argued that most of the leadership literature relating to authenticity refers to "theoretical 'recipes' that prescribe authenticity as a universal concept or solution with limited engagement with local discourses." They point out that recent critiques raise questions concerning the claim that it is actually possible "to know and consistently express one's inherent traits" (ibid., p.4), thus they question the "natural good of authentic leadership." Tourish (2012) is similarly critical of current authentic leadership theory, arguing that authentic leaders are merely expected to align their inner values with the organization's aims and still retain all the power expected in their corporate cultures.

The whole notion of authentic leadership is problematic on two counts. First, as suggested above, authenticity is a contested notion. Guignon (2004, p.151) suggested that "the problems running through the standard idea of authenticity result from thinking of it solely as a personal virtue," and proposed that authenticity should be thought of fundamentally and irreducibly as a social virtue: "it is only through our social interactions that we become selves whose inner episodes are given enough steadiness and cohesiveness so that our relations to others can be built on cooperation and trust" (ibid., p.155). Second, leaders are still placed in positions where they are expected to demonstrate choice and agency over followers. Eagly (2005) suggests that authentic leadership may overreach itself in situations where leaders who have openly behaved in a way that was congruent with their stated core values fail to reach what she describes as "relational authenticity" with followers, perhaps because these particular values have not been built in collaboration and do not match those of the followers. In addition, if the values that are espoused by the authentic leader are inappropriate to reinforce in a particular situation, then it is likely that there would be some internal conflict. It could also transpire that due to some extenuating set of circumstances, the leader's values were actually incompatible with an ethical path, or even a humanitarian path (both of which are socially constructed). This is a particular concern for ethical leadership, discussed in more detail below, as one can imagine a potential impasse between the perceived ethical values of leaders and the values of followers. So the socially constructed idea of leadership could be seen as the only way to achieve truly ethical leadership.

More recently, Gardner et al. (2011) and Nyberg and Sveningsson (2014) have clarified how the idea of authenticity is not the search for one true, atomistic self that might guide authentic action, but rather it is to immerse oneself in the never-ending *process* of becoming. For existentialists, authenticity is a social virtue, something that comes through awareness of alternative perspectives, critical thinking and the making of informed and committed choices: "there is no need to search for an authentic identity—we touch authenticity when we make choices from an informed place, when we author our lives" (Cox, 2013, p.55). The existential journey that involves becoming a creator in our own lives, moment by moment, can be seen as quite a brave expedition, involving countless others, and is one that almost certainly would benefit from the support of an experienced coach.

iii) Ethical leadership

Ethical leadership concerns leaders' behaviors, their conduct and character. These elements are seen as important because leaders have considerable responsibility for their organizations and the people they are leading. As Northouse (2013, p.428) has explained, "ethics is central to leadership because of the nature of the process of influence, the need to engage followers in accomplishing mutual goals, and the impact leaders have on the organization's values." Ciulla (2011, p.239) has further proposed that "an ethical and effective leader is someone who does the right thing, the right way, for the right reasons," pointing out that "the ethics of leaders are not different from the ethics of everyone else, but because their actions take place in public and affect larger numbers of people morality and immorality are magnified in everything they do" (ibid., p.239).

Northouse (2013) outlined two types of ethical leadership theories: those that stress the consequences of action on others and those that stress the duty or rules governing those actions (p.424). He also highlighted five principles of ethical leadership: respect for others, serving others, showing justice, manifesting honesty and building community, pointing out that leadership is not an amoral phenomenon. Northouse further suggested that although only transformational, authentic and servant leadership theories appear to incorporate an ethical dimension, leadership is "a process of influencing others; it has a moral dimension that distinguishes it from other types of influence" (ibid., p.438).

Key scholars writing about ethical leadership have emphasized the need for leaders to engage with the consequences of their actions and to assess followers' needs, values and morals. Burns (1978) took this position in his theory of transformational leadership, rooting his thinking in the works of Maslow and Kohlberg. According to Ciulla (2004, 2011), ethical leadership is essentially the art of leading others in such a way that those being led, "the followers," feel that their rights are being respected and that they are being treated with dignity. Indeed, De Wolde et al. (2012) suggested that ethical leaders do not merely have more influence due to their leadership style, as argued in earlier research by Mayer et al. (2009) and others, but because their leadership fits more closely with the norms and values of followers.

Whilst not as commonly discussed as ethical leadership within the business community, we would include spiritual leadership in this family of leading approaches. Indeed, many authors have linked the two (e.g. Brown & Trevino, 2006). Reave (2005, p.663) stated that spiritual leadership can be seen as occurring "when a person in a leadership position embodies spiritual values such as integrity, honesty, and humility, creating the self as an example of someone who can be trusted, relied upon, and admired." She goes on to say that it is also demonstrated "through behaviour, whether in individual reflective practice or in the ethical, compassionate, and respectful treatment of others." Thus, ethical decisions and action in the leadership context require moral courage and a certain amount of bravery to fulfill.

We believe that coaches can support leaders to become much more context sensitive, and to really wrestle with values—what they actually mean and what weighting they should be given in a particular situation. The leader can then ultimately become less "label driven," less prone to wonder if a particular situation lends itself to an ethical, authentic or transformational approach. It may be more productive to think that leadership is, in fact, all approaches and none: all, in the sense that every situation presents an opportunity to choose an approach and not be bound by an approach; and none, in the sense that these theoretical "hats" might just be informing decision making and behaviors like sub-routines in the background. Coaching can be helpful in this regard: Schaubroeck et al. (2012) mentioned coaching as among the embedding mechanisms that a leader may choose to use to support an ethical approach.

What approaches are used is, of course, a matter of cultural and individual choice, but we would suggest that the idea of suddenly switching on the ethical light, and rounding up the committee, or deciding to put on the authentic jacket is perhaps one way in which things have gone awry. This is partly because leaders in the moment, feeling isolated and pressured, can view ethics, authenticity or transformation as something other than what they are hired to do, and also partly because some leaders do not consider these "labels" to be truly part of their vision of themselves—they may see themselves more in the "hero," "tough," "charismatic" range of leadership. In fact, they may regard ethics as being something that the ethics group might consider at one of their meetings, something that has a process, a time, a place, but which is not intrinsically connected to their role.

iv) Situational leadership

The idea of a situational component in leadership has its origins in contingency theory, where it is suggested that the context of a situation should determine how leaders respond. Fiedler (1967) and House and Dessler (1974) proposed that the leader's response is greatly determined by followers' readiness to perform a task, and leaders need to adjust their style accordingly. In their theory of situational leadership, Hersey and Blanchard (1982) similarly considered that there is no one best way to lead—rather, the leader's task is to gauge their interaction with followers according to their needs or maturity levels. This, in turn, is thought to increase effectiveness. Such leadership is seen as involving both direction and support.

Situational leadership theory views follower maturity as an evolutionary progression, suggesting that when people approach tasks for the first time, they start out with little knowledge, ability or skill, but have a high level of enthusiasm, motivation and commitment. As they grow in experience, particularly if this is appropriately supported by the leader, they reach the next level of competence. However, their commitment may drop since the task might turn out to be more difficult or complex than originally anticipated. Thus maturity levels relate to varying degrees of capability and confidence in relation to the task at hand, the situation. Blanchard, Zigarmi and Zigarmi (1985) introduced the terms "competence" (ability, knowledge and skill) and "commitment" (confidence and motivation) to explain these different levels of maturity, and proposed that with continued direction, support and leadership, people move gradually to even higher levels of competence as they gain mastery of the task or role. Situational leadership thus requires that leaders identify other people's working styles to enable them to flex their approach.

The situational leadership model is deemed useful when coaching is undertaken by leaders with their employees, since its goal is to "develop the follower by using successive leadership styles as the leader moves on the continuum from prescribe to develop, to reinforce, and then follow up" (Hersey & Blanchard, 1982, p.253). Hersey and Blanchard also considered leadership in terms of the amount of relationship behavior or task behavior the leader offers to followers. They categorized all leadership into four behavior types or styles—telling (directive), selling (supportive), participating (participative), and delegating (achievement oriented)—suggesting that effective leaders need to be adaptable and adjust their style to suit the situation. Hersey, Blanchard and Johnson (2001) further confirmed that leadership style should change depending on the situation and the readiness of the follower, while Fry (2003) argued that leaders can create a context for building employee motivation by selecting specific leadership behaviors. The suggestion is that the right behavior can provide what is missing for employees in a particular work setting (Northouse, 2013).

Hersey and Chevalier (2000, pp.247–256) usefully presented ideas of how situational leadership might also be beneficial as a framework to guide coaching during the performance cycle, the leader acting as coach to steer the interaction with followers at each stage. Again, leaders would adjust their style to their followers' levels of readiness (ability and/or willingness) and provide the right amount of direction or support, dependent on need. These authors argue that the assessment phase is critical particularly for the coaching process and that the "leader must prepare, assess, and diagnose prior to making the actual intervention." However, Hersey and Chevalier suggested that the leader must "'earn the right' to intervene" (ibid., p.253).

It would seem to us that the situational approach has some affinity with brave leadership. It might require more time to respond according to individual need, but this demonstrates integrity and cultural sensitivity, and arguably requires a kind of situational courage to follow through.

v) *Servant leadership*

Van Dierendonck (2011) explained how in recent years leadership studies have shifted away from the strong focus on transformational leadership towards a greater emphasis on "shared, relational, and global perspectives where especially the interaction between leader and follower are key elements" (p.1229). The move has been away from an individualistic, opportunistic and self-serving focus, toward "governance based on viewing individuals as pro-organizational, self-actualizing, and trustworthy" (ibid., p.1229). Proposed by Greenleaf in the 1970s, servant leadership is suggested by Van Dierendonck as being of particular relevance in the modern era in that it adds an element of social responsibility to transformational leadership and "more than any other leadership theory, it explicitly emphasizes the needs of followers" (ibid., p.1229).

Based on his work with Greenleaf, Spears (1995) had earlier identified ten characteristics of the servant-leader:

- listening, emphasizing the importance of communication and seeking to identify the will of the people;
- empathy, understanding others and accepting how and what they are;
- healing, the ability to help make whole;
- awareness, being awake;
- persuasion, seeking to influence others relying on arguments, not on positional power;
- conceptualization, thinking beyond the present-day need and stretching it into a possible future;
- foresight, foreseeing outcomes of situations and working with intuition,
- stewardship, holding something in trust and serving the needs of others;
- commitment to the growth of people, nurturing the personal, professional and spiritual growth of others; and
- building community, emphasizing that local communities are essential in a person's life.

Later, Russell and Stone (2002, p.146) described nine functional attributes of servant leadership (classified as functional attributes due to their repetitive prominence in the literature). These are: vision, honesty, integrity, trust, service, modeling, pioneering, appreciation of others, and empowerment. Other models have been proposed, resulting in, as Van Dierendonck reported, 44 overlapping characteristics (it should be noted that these characteristics are distinct from Western's 44 types of leadership). Van Dierendonck (2011) also suggested that combining the conceptual models with empirical evidence from different measures of servant leadership, it might be possible to distinguish key characteristics of servant-leader behavior. The resulting six key characteristics, he says, give a good overview of servant leadership behavior as experienced by followers: "Servant-leaders empower and develop people; they show humility, are authentic, accept people for who they are, provide direction, and are stewards who work for the good of the whole" (ibid., p.1232). Core elements of servant leadership thus include self-awareness, responsibility, authenticity and moral courage. These constitute a values system rather than a set of specific leadership practices (Wheeler, 2012).

According to Luthans and Avolio (2003), the servant-leader is governed by creating opportunities within the organization to help followers grow.

Thus, servant leaders go beyond self-interest and are motivated by something more important than the need for power—namely, the need to serve (ibid.). In comparison with other leadership theories where the goal is the wellbeing of the organization, a servant-leader is genuinely concerned with serving his/her followers (Greenleaf, 1977).

Van Dierendonck also pointed out how, according to Greenleaf, "the servant-leader is 'primus inter pares' (i.e., first among equals), who does not use his or her power to get things done but who tries to persuade and convince staff" (Van Dierendonck, 2011, p.1231). In these circumstances the leader's power becomes a possibility only to serve others and is considered a prerequisite. Leading and serving in this model are almost interchangeable: "Being a servant allows a person to lead; being a leader implies a person serves" (ibid., p.1231).

Stone et al. (2003) compared transformational and servant leadership and suggested that even though they use different means, they can each produce real change in organizations. These authors went on to note what they consider to be the similarities between the frameworks of servant leadership and transformational leadership, notably: influence; vision; trust; respect or credibility; risk-sharing or delegation; integrity; and modelling (ibid., p.4), and suggest that the two theories are probably most similar because of their emphasis on considering the individual and taking account of follower needs.

Servant leadership, we would argue, also requires a certain amount of bravery to operationalize. Serving followers is a novel and potentially dangerous stance to adopt in many organizations and may run counter to customary and accepted practice. We consider that a coach would be vital for leaders planning to work this way.

vi) *Relational leadership*

Contrary to other studies of leadership, which focus on leadership effectiveness, Uhl-Bien (2006) clarifies that relational leadership theory "focuses on the relational processes by which leadership is produced and enabled" (p.667). She explains how the theory does not define the leader as holding a managerial position, nor does it use the terms "manager" and "leader" interchangeably, but rather it sees leadership as able to occur in any direction. Uhl-Bien also highlights that a relational approach should result in the breakdown of any distinction between who is leading and who is following, instead reflecting a mutual influencing process. This emphasis on mutuality is one of the differentiators between servant and relational leadership.

Uhl-Bien has further suggested that relational leadership theory draws from both entity and relational theory. The entity perspective is perhaps best illustrated by the Leader-Member Exchange (LMX) theory. According to Graen and Uhl-Bien (1995), the central concept of LMX theory is that leadership occurs when leaders and followers, as separate entities, are able to develop effective partnerships that result in incremental difference. This entity perspective assumes "individual agency"; it presupposes that organizational life is as a result of individual action (Hosking et al., 1995). Individuals are thought of as entities with some form of clear separation between their normal selves and the external environment, and leadership consists of a two-way influence between leader and follower, primarily aimed at attaining mutual goals.

Uhl-Bien (2006), however, concludes that the relationship is a separate unit of analysis. She argues that the key difference between relational and entity perspectives is that "relational perspectives identify the basic unit of analysis in leadership research as relationships, not individuals" (p.662). It seems that relationships have quite a different meaning from entity perspectives. This viewpoint is echoed by Murrell (1997), who regarded leadership as a shared responsibility: "Leadership is a social act, a construction of a 'ship' as a collective vehicle to help take us where we are as a group, organisation ... more parties to the process than just the leaders ... more than just the leader-follower exchange relationship" (pp.35–37). Murrell's argument is that by studying leadership that occurs relationally, we have the opportunity to account for many more of the social forces that work to influence group and social behavior. In relational leadership theory it is as if relationships between people are themselves "force multipliers" which enable or enhance incremental steps towards shared goals. Much in the same way that a lever can allow a person to move a greater weight than they may have considered possible, the ability of people in the organization to recognize and utilize their relationships is where the power may lie. In this model, who the leader is is of less importance than the combined actors involved and their ability through productive relationships, to achieve their collective purpose.

Just as relational leadership is concerned with the social interaction in leadership, distributed leadership is also less concerned with the leader as "the personality" and more the interaction between individuals. We believe, therefore, that it warrants inclusion here as a sub-set of relational leadership. As Barry (1991, p.4) noted, "[d]istributed leadership requires that attention be given not only to the type of leader behaviour required at a given time, but also to the interrelatedness and availability of leader behaviours." Harris (2008) suggested that distributed leadership exists when leadership is dispersed throughout a given community and that it is especially prevalent and popular in educational settings.

We thus support Grint (2010), who suggests that what is important is not so much "leadership," but what kind of leadership (p.90). The brave leader needs to recognize the benefits of this distributed power to the organization:

> in which the whole of distributive leadership is greater than the sum of its parts; second, the boundaries of leadership become more porous encouraging many more members of the community to participate in leading their organizations; third, it encourages a reconsideration of what counts as expertise within organizations and expands the degree of knowledge available to the community.
>
> *(Grint, 2010, p.90)*

Again, the role of coaching for a leader keen to adopt a relational strategy is in supporting the decisions needed to change the organizational culture to one that accepts a relational approach and can provide ongoing support for problems arising from the multi-reality construction that is created as a result (Fulop & Mark, 2013).

It is important at this point to reiterate that we are not championing any one of the pre-existing leadership theories; quite the reverse. These are all fundamental leadership ideas which should be more fully and appropriately considered. Our goal here is to make them "center stage" in this chapter in order to juxtapose their key features alongside the idea of brave leadership. It is hoped that such comparison will enable coaches to encourage leaders to act according to their particular values and ethos, even when the pressure is most certainly on.

2 Brave Leadership Informs All Leadership Approaches

Empirical research into the different leadership theories outlined above is still at an early stage and most approaches lack a strong theoretical framework or reliable measures to confirm the theory (Copeland, 2014). Our research found that leaders placed more emphasis on the trait- or values-based leadership theories, such as being authentic and ethical, and this probably reflects the current zeitgeist in most organizations.

Having reviewed the leadership theories in this chapter, it becomes evident that a synergy exists between brave leadership and the different theories. We have considered each theory in turn and it appears that they are each promoting an idea of what is important about leadership.

Relational leadership in broad terms promotes the idea that relationships between people in the organization are key, and that, particularly when linked to distributed leadership, the role of leader may shift between individuals. Situational leadership supports the need to adapt one's style in different situations. Servant leadership advances the idea that self-interest should not motivate the servant leader, but rather the leader should focus on creating the best environment for the followers. Ethical leadership promotes a sense of ethical duty to the followers, to ensure that they feel their rights are being respected and that they are being treated with dignity. Authentic leadership encourages the alignment of the leader's (or in some interpretations, the organization's) core and espoused values, and thus his/her authentic actions. Transformational leadership advocates the encouragement of intellectual stimulation through inspiration of the follower, and so any transformation that takes place is likely to do so within the follower.

It is also possible to link the key concepts from each of the theories. It could be argued, for instance, that transformational leadership requires acuity from the leader about the situation at hand, it requires the need to flex approaches appropriately and pay attention to the importance of relationships; the loyalty and inspiration of followers may be gained not only by intellectual stimulation but also by adopting, where suitable, an ethical, authentic and/or servant stance.

We also believe that by looking at the leadership theories from what we call a "core theme" perspective, a more fundamental synthesis can be achieved. From the core theme perspective it appears that each of the leadership theories is "selling" the idea of considering doing things differently, in relation to ideas such as change, or self-awareness. Below we consider each of these main leadership theories first viewed through the lens of a core theme of change:

- Transformational leadership: Change in relation to transforming people and cultures. Coaching can help leaders think about how they provide vision, stimulation and inspiration.
- Authentic leadership: Change in relation to what they perceive as being authentic, which is often linked to values. Leaders may need challenging to consider their values and purpose and how to act from the heart.
- Ethical leadership: Change in relation to the perceived ethics of the situation. Leaders must consider changing their approach or the culture of the organization and be aware of the consequences of action based on current espoused ethical values.

- Situational leadership: Change in relation to meeting the needs of the situation. Leaders need help to consider changing and flexing their style to meet follower maturity needs.
- Servant leadership: Change in relation to adopting a servant approach. Leaders need support while they consider what generates the best environment for followers and how best they can serve the needs and the culture of the organization.
- Relational leadership: Change in relation to the dynamic of relationships. Leaders need cognitive and practical support in order to break down the distinctions between leader and followers in order for mutuality to flourish. They need help in shifting the role they play from leader to team member, allowing the relationships created to produce leadership decisions.

The idea expressed here is that the leader is an agent of change and the coach supports the leader through the process of change. Each theory promotes the idea of change based on its own value system; each promotes change, or the resistance to it. Each promotes an idea that demands attention and, where applicable, appropriate action. It is likely that there would be periods of time within an organization when there is little change. However, the corporate environment of global market forces, the demands of shareholders, economic conditions and politics, both organizational and governmental, are unlikely to allow the status quo to exist for long. Coaches are not usually considered to be agents of change in the broad sense of the term, but they are change agents in a limited sense, assisting leaders in understanding the need for change and what is entailed.

Another core theme running through all these leadership theories is that of self-awareness. For relational leadership the leader must be self-aware to identify where the balance of power lies, within them or with others. In situational leadership the leader must be aware of what approach they need to be taking. In servant leadership leaders need to be aware of when they deviate from a servant mindset. For ethical leadership the leader must be aware of ethical tensions. In authentic leadership leaders must always be aware of their internal dialogue, and for transformational leadership it is essential to be aware of how self-interest might impede the values base underpinning the vision.

We propose that a core theme perspective (for example, of change or self-awareness) allows brave leadership coaching to be linked practically and conceptually to each of the leadership theories, and by extension to all other theories that sit on the suggested continuum. We would argue, in fact, that bravery must be exhibited in order for leadership approaches to manifest at all in the organization. Relational leaders, for example, may have a comfort zone challenge as they encourage followers to become the leader. For the situational leader it may be the brave step of moving out of the comfort zone to flex his/her style. The ethical and authentic leader may need to be brave in standing up for what s/he believes is right and the servant leader may have to take the brave step of adopting a less authoritarian and/or self-serving approach. Similarly, transformational leaders may have to make the brave move to adopt a coaching style.

Although these are generalized examples, in essence for any of these leadership theories to be realized in an organization, the leader is highly likely, at some point, to need to do something that requires bravery. We therefore believe that the idea of bravery has necessarily to be subsumed within each theory rather than be posited as a separate theory. However, we also believe that its potential importance in helping to address the leadership gap, and in weaving together some previously disparate theories, suggests that it deserves its own nomenclature, and its own particular place in the literature. The consideration of bravery as a common element or catalyst might even encourage a broader reflection of what other leadership ideas and approaches might be applicable in any given situation. Certainly coaches might encourage leaders to consider a range of approaches.

To highlight how the idea of brave leadership might link to each of the six leadership theories, a map is shown in Figure 10.2, showing brave leadership as a common aspect of each theory. We suggest that for a leader to be consistently ethical, authentic and transformational, there are times when an element (either large or small) of bravery is required. This we believe also holds true for relational, servant and situational leadership. To be truly effective the leader must be able to be brave when the situation dictates, to consider all the factors and to make the right choices, despite potentially feeling fear, and despite personal consequences. An example is given by Dutton et al. (2002), who suggested that during times of trauma, leaders who demonstrate compassion and humanity may help promote personal and organizational healing. Such expressions of empathy incorporate an element of self-sacrifice in the sense that the leader may be emotionally, as well as authoritatively, "exposed." Self-sacrifice can also be a component of transformational leadership. As mentioned earlier, Bass (1990) views transformational leadership as encouraging others to transcend their own self-interest for the good of the organization, and, interestingly, Quinn (2010) notes that transformational leaders are able to turn even scandalous organizations into virtuous ones by demonstrating

Positioning Braver Leadership Coaching 217

courage. We would suggest that it is likely that the brave leader, by demonstrating emotional courage and brave action, particularly in a difficult situation, may be inspirational, and that this contextualized response has echoes of situational, relational and transformational leadership.

Figure 10.2 shows that leadership theories are not mutually exclusive, since in reality there is likely to be interplay between them and some overlaps in philosophies. In the figure, not only are links from brave leadership to other leadership theories made, but we also include what we consider to be the important similarities between them. For example, we believe that the idea of flexing style or approach is common to both transformational leadership and situational leadership, albeit that transformational leadership sounds more far reaching and visionary in nature and situational leadership more transactional. We have also shown links between authentic and ethical leadership, as they both tend to promote the need to do "what is right," in relation to values in the case of authentic leadership and the perceived rights of individuals in the case of ethical leadership. A link between servant and relational leadership is also illustrated as both approaches suggest a less autocratic leadership stance.

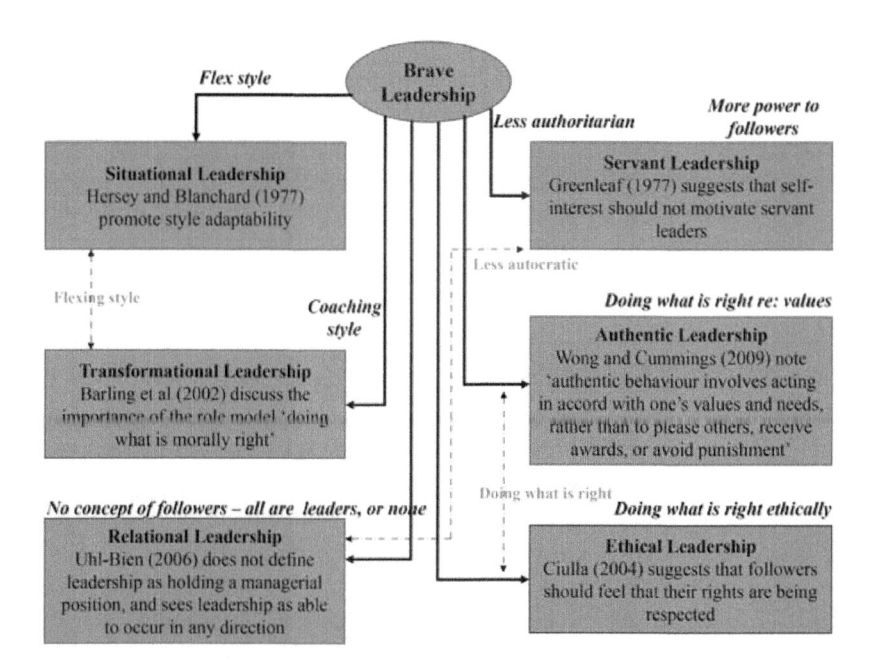

FIGURE 10.2 Brave leadership spans all leadership approaches

3 Coaching As A Form Of Brave Leader Development

Traditional leadership development takes many different forms and there is a multiplicity of literature, interventions and theories for individuals and organizations aiming to enhance leadership capability (Hanson, 2013). However, as suggested earlier, leadership theory and leadership development has conventionally been concerned with identifying and addressing the specific traits and competencies that leaders lack. Of course, the focus on theories, especially those that incorporate an understanding of relational and situational factors, as described above, are extremely useful, but, as mentioned earlier in this chapter, a deficit mindset exists. This way of thinking has a continuing effect on the way coaching is perceived by leaders.

In a study undertaken by the Stanford Graduate School of Business (2013), it was found that nearly two thirds of CEOs and almost half of executives did not receive executive coaching or leadership advice from outside coaches or consultants. Paradoxically, nearly all those surveyed said they would enjoy the experience of coaching to enhance their development. So, it is interesting to consider why CEOs and other senior leaders say they like coaching but fail to seek it. The reason appears to lie in a misunderstanding about what leaders think they need and what they think coaching can offer. According to LaBier (2013):

> most omit or misconstrue the core coaching element that CEOs need to grow their skills and effectiveness: Increased self-awareness, honest self-knowledge, about one's motives, personality capacities and values. The consequences of this absence play out in ways that diminish the relevance of coaching in the eyes of most senior leaders.

Many CEOs still see coaching as remedial, filling a gap in skill or ability, rather than as something that can promote high performance. They still cling to the traditional deficit model of leadership development transmitted through their business school education and training organizations.

The Stanford Graduate School of Business (2013, p.1) report goes on to point out that almost 43 percent of CEOs rated "conflict management skills" as their highest development need. How to manage effectively through conflict was identified as one of the top priorities for CEOs, which illustrates that they are concerned about the difficult decisions that they have to make and that these inevitably involve an element of disagreement. However, the Stanford report suggests that CEOs see the need for compassion or persuasion skills as less of a priority. Presumably they think that they already have these soft skills or that they are less important. These results reflect leaders' perceptions, but they also reflect the failure of coaching, and/or a broader societal awareness, to highlight that successful leadership is achieved through greater self-awareness about motivation, values and decision making. Relationship competencies or soft skills are built on a constructed foundation of self-knowledge combined with organizational awareness and are key for a leader to be able to articulate vision and leadership for the organization:

> Self-knowledge builds clarity about objectives; it fine-tunes one's understanding [of] the perspectives, values, aims and personality traits of others. When that's lacking, you often see discord and conflict among members of the senior management team; or between some of its members and the CEO.
>
> *(LaBier, 2013)*

Another example of a leadership development process that has become popular is the idea of peer, subordinate and managerial feedback to improve performance. This has become prevalent in many different organizations and cultures. Indeed, Sones (2009) discusses the merits of a bespoke 360° feedback and assessment tool for Army Captain-level development. Hill and Stephens (2005) also describe how they undertook to design a program for leaders in medical education, which appeared to offer, amongst other things, team-building exercises and exposure to change management theory. Their approach appears to have been informed, at least in part, by the theory of relational leadership. Intriguingly, however, Van de Valk and Constas (2011) suggest that the social aspect of leadership (one of the main ideas behind relational leadership theory) and in particular social capital (Balkundi & Kilduff, 2006) may not be enhanced by some existing leadership development strategies. Similarly, Thornton (2009) reports that ethical leadership development is fraught with difficulties mainly because the definition is unclear; they argue that it is a moving target and it is often company specific.

In many ways, this sums up why leadership development is so diversified and sometimes so ineffectual. We have a variety of leadership theories, which may be interesting from an academic perspective, but which, unless a pragmatic approach is adopted, can be diluted to become simply a veneer applied over existing paradigms and behaviors, in the vague hope that some uptake of situational, transformational, authentic, ethical, relational or servant leadership ideas, for example, is attained.

Turnbull James and Collins (2008, p.3) have also argued that development interventions for leaders need to be designed differently, with a focus beyond the individual capabilities of program delegates and, we would suggest, beyond immediate organizational needs. A more holistic approach would seem appropriate—one that embraces the wider systemic and cultural context in which leaders are connected, as well as addressing individual development needs. As mentioned earlier, Turnbull James and Collins (2008, p.20) are of the view that "the equating of leadership and leader has enabled leadership development to focus on the deficits an individual has in leadership terms and creating learning opportunities for the leader to correct these deficits." They consider that there are limitations to this "deficit" approach, since the focus is on "fixing problem areas or adding new pre-determined competences," which because of the focus on specific learning objectives or the need for immediate application, may stifle developmental aims. Coaching provides a different approach—one that exploits the possibility of experiential learning for development (Cox, 2013), especially in the context of current leadership concerns.

Summary

In this chapter we highlighted how leaders have traditionally been developed and we linked this discussion to some recognized leadership theories, including transformational, authentic, situational and relational leadership. We then argued that bravery is an essential core theme cutting across these approaches and making them more effective, especially, we would suggest, in the "wicked" contexts discussed in Chapters 7 and 8. Toward the end of the chapter we synthesized the main arguments for a coaching approach to leader development, suggesting that there are many leadership programs available, but that executive education often does not translate into the type of leader development that leaders need. We proposed that coaching is the right intervention to help leaders to experiment with the wide variety of theories and approaches and to be braver in support of their brave mission.

11
THE BRAVE AGENDA

We began this book by highlighting Martin Luther King's assertion that the measure of a man is where he stands in times of challenge, not where he stands in moments of comfort. Throughout the book we considered how leaders can find the control and direction they need in times of challenge by calling on the support of a leadership coach. A coach can facilitate a range of sense-making strategies that promote development and understanding for leaders as they brave the problems presented in our complex global workplaces. A coach can encourage the kinds of pro-social workplace behaviors discussed by Hannah et al. (2011), aimed at supporting and promoting wellbeing, positivity and environmental concern.

In Chapter 1 we introduced a model of leadership coaching that can enable coaches to support leaders in times of challenge. It is aimed first and foremost at facilitating leaders to make braver decisions and position themselves successfully within their organizations. We argued that the world needs its leaders to be braver in the face of the challenges they encounter in order to create and sustain both successful and ethical businesses. In our introduction we highlighted dysfunctions in leadership that can lead to debacles such as those in the finance sector in recent years. We made a case for how the brave leadership coaching model can raise and maintain an awareness of context, values and ethical decision making that might avoid such misfortunes in future.

In the introduction we also underscored what Schein (2006) holds as the ultimate skill of the coach, the assessment of each moment in order to be in the most appropriate role at that time. We suggested ways in which through using a model for braver leadership coaching the coach can ensure the coaching intervention is absolutely relevant to the current situation, and is appropriate for the development needs of the leader. Accordingly, the brave leadership coaching model focuses on coaching to promote change for the benefit of leaders, their organizations, and society.

We also defined early on what we mean by brave, arguing that being brave involves being ready to face fear and bear danger or pain. We suggested that a brave leader is one who has mastered his or her emotions and is ready and able to take action even in the face of adversity from whatever quarter. Brave leaders, we argued, are those who *act* in accordance with their courage. Inspired by Grint (2010), we also made the point that brave leaders are not necessarily heroic. They can be working in any walk of life, but are those people who inspire by taking a stand on issues that they value, such as equality, sustainable development or environmental justice.

In Chapter 2 we introduced the first part of our leadership coaching approach, where the coach begins with a task for the leader to consider his or her ideas about bravery in relation to leadership. The coach asks for definitions and stories about who has been brave, helps the leader unpack the values inherent in those stories and focus on how to bring similar values to the challenges that they might face in their own organization. The chapter stressed the need for leaders to be in touch with their values and for coaches to be able to support that self-awareness. Using examples from our coaching practice we introduced four leaders—John, Ron, Matt and Christine—who were asked to define bravery through the identification of their own role models. This in turn led to the construction of their own brave story of what bravery means to them, and subsequently enabled them to get in touch with their ideals, their passions and their hopes.

In Chapter 3 we explained the approach used to support leaders in developing situational awareness, enabling them to make sense of their organizational challenges, and to consider what is pulling on them in their current environment. This identification allows leaders to understand the interdependencies inherent within the challenges they face, and the subsequent pulling factors analysis highlights contextual elements of leaders' work that can have the tendency to polarize and pull them in all kinds of different directions, causing tension and stress. The chapter provided examples of how the coach can help leaders analyze their pulling factors.

Chapter 4 led to the exploration of the psychological factors, or psychological capital, that ground leaders. We explained how what we call the gravitational factors are a key aspect of brave leadership coaching, helping leaders to remain grounded despite the organizational demands made on them. We argued that the heightened awareness of personal power that exploring psychological capital creates allows leaders to consider what is most important to them, including not only their professional goals and values but also wider family, societal and environmental concerns. We established ways in which gravitational factors can be developed, supported or challenged through coaching and introduced a retroductive technique as a way of tracing and understanding habits or practices and so reducing blind spots. We also explained the need to have a clearly formulated and articulated vision or mission for the company in order to position decision making and ultimately achieve optimal performance in all aspects of the organization.

In Chapter 5 we discussed the need for leaders to find balance using their gravitational factors to ensure that equilibrium is achieved. We suggested that in order to achieve a balance it is necessary to take stock in four key areas that support a strong "core": emotional awareness, reflective pause, self-regulation and moral preparation. We explained how coaches can bolster calibration of the client's current emotional landscape, through techniques such as mindfulness, in order to balance thinking and behaviors. This process can help leaders manage their specific pulling factors— the organizational pressures and tensions that might otherwise thrust them out of alignment.

The brave sphere introduced in Chapter 6 embraced the idea that it is vital for leaders to consider organizational situations and perspectives calmly and from a "safe distance." We suggested that holding tensions calmly and in balance requires a certain amount of bravery in itself. We thus proposed that using a metaphorical sphere can perform three functions for the leader: i) providing a place of calm and sanctuary to reflect on problems; ii) enabling a focus on different perspectives and needs within the organizational landscape; and iii) giving the opportunity to analyze feelings in relation to the observations, and so hold what they find as a resource for sustainable decision making. Using the framework of the sphere we saw how coaches can guide leaders as they negotiate wicked problems and conflicting environmental tensions.

Chapter 7 focused on how brave leadership coaching with its emphasis on values and emotions in addition to situational sense making, actually facilitates the leader to come to a brave decision. Whereas in Chapter 6 we played with the idea of moving the sphere through each of the pulling factors and testing how moving the sphere towards or away from the gravitational factors is experienced, in this chapter we examined how precise options for problem solving might be identified and evaluated.

224 The Brave Agenda

After introducing the different types of problems that organizations face, we explained how the depth of awareness that can be achieved using brave leadership coaching supports the kind of reflection and decision making necessary to address the complexity of the specifically wicked problems that leaders most often encounter.

In Chapter 8 we completed our presentation of the brave leadership coaching process by discussing how coaching can help leaders to implement their decisions. Action, we argued, also requires bravery to overcome tensions relating to decision implementation in the organization, some of which are inherent in the leader as an individual, while others relate more to the pressures created through differing agendas of stakeholders. In the chapter, with the help of examples from our four leaders, we examined a number of tensions and provided a range of potential responses and strategies which, with the help of the coach, leaders can use to begin to address implementation issues and create brave actions. Crucially, we identified a need for communication of plans and appropriate supporting structures.

Chapter 9 examined the important issue of trust. We stressed how trust is linked to the development of a working coaching alliance with the leader, and is also connected to coach credibility and integrity. As well as supporting the brave agenda, we argued the importance for the coach of recognizing the trust issues that confront them, suggesting it is imperative for them to consider their own boundaries and ethical positions. Coach supervision was highlighted as vital for ongoing personal development.

Chapter 10 evaluated the braver leadership concept in relation to familiar leadership theories, such as transformational, authentic, situational and relational leadership, suggesting that bravery is essential across these approaches for them to be effective. We also synthesized the key arguments for a coaching approach to leader development, to augment traditional executive education. We reinforced how leaders need individual support to be braver and to have the resolve to prove to followers and stakeholders that they are worthy of respect. To sustain them in this endeavor we argued that coaching is the right development intervention.

One of the issues that leadership development has faced is what we call the "identikit" approach. When witnesses to a crime are asked to recollect what the perpetrator may have looked like, often they are helped to build up a picture of the suspect's appearance by using pre-existing features, like eyebrows, a nose, the shape of the eyes, and so forth. The images form a semblance of the appearance of an individual, but rarely do they end up as an exact likeness. We would suggest that those leadership development approaches which seek to piece together parts of leadership theory, or leadership traits, to which the leader should somehow shape themselves, is a little bit like the identikit process. At first glance individuals can look like leaders, but they are simply an impression of an actual leader.

Implementing A Brave Agenda

As discussed in Chapter 1, there appears to be a distinct gap between where we are in terms of leadership capability, and where we need to be, both in relation to public expectation, and employee expectation. It seems unlikely that any potential leader enters an organization or even politics with the express desire to become an environmental, corporate or political rogue. There are no doubt people who just want to "keep their head down" and make money, or are interested only in the power and prestige that their position may bring them. However, there are many who want more; they really do want to make a difference. They approach their work, at least initially, with a professional moral code, a set of values and beliefs that motivate them. Therefore the questions that must be asked are "Why the gap?" and "What can we do about it"?

Throughout this book we have supported the view that coaches have a particular role to play in the development of leaders. This view was driven by a strong sense that things are not as they could or should be. Since beginning writing this book, we could easily have gone back and rewritten our examples of leadership and corporate fiascos probably at least half a dozen times over: either things are getting worse, or things that were not getting much exposure before, are now, or both. In any event, the good news is that people are generally more aware of the shortcomings of some leaders, some corporations and some politicians. That awareness is important, but so is the pressing need to do things differently.

We also believe that there is much that is right and good in the corporate world and that we should embrace the wonderful and positive elements of business and its leaders, and celebrate the genuine successes that are possible when things are done the "right way." There is much work to be done, however, to make it more acceptable for individuals to testify to or disclose the darker behaviors that they observe in their organizations. We must all become more comfortable at pointing out where things could be better or where a braver solution is possible. Businesses can, of course, offer individuals a way to earn money and to survive and sometimes thrive in a complex world. They can also help people on their road to a purposeful and meaningful life. However, when we begin to blur the line between being efficient as a business and being greedy, or between being ambitious and being utterly ruthless, we are getting into a dangerous space. For the sake of the environment and humanity, short-term greed and short-term thinking need, we would argue, to be discouraged and replaced with a morally sustainable approach to business. Coaches, we would argue, have a role to play here.

Coaching leaders to be brave is not something we can do on every assignment. Coaching is all about the client agenda and if the client does not want to focus on taking brave action, but is stuck on another issue or is focused in a more individualistic paradigm of profit and efficiency, it may be that the coach pays no heed to bravery at all, or, if the individualistic concerns are too heavily rooted in the ego, a coach may even decide to disengage.

However, we would suggest that coaches may wish to do some good in a potentially toxic environment, and to help clients in those environments become the braver leaders they probably want to be but are currently unable to be. Coaches could make a conscious decision to engage with that important work, and do so mindfully, rather than being swept along on a wave of financial necessity. Our hope is that we have given those coaches who want to engage with the braver agenda, a model of coaching to inspire them.

We know that some coaches have been taught to eschew giving advice and to work within the client's world, but that will not always work. However, rather than have the coach work as a mere reflective glass, or testament to the leader's position in the organization ("I've made it, I have a personal coach"), we propose the time has come for the coach to be connected to the wider need for change: in those quiet and confidential meetings between leader and coach, we would suggest that there may be times where the coach must hold the leader accountable. We have seen in Chapters 5 and 6 how mindfulness and other strategies for increasing awareness can provide leaders with the wherewithal to maintain their early values and motivations, and to stand up for what they believe in.

So we contend that coaching can be part of a change for the better. We suggest that if coaches do not care about humanity or do not have moral fiber, and feel able to challenge their clients on these issues, perhaps they should not be in the role. However, we cannot recall meeting a coach who did not display humility, humanity and decency, so they are well placed to be part of this change process.

This book is fundamentally about coaches and leaders, and yet it is also about all of us. It does not serve us any more, if it ever did, to turn a blind eye, to walk away, to hope or presume that whatever we see that disturbs us will never impact us. We look to the leaders to change, but so must we. We should not encourage organizations or leaders who display no humanity, or compassion or moral fiber or environmental responsibility. If the environment that we coach or work in is toxic in any of these areas, it would probably be best for all of us to agree not to work in such environments at all. As coaches, or as employees, we could walk away: we could all uphold our own values and decline any work that does not allow us to do so. So this book is a clarion call for leaders and coaches, but also for anyone else who wants to think about change in the way leaders and organizations function. I suppose it is for our children and their future, too. It is about every coach being brave enough to bring sustainability in all its complexity and guises into the coaching room as a challenge to the next, long-awaited, generation of brave leaders.

REFERENCES

Adler, N.J. (2010) Going beyond the dehydrated language of management: Leadership insight. *Journal of Business Strategy*, 31(4): 90–99.
Allen, J.H., Beaudoin, F., Lloyd-Pool, E. & Sherman, J. (2014) Pathways to sustainability careers: Building capacity to solve complex problems. *Sustainability: The Journal of Record*, 7(1): 47–53.
Alvey, S. & Barclay, K. (2007) The characteristics of dyadic trust in executive coaching. *Journal of Leadership Studies*, 1(1): 18–27.
Andrews, W., Twigg, E., Minami, T. & Johnson, G. (2011) Piloting a practice research network: A 12-month evaluation of the Human Givens approach in primary care at a general medical practice. *Psychology and Psychotherapy: Theory, Research and Practice*, pp. 1–17.
Annas, J. (2003) *Virtue ethics and social psychology*. Ohio State University. Mershon Center for International Security Studies. Available at: kb.osu.edu/dspace/handle/1811/32006 (accessed September 30, 2014).
Annas, J. (2005) Lack of character: Personality and moral behavior by John M. Doris, book review. *Philosophy and Phenomenological Research*, 71(3): 636–642.
April, K., Kukard, J. & Peters, K. (2013) *Steward Leadership: A Maturational Perspective*. Claremont: UCT Press.
Argyris, C. (2012) *Organizational Traps*. Oxford: Oxford University Press.
Argyris, C. & Schön, D.A. (1974) *Theory in Practice: Increasing Professional Effectiveness*. San Francisco, CA: Jossey-Bass.
Aristotle (1980) *Nicomachean Ethics*. Trans. by D. Ross. Oxford University Press.
Atkinson, T. & Claxton, G. (eds). (2000) *The Intuitive Practitioner: On the Value of Not Always Knowing What One is Doing*. Abingdon: Taylor & Francis.

Avey, J.B., Luthans, F. & Jensen, S.M. (2009) Psychological capital: A positive resource for combating employee stress and turnover. *Human Resource Management*, 48(5): 677–693.

Avolio, B.J., Gardner, W.L. & Walumbwa, F.O. (2005) *Authentic Leadership Theory and Practice: Origins, Effects and Developments*. Amsterdam: Elsevier.

Bachkirova, T. (2011) *Developmental Coaching: Working with the Self*. Columbus, OH: McGraw-Hill International.

Bachkirova, T. & Cox, E. (2007) Coaching with emotion in organisations: Investigation of personal theories. *Leadership & Organization Development Journal*, 28(7): 600–612.

Bachkirova, T., Cox, E. & Clutterbuck, D. (2014) Introduction. In E. Cox, T. Bachkirova & D. Clutterbuck (eds), *The Complete Handbook of Coaching* (2nd edn), London: Sage, pp. 1–17.

Balkundi, P. & Kilduff, M. (2006) The ties that lead: A social network approach to leadership. *The Leadership Quarterly*, 17(4): 419–439.

Bandura, A. (1991) Social cognitive theory of moral thought and action. In W.M. Kurtines & J.L. Gewitz (eds), *Handbook of Moral Behavior and Development, Vol. 1*. Hillsdale, NJ: Lawrence Erlbaum Associates, pp. 45–103.

Bandura, A. (1998) Personal and collective efficacy in human adaptation and change. In J.G. Adair, D. Belanger & K.L. Dion (eds), *Advances in Psychological Science, Vol. 1: Personal, Social and Cultural Aspects*. Hove: Psychology Press, pp. 51–71.

Bargh, J.A., Gollwitzer, P.M., Lee-Chai, A., Barndollar, K. & Troetschel, R. (2001) The automated will: Unconscious activation and pursuit of behavioral goals. *Journal of Personality and Social Psychology*, 81: 1004–1027.

Barling, H., Kelloway, E.K. & Loughlin, C. (2002) Development and test of a model linking safety-specific transformational leadership and occupational safety. *Journal of Applied Psychology*, 87: 488–496.

Barnard, J.W. (2008) Narcissism, over-optimism, fear, anger, and depression: The interior lives of corporate leaders. *University of Cincinnati Law Review*, 77: 405.

Barner, R. & Higgins, J. (2005) A social constructionist approach to leadership coaching. *The OD Practitioner*, 37(4): 37–41.

Baron, L., Morin, L. & Morin, D. (2011) Executive coaching: The effect of working alliance discrepancy on the development of coachees' self-efficacy. *Journal of Management Development*, 30(9): 847–864.

Barry, D. (1991) Managing the bossless team: Lessons in distributed leadership. *Organizational Dynamics*, 20(1): 31–47.

Bass, B.M. (1985) *Leadership and Performance Beyond Expectations*. New York: Free Press.

Bass, B.M. (1990) From transactional to transformational leadership: Learning to share the vision. *Organizational Dynamics*, 18: 19–31.

Bass, B.M. & Avolio, B.J. (1989) Potential biases in leadership measures: How prototypes, leniency, and general satisfaction relate to ratings and rankings of transformational and transactional leadership constructs. *Educational and Psychological Measurement*, 49(3): 509–527.

Bass, B. & Riggio, R. (2006) *Transformational Leadership* (2nd edn). Hove: Psychology Press.
Baumeister, R.F. & Vohs, K.D. (2007) *Handbook of Self-regulation*. New York: Guilford.
Bayramoğlu, G. & Şahin, M. (2015) Positive psychological capacity and its impacts on success. *Journal of Advanced Management Science*, 3(2).
Benjamin, D.J., Choi, J.J. & Strickland, A.J. (2010) Social identity and preferences. *American Economic Review*, 100(4): 1913–1928.
Bennet, A. & Bennet, D. (2007) From stories to strategy: putting organizational learning to work, *VINE*, 37(4): 404–409.
Bennet, A. & Bennet, D. (2008a) The decision-making process for complex situations in a complex environment. In F. Burstein & C.W. Holsapple (eds), *Handbook on Decision Support Systems*. Berlin: Springer-Verlag, pp. 3–20.
Bennet, D. & Bennet, A. (2008b) The depth of knowledge: surface, shallow or deep? *VINE*, 38(4): 405–420.
Bitbol, M. & Petitmengin, C. (2011) On pure reflection: A reply to Dan Zahavi, *Journal of Consciousness Studies*, 18(2): 24–37.
Black, D.S. (2010) Defining mindfulness. In *Mindfulness Research Guide*. Available at: www.mindfulexperience.org/resources/files/defining_mindfulness.pdf (accessed February 18, 2015).
Blanchard, K. & O'Connor, M.J. (1997) *Managing by Values*. San Francisco, CA: Berrett-Koehler Publishers.
Blanchard, K.H., Zigarmi, P. & Zigarmi, D. (1985) *Leadership and the One Minute Manager: Increasing Effectiveness through Situational Leadership*. New York: Morrow.
Blanchette, I. & Richards, A. (2004) Reasoning about emotional and neutral materials is logic affected by emotion? *Psychological Science*, 15(11): 745–752.
Bluckert, P. (2005) Critical factors in executive coaching—the coaching relationship. *Industrial and Commercial Training*, 37(7): 336–340.
Bogardus, E.S. (1927) Leadership and social distance. *Sociology and Social Research*, 12(1): 173–178.
Bordin, E.S. (1979) The generalizability of the psychoanalytic concept of the working alliance. *Psychotherapy: Theory, Research & Practice*, 16(3): 252.
Boyatzis, R.E., et al. (2013) Developing resonant leaders through emotional intelligence, vision and coaching. *Organizational Dynamics*, 42: 17–24.
Boyatzis, R.E. & Akrivou, K. (2006) The ideal self as the driver of intentional change. *Journal of Management Development*, 25(7): 624–642.
Boyatzis, R.E., Smith, M.L., Van Oosten, E. & Woolford, L. (2013) Developing resonant leaders through emotional intelligence, vision and coaching. *Organizational Dynamics*, 42(1): 17–24.
Boyce, L.A., Jackson, R.J. & Neal, L.J. (2010) Building successful leadership coaching relationships: Examining impact of matching criteria in a leadership coaching program. *Journal of Management Development*, 29: 914–931.
Bozer, G., Sarros, J.C. & Santora, J.C. (2014) Academic background and credibility in executive coaching effectiveness. *Personnel Review*, 43(6): 881–897.

Brewer, A.M. (2014) Leadership, followership and coaching: Asking the questions. In *Leadership, Coaching and Followership: An Important Equation*. Amsterdam: Springer, pp. 1–14.

Bright, D.S., Cameron, K.S. & Caza, A. (2006) The amplifying and buffering effects of virtuousness in downsized organisations. *Journal of Business Ethics*, 64: 249–269.

Brockbank, A. & McGill, I. (2006) *Facilitating Reflective Learning through Mentoring and Coaching*. London: Kogan Page Publishers.

Brown, K.H. & Gillespie, D. (1997) We become brave by doing brave acts: Teaching moral courage through the theater of the oppressed. *Literature and Medicine, Special Issue: Unruly Texts*, 16(1): 108–120.

Brown, K.W. & Ryan, R.M. (2003) The benefits of being present: Mindfulness and its role in psychological wellbeing. *Journal of Personality and Social Psychology*, 84: 822–848.

Brown, K.W. & Ryan, R.M. (2004) Fostering healthy self-regulation from within and without: A self-determination theory perspective. In P.A. Linley & S. Joseph (eds), *Positive Psychology in Practice*. Oxford: Wiley.

Brown, K.W., Ryan, R. & Creswell, J.D. (2007) Addressing fundamental questions about mindfulness. *Psychological Inquiry*, 18(4): 272–281.

Brown, M.E. & Trevino, L.K. (2006) Ethical leadership. A review and future directions. *Leadership Quarterly*, 17: 595–616.

Brown, M.E., Trevino, L.K. & Harrison, D.A. (2005) Ethical leadership: A social learning perspective for construct development and testing. *Organizational Behavior and Human Decision Processes*, 97: 117–134.

Buckingham, M. & Clifton, D. (2004) *Now, Discover Your Strengths*. New York: The Free Press.

Burford, G., Hoover, E., Dahl, A. & Harder, M.K. (2015) Making the invisible visible: Designing values-based indicators and tools for identifying and closing "value-action gaps." In *Responsible Living*. Amsterdam: Springer, pp. 113–133.

Burns, J.M. (1978) *Leadership*. New York: Harper & Row.

Caligiuri, P. (2014) Many moving parts: Factors influencing the effectiveness of HRM practices designed to improve knowledge transfer within MNCs. *Journal of International Business Studies*, 45: 63–72.

Cameron, K.S. (2011) Responsible leadership as virtuous leadership. *Journal of Business Ethics*, 98: 25–35.

Cameron, K.S., Mora, C., Leutscher, T. & Calarco, M. (2011) Effects of positive practices on organizational effectiveness. *The Journal of Applied Behavioral Science*, 20: 1–43.

Camillus, J.C. (2008) Strategy as a wicked problem. *Harvard Business Review*, 86(5): 99–106.

Carver, C.S. & Scheier, M.F. (1998) *On the Self-regulation of Behaviour*. New York: University of Cambridge.

Carver, C.S. (2007) Self-regulation of action and affect. In K.D. Vohs & R.F. Baumeister (eds), *Handbook of Self-regulation* New York: Guilford, pp. 13–39

Carver, C.S. & Scheier, M.F. (2011) Self-regulation of action and affect. In K.D. Vohs & R.F. Baumeister (eds), *Handbook of Self-regulation: Research, Theory, and Applications* (2nd edn). New York: Guilford, pp. 3–21.

Chartered Institute of Purchasing and Supply (2007) *Contract Management Guide*. Available at: www.cips.org/documents/CIPS_KI_Contract%20Management%20Guidev2.pdf (accessed May 10, 2015).

Checkland, P. & Poulter, J. (2006) *Learning for Action: A Short Definitive Account of Soft Systems Methodology and its Use for Practitioner, Teachers, and Students, Vol. 26*. Chichester: Wiley.

Chhetri, P. (2014) The role of cognitive and affective trust in the relationship between organizational justice and organizational citizenship behavior: a conceptual framework. *Business: Theory and Practice*, 15(2): 170–178.

Churchman, C.W. (1967) Wicked problems. *Management Science*, 14(4): B141–B142.

Chung, K.-S. (2000) Role models and arguments for affirmative action. *American Economic Review*, 90(3): 640–648.

Ciulla, J.B. (2004) Ethics and leadership effectiveness. *The Nature of Leadership*: 302–327.

Ciulla, J.B. & Forsyth, D.R. (2011) Leadership ethics. In A. Bryman, D. Collinson, K. Grint, B. Jackson & M. Uhl-Bien, *The Sage Handbook of Leadership*. London: Sage, pp. 229–241.

Claxton, G. (1999) Whodunnit? Unpicking the "seems" of free will. *Journal of Consciousness Studies*, 6(8–9): 8–9.

Cohen, L. & Manion, L. (1994) *Research Methods in Education* (4th edn). London: Routledge.

Collard, P. and Walsh, J. (2008) Sensory awareness mindfulness training in coaching: Accepting life's challenges. *Journal of Rational-Emotional Cognitive Behavioral Therapy*, 26: 30–37.

Collins, J.C. & Porras, J.I. (2005) *Built to Last: Successful Habits of Visionary Companies*. New York: Random House.

Conan Doyle, A. (1887) *A Study in Scarlet*. Project Gutenberg Ebook #244 (2008). Available at: www.gutenberg.org/ebooks/244 (accessed May 10, 2015).

Conger, J.A. & Kanungo, R.N. (1998) *Charismatic Leadership in Organizations*. London: Sage Publications.

Copeland, M.K. (2014) The emerging significance of values based leadership: A literature review. *International Journal of Leadership Studies*, 8(2): 105–135.

Coutu, D. (2002) How Resilience Works. *Harvard Business Review*, 80(5), May.

Covey, S.R. (1992) *Principle Centered Leadership*. New York: Simon and Schuster.

Cox, E. (2006) An adult learning approach to coaching. In D. Stober & A.M. Grant (eds), *Evidence Based Coaching Handbook*. New York: Wiley, pp. 193–217.

Cox, E. (2012) Individual and organisational trust in a reciprocal peer coaching context. *Mentoring & Tutoring: Partnership in Learning*, 20(3), August: 427–443.

Cox, E. (2013) *Coaching Understood*. London: Sage.

Croskerry, P. (2013) From mindless to mindful practice—Cognitive bias and clinical decision making. *New England Journal of Medicine*, 368: 2445–2448.

Available at: www.oklahomahealthcaresummit.com/sites/default/files/files/From%20Mindless%20to%20Mindful%20Practice%20%E2%80%94%20Cognitive%20Bias.pdf (accessed February 23, 2015).
Cunha, M.P., Clegg, S. & Rego, A. (2013) Lessons for leaders: Positive organization studies meets Niccolò Machiavelli. *Leadership*, 9(4): 450–465.
Cutuli, J.J. & Masten, A.S. (2009) Resilience. In S.J. Lopez (ed.), *The Encyclopedia of Positive Psychology*. Oxford: Wiley-Blackwell, p.837.
Czołczyński, K., Perlikowski, P., Stefański, A. & Kapitaniak, T. (2011) Why two clocks synchronize: Energy balance of the synchronized clocks. *Chaos: An Interdisciplinary Journal of Nonlinear Science*, 21(2): 023129.
Dahlsgaard, K., Peterson, C. & Seligman, M.E. (2005) Shared virtue: The convergence of valued human strengths across culture and history. *Review of General Psychology*, 9(3): 203.
Damasio, A.R. (2000) *The Feeling of What Happens: Body and Emotion in the Making of Consciousness*. New York: Random House.
Dane, E. & Pratt, M.G. (2007) Exploring intuition and its role in managerial decision making. *Academy of Management Review*, 32(1): 33–54.
Day, D. (2001) Leadership development: A review in context. *Leadership Quarterly*, 11(4): 5641–5613.
Day, D., Harrison, M.M. & Halpin, S.M. (2009) *An Integrative Approach to Leader Development: Connecting Adult Development, Identity and Expertise*. London: Routledge.
Day, G.S. & Schoemaker, P.J. (2005) Scanning the periphery. *Harvard Business Review*, 83(11): 135.
De Haan, E. (2008) *Relational Coaching: Journeys Towards Mastering One-to-one Learning*. Oxford: Wiley.
De Martino, B., Kumaran, D., Seymour, B. & Dolan, R.J. (2006) Frames, biases, and rational decision-making in the human brain. *Science*, 313: 684–687.
Densten, I.L. & Gray, J.H. (2001) Leadership development and reflection: what is the connection? *International Journal of Educational Management*, 15(3): 119–124.
Dewey, J. (1933) *How We Think: A Restatement of the Relation of Reflective Thinking to the Educative Process*. Chicago, IL: Henry Regnery.
De Wolde, A., Groenendaal, J., Helsloot, I. & Schmidt, A. (2012) An explorative study on the connection between ethical leadership, prototypicality and organizational misbehavior in a Dutch fire service. *International Journal of Leadership Studies*, 8(2): 18–43.
Diaz, F. (2010) *A preliminary investigation into the effects of a brief mindfulness induction on perceptions of attention, aesthetic response, and flow during music listening*. Unpublished doctoral thesis. Available at: etd.lib.fsu.edu/theses/available/etd-05072010-130110/unrestricted/Diaz_F_Dissertation_2010.pdf (accessed January 29, 2012).
Dibben, M.R., Eley-Morris, S. & Lean, M.E.J. (2000) Situational trust and co-operative partnerships between physicians and their patients: A theoretical

explanation transferable from business practice. *QJM: An International Journal of Medicine*, 93(1): 55–61.

Dirks, K.T. & Skarlicki, D.P. (2004) Trust in leaders: Existing research and emerging issues. *Trust and Distrust in Organizations: Dilemmas and Approaches*, 7: 21–40.

Doidge, N. (2007) *The Brain that Changes Itself*. New York: Viking Press.

Dolan, S.L. (2011) *Coaching by Values*. Bloomington, IN: iUniverse Publishing.

Doris, J.M. (2002) *Lack of Character: Personality and Moral Behavior*. New York: Cambridge University Press.

Doris, J.M. (2005) Précis of lack of character. *Philosophy and Phenomenological Research* 71(3): 632–635.

Doval, H.C. (2008) Attributes of a doctor. *Rev. argent. Cardiol.* Autonomous City of Buenos Aires, 76(6), December. Available at: www.scielo.org.ar/scielo.php?script=sci_arttext&pid=S1850-37482008000600018&lng=es&nrm=iso (accessed May 10, 2015).

Dowling, G.R. (2004) *The Art and Science of Marketing*. Oxford: Oxford University Press.

Drake, D. (2010) Narrative coaching. In E. Cox, T. Bachkirova & D. Clutterbuck (eds), *The Complete Handbook of Coaching*. London: Sage, pp. 120–131.

Drucker, P.F. (1970) *The Effective Executive*. London: Pan Books.

Drucker, P.F. (2004) What makes an effective executive? *Harvard Business Review*: 14–22.

Dufault, K. & Martocchio, B.C. (1985) Symposium on compassionate care and the dying experience. Hope: its spheres and dimensions. *The Nursing Clinics of North America*, 20(2): 379–391.

Dugan, J.P., Bohle, C.W., Woelker, L.R. & Cooney, M.A. (2014) The role of social perspective—Taking in developing students' leadership capacities. *Journal of Student Affairs Research and Practice*, 51(1): 1–15.

Dutton, J.E., Frost, P.J., Worline, M.C., Lilius, J.M. & Kanov, J.M. (2002) Leading in times of trauma. *Harvard Business Review*, 80(1): 54–61.

Duymedjian, R. & Rüling, C.C. (2010) Towards a foundation of bricolage in organization and management theory. *Organization Studies*, 31(2): 133–151.

Eagly, A.H. (2005) Achieving relational authenticity in leadership: Does gender matter? *The Leadership Quarterly*, 16(3): 459–474.

Echols, M., Gravenstine, K. & Mobley, S. (2008) Using story in coaching. *On Becoming a Leadership Coach: A Holistic Approach to Coaching Excellence*: 53–60.

Elston, F. & Boniwell, I. (2011) A grounded theory study of the value derived by women in financial services through a coaching intervention to help them identify their strengths and practice using them in the workplace. *International Coaching Psychology Review*, 6(1): 16–32.

Ely, K., Boyce, L.A., Nelson, J.K., Zaccaro, S.J., Hernez-Broome, G. & Whyman, W. (2010) Evaluating leadership coaching: A review and integrated framework. *The Leadership Quarterly*, 21(4): 585–599.

Evans, J.S.B. (2003) In two minds: dual-process accounts of reasoning. *Trends in Cognitive Sciences*, 7(10): 454–459.

Fiedler, F.E. (1967) *A Theory of Leadership Effectiveness*. New York: McGraw-Hill.
Finkelstein, S., Hambrick, D.C. & Cannella, A.A. (2009) *Strategic Leadership: Theory and Research on Executives, Top Management Teams and Boards*. Oxford: Oxford University Press.
Flavell, J. (1979) Metacognition and cognitive monitoring: A new area of cognitive-developmental inquiry. *American Psychologist*, 34: 906–911.
Francisco, J.M. & Burnett, C.A. (2008) Deliberate intuition: giving intuitive insights their rightful place in the creative problem solving thinking skills model. In *Creativity and Innovation Management Journal Conference*. Available at: bridgepointeffect.com/wp-content/uploads/2012/12/Deliberate-Intuition-CIM.pdf (accessed February 19, 2015).
Franco, Z.E., Blau, K. & Zimbardo, P.G. (2011) Heroism: A conceptual analysis and differentiation between heroic action and altruism. *Review of General Psychology*, 15(2): 99–113.
Fredrickson, B.L. (2004) The broaden-and-build theory of positive emotions. *Philosophical Transactions-Royal Society of London Series B Biological Sciences*: 1367–1378.
Fredrickson, B. (2009) *Positivity: Top-notch Research Reveals the 3 to 1 Ratio that will Change Your Life*. New York: Three Rivers Press.
Fry, L.W. (2003) Toward a theory of spiritual leadership. *The Leadership Quarterly*, 14: 693–727.
Fryer, M. (2011) *Ethics and Organizational Leadership: Developing a Normative Model*. Oxford: Oxford University Press.
Fulop, L. and Mark, A. (2013) Relationship coaching, decision making. *Leadership* 9: 254.
Galinsky, A.D., Ku, G. & Wang, C.S. (2005) Perspective-taking and self-other overlap: Fostering social bonds and facilitating social coordination. *Group Processes & Intergroup Relations*, 8(2): 109–124.
Gallwey, T. (2010) Foreword: The inner game of coaching. In J. Passmore (ed.), *Leadership Coaching: Working with Leaders to Develop Elite Performance*. London: Kogan Page.
Gardner, W.L., Avolio, B.J. & Walumbwa, F.O. (eds) (2005) *Authentic Leadership Theory and Practice: Origins, Effects and Development, Vol. 3*. Oxford: Elsevier.
Gardner, W.L., Cogliser, C.C., Davis, K.M. & Dickens, M.P. (2011) Authentic leadership: A review of the literature and research agenda. *The Leadership Quarterly*, 22(6): 1120–1145.
Gardner, W.L., Lowe, K.B., Moss, T.W., Mahoney, K.T. & Cogliser, C.C. (2010) Scholarly leadership of the study of leadership: A review of The Leadership Quarterly's second decade, 2000–2009. *The Leadership Quarterly*, 21(6): 922–958.
Garland, E.L., Fredrickson, B., Kring, A.M., Johnson, D.P., Meyer, P.S. & Penn, D.L. (2010) Upward spirals of positive emotions counter downward spirals of negativity: Insights from the broaden-and-build theory and affective neuroscience on the treatment of emotion dysfunctions and deficits in psychopathology. *Clinical Psychology Review*, 30(7): 849–864.

Garratt, B. (2011) *The Fish Rots from the Head: Developing Effective Board Directors*. London: Profile Books.
George, B. (2003) *Authentic Leadership: Rediscovering the Secrets to Creating Lasting Value*. Oxford: John Wiley & Sons.
Glunk, U. & Follini, B. (2011) Polarities in executive coaching. *Journal of Management Development*, 30(2): 222–230.
Goleman, D. (1998) *Working with Emotional Intelligence*. London: Bloomsbury.
Govindji, R. & Linley, P.A. (2007) Strengths use, self-concordance and well-being: Implications for strengths coaching and coaching psychologists. *International Coaching Psychology Review*, 2(2): 143–153.
Gowri, A. (2007) On corporate virtue. *Journal of Business Ethics*, 70(4): 391–400.
Graber, D.R. & Kilpatrick, A.O. (2008) Establishing values-based leadership and value systems in healthcare organizations. *Journal of Health and Human Services Administration*: 179–197.
Graen, G.B. & Uhl-Bien, M. (1995) Relationship-based approach to leadership: Development of leader-member exchange (LMX) theory of leadership over 25 years—Applying a multi-level multi-domain perspective. *The Leadership Quarterly*, 6(2): 219–247.
Greenleaf, R. (1977) *Servant Leadership*. mahwah, NJ: Paulist Press.
Gregory, J.B., Beck, J.W. & Carr, A.E. (2011) Goals, feedback, and self-regulation: Control theory a natural framework for executive coaching. *Consulting Psychology Journal: Practice and Research*, 63(1): 26.
Griffin, J. & Tyrrell, I. (2004) *Human Givens: A New Approach to Emotional Health and Clear Thinking*. Chalvington: Human Givens Publishing Ltd.
Griffin, J. & Tyrrell, I. (2008) *An Idea in Practice: Using the Human Givens Approach*. Chalvington: Human Givens Publishing Ltd.
Grint, K. (2005) Problems, problems, problems: The social construction of leadership. *Human Relations*, 58(11): 1467–1494.
Grint, K. (2008) Wicked problems and clumsy solutions: The role of leadership. *Clinical Leader*, 1(2): 54–68.
Grint, K. (2010) The cuckoo clock syndrome: addicted to command, allergic to leadership. *European Management Journal*, 28(4): 306–313.
Groysberg, B. & Slind, M. (2012) Leadership is a conversation. *Harvard Business Review*, 90(6): 76–84.
Guignon, C.B. (2004) *On Being Authentic*. Hove: Psychology Press.
Guttel, W.H. & Konlechner, S.W. (2009) Continuously hanging by a thread: Managing contextually ambidextrous organizations. *Schmalenbach Business Review: ZFBF*, 61: 150.
Haidt, J. (2006) *The Happiness Hypothesis: Finding Modern Truth in Ancient Wisdom*. New York: Basic Books.
Hannafey, F.T. & Vitulano, L.A. (2013) Ethics and executive coaching: An agency theory approach. *Journal of Business Ethics*, 115: 599–603.

Hannah, S.T., Avolio, B.J. & Walumbwa, F.O. (2011) Relationships between authentic leadership, moral courage, and ethical and pro-social behaviors. *Business Ethics Quarterly*, 21(4): 555–578.

Hannah, S.T., Sweeney, P.J. and Lester, P.B. (2007) Toward a courageous mindset: The subjective act and experience of courage. *The Journal of Positive Psychology*, 2(2): 129–135.

Hanson, B. (2013) The leadership development interface: Aligning leaders and organizations toward more effective leadership learning. *Advances in Developing Human Resources*, 15(1): 106–120.

Harris, A. (2008) Distributed leadership: According to the evidence. *Journal of Educational Administration*, 46(2): 172–188.

Harris, J.C. (2012) Daw Aung San Suu Kyi: Freedom to Lead. *Archives of General Psychiatry*, 69(7): 657–659.

Harvey, M. (2014) *Interactional Leadership and How to Coach It: The Art of the Choice-focused Leader*. Abingdon: Routledge.

Hayward, M. (2007) *Ego Check: Why Executive Hubris is Wrecking Companies and Careers and How to Avoid the Trap*. Wokingham: Kaplan Publishing.

Heal, G. (2008) *When Principles Pay: Corporate Social Responsibility and the Bottom Line*. New York: Columbia University Press.

Heffernan, T. (2004). Trust formation in cross-cultural business-to-business relationships. *Qualitative Market Research: An International Journal*, 7(2): 114–125.

Heifetz, R.A. & Linsky, M. (2002) *Leadership on the Line*. Boston, MA: Harvard Business School Press.

Helsdingen, A.S., Van Gog, T. & Van Merriënboer, J.J. (2011) The effects of practice schedule on learning a complex judgment task. *Learning and Instruction*, 21(1): 126–136.

Heracleous, L. & Wirtz, J. (2014) Singapore Airlines: Achieving sustainable advantage through mastering paradox. *The Journal of Applied Behavioral Science*, 50: 150–170.

Hersey, P. & Blanchard, K.H. (1982) Leadership style: Attitudes and behaviors. *Training and Development Journal*, 36(5): 50–52.

Hersey, P., Blanchard, K. & Johnson, D. (2001) *Management of Organizational Behavior* (8th edn). London: Prentice Hall.

Hersey, P. & Chevalier, R. (2000) Situational leadership and performance coaching. *Coaching for Leadership*. San Francisco, CA: Jossey-Bass, pp. 247–256.

Hill, F. & Stephens, C. (2005) Building leadership capacity in medical education: Developing the potential of course coordinators. *Medical Teacher*, 27(2): 145–149.

Hill, P.L. & Roberts, B.W. (2010) Propositions for the study of moral personality development. *Current Directions in Psychological Science*, 19: 380–383.

Hofstede, G. (1980) Motivation, leadership, and organization: Do American theories apply abroad? *Organizational Dynamics*, 9(1): 42–63.

Hoover, E. & Harder, M. (2014) The hidden complexities of organizational change for sustainability in higher education. *Journal of Cleaner Production*, online February 7.

Hosking, D.M.E., Dachler, H. & Gergen, K.J. (1995) *Management and Organization: Relational Alternatives to Individualism*. Avebury: Ashgate Publishing Co.

House, R.J. & Dessler, G. (1974) The path-goal theory of leadership: Some post hoc and a priori tests. *Contingency Approaches to Leadership*, 29: 55.

Huffington, C. (2006) A contextualised approach to coaching. In H. Brunning (ed.), *Executive Coaching: Systems-psychodynamic Perspective*. London: Karnac Books.

Hunt, J. & Weintraub, J. (2007) *The Coaching Organization: A Strategy for Developing Leaders*. Thousand Oaks, CA: Sage.

Isaacson, W. (2011) *Steve Jobs*. New York: Simon and Schuster.

Ives, Y. & Cox, E. (2012) *Goal-focused Coaching: Theory and Practice*. New York: Routledge.

Janis, I. & Mann, L. (1977) *Decision Making: A Psychoanalysis of Conflict, Choice and Commitment*. New York: The Free Press.

Jenlink, P.M. (2014) The moral nature of educational leadership: Examining the dispositional aims of moral leadership. *Educational Leadership and Moral Literacy: The Dispositional Aims of Moral Leaders*, 17.

Jessop, B. (2005) Critical realism and the strategic-relational approach. *New Formations, London*, 56: 40–53.

Johnson, D. & Grayson, K. (2005) Cognitive and affective trust in service relationships. *Journal of Business Research*, 58(4): 500–507.

Johnson, D.D.P. & Tierney, D. (2011a). The Rubicon theory of war: How the path to conflict reaches the point of no return. *International Society*, 36(1): 7–40.

Johnson, D.D. & Tierney, D. (2011b). *Crossing the Rubicon: The Perils of Committing to a Decision*. Cambridge, MA: Belfer Center for Science and International Affairs, Harvard Kennedy School.

Johnson, B. (2014) Reflection: A perspective on paradox and its application to modern management. *The Journal of Applied Behavioral Science*, 50(2): 206–212.

Jones, G. & Spooner, K. (2006) Coaching high achievers. *Consulting Psychology Journal: Practice and Research*, 58(1): 40–50.

Kaiser, R.B. & Overfield, D.V. (2011) Strengths, strengths overused, and lopsided leadership. *Consulting Psychology Journal: Practice and Research*, 63(2): 89.

Katoch, D. (2013) Decision-making and the leadership conundrum. *CLAWS Journal*, Summer, 161–173.

Kemp, T. (2009) Is coaching an evolved form of leadership? Building a transdisciplinary framework for exploring the coaching alliance. *International Coaching Psychology Review*, 4(1): 105–110.

Kemp, T. (2010) Building the coaching alliance. In G. Hernez-Broome & L.A. Boyce (eds), *Advancing Executive Coaching: Setting the Course for Successful Leadership Coaching, Vol. 29*. Oxford: John Wiley & Sons, pp. 151–176.

King, M.L. (1963) *Strength to Love*, Vol. 27. K. Kasegawa & T. Amemiya (eds), New York: Harper & Row.

Knapp, M.S., Copland, M.A. & Swinnerton, J.A. (2007) Understanding the promise and dynamics of data-informed leadership. *Yearbook of the National Society for the Study of Education*, 106(1): 74–104.

Kohlberg, L. (1963) Moral development and identification. In H. Stevenson (ed.), *Child Psychology: 62nd Yearbook of the National Society for the Study of Education*. Chicago, IL: University of Chicago Press, pp. 277–332.

Kollmuss, A. & Agyeman, J. (2002) Mind the gap: Why do people act environmentally and what are the barriers to pro-environmental behavior? *Environmental Education Research*, 8(3): 239–260.

Kouzes, J.M. & Posner, B.Z. (2009) The five practices of exemplary leadership. *The Jossey-Bass Reader on Educational Leadership*, 63.

LaBier, D. (2013) Why CEOs don't want executive coaching. *Huffington Post*, August 16. Available at: www.huffingtonpost.com/douglas-labier/why-ceos-dont-want-execut_b_3762704.html (accessed November 2, 2014).

Ladegard, G. & Gjerde, S. (2014) Leadership coaching, leader role-efficacy, and trust in subordinates. A mixed methods study assessing leadership coaching as a leadership development tool. *The Leadership Quarterly*.

Lanctot, J.D. & Irving, J.A. (2010) Character and leadership: Situating servant leadership in a proposed virtues framework. *International Journal of Leadership Studies*, 6(1): 28–50.

Laszlo, C. & Zhexembayeva, N. (2011) *Embedded Sustainability: The Next Big Competitive Advantage*. Sheffield and Stanford, CA: Greenleaf Publishing and Stanford University Press.

Lee, G. (2003). *Leadership Coaching: From Personal Insight to Organisational Performance*. London: CIPD Publishing.

Lee, R.J. & Frisch, M.H. (2011) Learning to coach leaders. In G. Hernez-Broome and L.A. Boyce (eds), *Advancing Executive Coaching*. San Francisco, CA: Jossey Bass, pp. 47–81.

Lévi-Strauss, C. (1966) *The Savage Mind*. Chicago, IL: University of Chicago Press.

Levy, B.R. (2003) Mind matters: Cognitive and physical effects of aging self-stereotypes. *Journals of Gerontology: Psychological Sciences*, 58: 203–211.

Lewin, K. (1951) *Field Theory in Social Science*. London: Tavistock.

Lewin, K. (1996) *Resolving Social Conflicts: Field Theory in Social Science*. Washington, DC: American Psychological Association.

Linley, P.A. (2008) *Average to A+: Realising Strengths in Yourself and Others*. Coventry: CAPP Press.

Lipman-Blumen, J. (2005) The allure of toxic leaders: Why followers rarely escape their clutches. *Ivey Business Journal*, 69(3): 1–40.

Lofting, H. (1922) *The Voyages of Dr. Dolittle*. New York: Grosset & Dunlap.

Louis, C., Lawrence, M. & Keith, M. (1994) *Research Methods in Education*. London: Routledge, pp. 365–370.

Lovallo, D. & Kahneman, D. (2003) Delusions of success. *Harvard Business Review*, 81(7): 56–63.

Luft, J. & Ingham, H. (1955) *The Johari Window: A Graphic Model for Interpersonal Relations*.

Luthans, F. (2002). The need for and meaning of positive organizational behavior. *Journal of Organizational Behavior*, 23: 695–706.

Luthans, F. & Avolio, B. (2003) Authentic leadership development. *Positive Organizational Scholarship*, 241: 258.

Luthans, F., Luthans, K.W. & Luthans, B.C. (2004) Positive psychological capital: Beyond human and social capital. *Business Horizons*, 47(1): 45–50.

Luthans, F., Youssef, C.M. & Avolio, B.J. (2007) *Psychological Capital*. New York: Oxford University Press.

Maak, T. & Pless, N.M. (2006) Responsible leadership in a stakeholder society—a relational perspective. *Journal of Business Ethics*, 66(1): 99–115.

Maddux, J.R. (2002) Self-efficacy: The power of believing you can. In C.R. Snyder & S.J. Lopez (eds), *Handbook of Positive Psychology*. New York: Oxford University Press, pp. 277–287.

Maiocchi, M. (2015) Emotions and design. In *The Neuroscientific Basis of Successful Design*Amsterdam: Springer, pp. 11–24.

Marianetti, O. & Passmore, J. (2010) Mindfulness at work: Paying attention to enhance well-being and performance. In *Oxford Handbook of Positive Psychology and Work*. Oxford: Oxford University Press, pp. 189–200.

Markovic, J., McAtavey, J.M. & Fischweicher, P. (2014) An integrative trust model in the coaching context. *American Journal of Management*, 14(1–2): 102–110.

Massey, G. & Kyngdon, A.S. (2005) The measurement of interpersonal trust between peer managers: A test of a specific item bank using factor analysis and Rasch modelling. *UTS Working Paper Series*, 3(05): 1–16.

Mayer, D.M., Kuenzi, M., Greenbaum, R., Bardes, M. & Salvador, R. (2009) How low does ethical leadership flow? Test of a trickle-down model. *Organizational Behavior and Human Decision Processes*, 108: 1–13.

Mayer, R. (2005) Restoring character and confidence in the workplace: A case for values-based leadership. Presentation at the Caribbean Corporate Governance Forum, Saint Kitts.

Mayer, R.C., Davis, J.H. & Schoorman, F.D. (1995) An integration model of organizational trust. *Academy of Management Review*, 20: 709–734.

McLaughlin, M. (2010) An in-depth phenomenological study of the effect that knowledge of Human Givens has within executive coaching. *International Journal of Evidence Based Coaching and Mentoring*, Special Issue (4): 83–94.

Mezirow, J. (1991) *Transformative Dimensions of Adult Learning*. San Francisco, CA: Jossey-Bass Publishers.

Miller, C.C. & Ireland, R.D. (2005) Intuition in strategic decision making: Friend or foe in the fast-paced 21st century? *The Academy of Management Executive*, 19(1): 19–30.

Miller, W.I. (2002) *The Mystery of Courage*. Cambridge, MA: Harvard University Press.

Mingers, J. (2003) *The Place of Statistical Modelling in Management Science: Critical Realism and Multimethodology*. Canterbury: Canterbury Business School. Working Paper Series No.45.

Mitchell, J.R., Shepherd, D.A. & Sharfman, M.P. (2011) Erratic strategic decisions: when and why managers are inconsistent in strategic decision making. *Strategic Management Journal*, 32(7): 683–704.

Mumford, M.D., Zaccaro, S.J., Harding, F.D., Jacobs, T.O. & Fleishman, E.A. (2000) Leadership skills for a changing world: Solving complex social problems. *The Leadership Quarterly*, 11(1): 11–35.

Murrell, K.L. (1997) Emergent theories of leadership for the next century: Towards relational concepts. *Organization Development Journal*, 15: 35–42.

Musselwhite, C. (2009) Good choices: Making better decisions by knowing how best to decide, *LIA*, 2 9(4): 3–7. Available at: www.ccl.org/leadership/pdf/publications/lia/lia29_4good.pdf (accessed January 21, 2015).

Neal, D.T., Wood, W. & Quinn, J.M. (2006) Habits—A repeat performance. *Current Directions in Psychological Science*, 15: 198–202.

Neck, C.P. & Moorhead, G. (1995) Groupthink remodeled: The importance of leadership, time pressure, and methodical decision-making procedures. *Human Relations*, 48(5): 537–557.

Neenan, M. & Palmer, S. (eds) (2013) *Cognitive Behavioural Coaching in Practice: An Evidence Based Approach*. London: Routledge.

Northouse, P.G. (2009) Transformational leadership. In *Leadership: Theory and Practice* (5th edn). Upper Saddle River, NJ: Pearson Education, pp. 171–204.

Northouse, P.G. (2013) *Leadership: Theory and Practice*. London: Sage.

Nyberg, D. & Sveningsson, S. (2014) Paradoxes of authentic leadership: Leader identity struggles. *Leadership*. Pre-published March 13. doi: 10.1177/1742715013504425.

Ophir, E., Nass, C.I. & Wagner, A.D. (2009) Cognitive control in media multitaskers. *Proceedings of the National Academy of Sciences*, 106: 15583–15587.

Pawar, B.S. (2003) Central conceptual issues in transformational leadership research. *Leadership & Organization Development Journal*, 24(7): 397–406.

Peterson, C. & Park, N. (2006) Characters strengths in organizations. *Journal of Organizational Behavior*, 27: 1149–1154.

Peterson, C. & Seligman, M. (2004) *Character Strengths and Virtues: A Handbook and Classification*. New York: Oxford University Press.

Pidd, M. & Woolley, R.N. (1980) Four views on problem structuring. *Interfaces*, 10(1): 51–54.

Pless, N.M. (2007) Understanding responsible leadership: Role identity and motivational drivers. *Journal of Business Ethics*, 74: 437–456.

Pritchard, G.M. (2009) *A grounded theory of the factors that mediate the effect of a strengths-based educational intervention over a four-month period*. PhD thesis, Azusa Pacific University.

Prochaska, J.O. & Velicer, W.F. (1997) The transtheoretical model of health behavior change. *American Journal of Health Promotion*, 12(1): 38–48.

Proust, M. (2006) *Remembrance of Things Past*. London: Wordsworth.

Pury, C.L.S. & Kowalski, R.M. (2007) Human strengths, courageous actions, and general and personal courage. *The Journal of Positive Psychology*, 2(2): 120–128.

Pury, C.L.S., Kowalski, R.M. & Spearman, J. (2007) Distinctions between general and personal courage. *The Journal of Positive Psychology*, 2(2): 99–114.

Quinn, R.E. (2010) *Deep Change: Discovering the Leader Within, Vol. 378*. Oxford: John Wiley & Sons.

Rafferty, A.E. & Griffin, M.A. (2004) Dimensions of transformational leadership: Conceptual and empirical extensions. *The Leadership Quarterly*, 15(3): 329–354.

Reave, L. (2005) Spiritual values and practices related to leadership effectiveness. *The Leadership Quarterly*, 16(5): 655–687.

Riddle, D. (2008) *Leadership Coaching: When it's Right, When You're Ready*. Greensboro, NC: CCL Press.

Rittell, H. & Webber, M. (1973) Dilemmas in a general theory of planning. *Policy Sciences*, 4: 155–169.

Robbins, B. (2014) The transformative practice of core centering: Hara, peak performance, and the integral movement. In E. Leskowitz (ed.), *Sports, Energy and Consciousness: Awakening Potential through Sport*. CreateSpace Independent Self-Publishing Platform.

Robinson, S.L. & Bennett, R.J. (1995) A typology of deviant workplace behaviors: A multidimensional scaling study. *Academy of Management Journal*, 38(2): 555–572.

Rosental, S.B. (1993) Peirce's ultimate logical interpretant and dynamical object: A pragmatic perspective. *Transactions of the Charles S. Peirce Society*, 29: 195–210.

Rousseau, D.M., Sitkin, S.B., Burt, R.S. & Camerer, C. (1998) Not so different after all: A cross-discipline view of trust. *Academy of Management Review*, 23(3): 393–404.

Ruch, W., Proyer, R.T., Harzer, C., Park, N., Peterson, C. & Seligman, M.E.P. (2010). Values in action inventory. *Journal of Individual Differences*, 31(3), 138–149.

Ruedy, N.E. & Schweitzer, M.E. (2010) In the moment: The effect of mindfulness on ethical decision making. *Journal of Business Ethics*, 95(1): 73–87.

Russell, R.F. & Stone, A.G. (2002) A review of servant leadership attributes: Developing a practical model. *Leadership & Organization Development Journal*, 23(3): 145–157.

Ryan, R.M. and Deci, E.L. (2000) Self-determination theory and the facilitation of intrinsic motivation, and well-being. *American Psychologist*, 55: 68–78.

Sadler-Smith, E. & Shefy, E. (2004) The intuitive executive: Understanding and applying "gut feel" in decision making. *Academy of Management Executive*, 18: 76–91.

Safran, J.D., Crocker, P., McMain, S. & Murray, P. (1990) Therapeutic alliance rupture as a therapy event for empirical investigation. *Psychotherapy*, 27(2): 154–165.

References 243

Schaefer Muñoz, S. & Colchester, M. (2012) Top officials at Barclays resign over rate scandal. *The Wall Street Journal*, July 4. Available at: www.wsj.com/articles/SB10001424052702304299704577503974000425002 (accessed May 10, 2015).

Scharmer, C.O. and Kaufer, K. (2013) *Leading from the Emerging Future: From Ego-system to Eco-system Economics*. Oakland, CA: Berrett-Koehler.

Schaubroeck, J.M., Hannah, S.T., Avolio, B.J., Kozlowski, S.W.J., Lord, R.G., Trevino, L.K., Dimotakis, N. & Peng, A.C. (2012) Embedding ethical leadership within and across organizational levels. *Academy of Management Journal*, 55: 1053–1078.

Scheier M.F. & Carver, C.S. (2009) Optimism. In S.J. Lopez (ed.), *The Encyclopedia of Positive Psychology*. Oxford: WileyBlackwell, p. 656.

Schein, E. (2006) Coaching and consultation revisited: Are they the same? In M. Goldsmith & M. Lyons (eds), *Coaching for Leadership* (2nd edn). San Francisco, CA: Wiley.

Schunk, D.H. (1991) Self-efficacy and academic motivation. *Educational Psychologist*, 26: 207–231.

Sekerka, L.E. (2010) Preserving integrity in the face of corruption: Exercising moral muscle in the path to right action. *Journal of Organizational Moral Psychology*, 1(3): 1–14.

Sekerka, L.E. (2011) Preserving integrity in the face of corruption: Exercising moral courage in the path to right action. *Journal of Moral Philosophy*, 1(3): 1–14.

Sekerka, L.E. & Bagozzi, R.P. (2007) Moral courage in the workplace: Moving to and from the desire and decision to act. *Business Ethics: A European Review*, 16: 132–149.

Sekerka, L.E., McCarthy, J.D. & Bagozzi, R. (2011) Developing the capacity for professional moral courage: Facing daily ethical challenges in today's military workplace. In D. Comer and G. Vega (eds), *Moral Courage in Organizations: Doing the Right Thing at Work*. New York: Routledge, pp. 130–141.

Seligman, M.E.P. (2002) *Authentic Happiness*. New York: Free Press.

Senge, P.M. (1990) *The Fifth Discipline: The Art and Practice of the Learning Organization*. New York: Currency.

Senge, P., Scharmer, C.O., Jaworski, J. & Flowers, B.S. (2004) *Presence*. Cambridge, MA: Society of Organizational Learning.

Shamir, B. & Eilam, G. (2005) What's your story? A life-stories approach to authentic leadership development. *The Leadership Quarterly*, 16(3): 395–417.

Shapiro, S.L., Oman, D., Thoresen, C.E., Plante, T.G. & Flinders, T. (2008) Cultivating mindfulness: effects on well-being. *Journal of Clinical Psychology*, 64(7): 840–862.

Shapiro, S.L., Schwartz, G.E. & Santerre, C. (2005) Meditation and positive psychology. In C.R. Snyder & S.J. Lopez (eds), *Handbook of Positive Psychology*. New York: Oxford University Press, pp. 632–645.

Shelp, E.E. (1984) Courage: A neglected virtue in the patient-physician relationship. *Social Science & Medicine*, 18(4): 351–360.

Simmons, A.L. & Sower, V.E. (2012) Leadership sagacity and its relationship with individual creative performance and innovation. *European Journal of Innovation Management*, 15(3): 298–309.

Simons, T. (2002) Behavioral integrity: The perceived alignment between managers' words and deeds as a research focus. *Organization Science*, 13(1): 18–35.

Singh, N. & Krishnan, V.R. (2008) Self-sacrifice and transformational leadership: mediating role of altruism. *Leadership & Organization Development Journal*, 29(3): 261–274.

Snyder, C.R. (2000). *Handbook of Hope*. San Diego, CA: Academic Press.

Snyder, C.R. (2002) Hope theory: Rainbows in the mind. *Psychological Inquiry*, 13: 249–275.

Snyder, C.R., Irving, L.M. & Anderson, J. (1991) Hope and health. In C.R. Snyder & D.R. Forsyth (eds), *Handbook of Social and Clinical Psychology: The Health Perspective*. Elmsford, NY: Pergamon Press.

Snyder, C.R., Shorey, H.S., Cheavens, J., Pulvers, K.M., Adams, V.H., III & Wiklund, C. (2002) Hope and academic success in college. *Journal of Educational Psychology*, 94(4): 820–826.

Sones, E. (2009) 360 assessment, an easier pill to swallow: Implementation of peer assessment for captain's career course students and staff. *U.S. Army Medical Department Journal*: 59–63.

Spears, L.C. (1995) *Reflections on Leadership: How Robert K. Greenleaf's Theory of Servant-Leadership Influenced Today's Top Management Thinkers*. New York: John Wiley.

Spreitzer, G.M. & Sonenshein, S. (2004) Toward the construct definition of positive deviance. *American Behavioral Scientist*, 47(6): 828–847.

Stacey, R. (2007) The challenge of human interdependence: Consequences for thinking about the day to day practice of management in organizations. *European Business Review*, 19(4): 292–302.

Stajkovic, A.D. (2003) Introducing positive psychology to work motivation: Development of a core confidence model. Paper presented at Academy of Management national meeting, Seattle, Washington (August).

Stajkovic, A. & Luthans, F. (1998) Social cognitive theory and self-efficacy. *Organizational Dynamics*, 26: 62–74.

Stanford Graduate School of Business (2013) *2013 Executive Coaching Survey*. Stanford Centre for Leadership Development and Research. Available at: www.gsb.stanford.edu/sites/default/files/2013-ExecutiveCoachingSurvey.pdf (accessed November 2, 2014).

Staw, B.M. & Boettger, R.D. (1990) Task revision: A neglected form of work performance. *Academy of Management Journal*, 33(3): 534–559.

Stephens, J.P., Heaphy, E.D., Carmeli, A., Spreitzer, G.M. & Dutton, J.E. (2013) Relationship quality and virtuousness: Emotional carrying capacity as a source of individual and team resilience. *The Journal of Applied Behavioral Science*, doi: 0021886312471193.

Stober, D.R. (2006) Coaching from the humanistic perspective. In D. Stober & A.M. Grant,*Evidence Based Coaching Handbook*. Hoboken, NJ: Wiley, pp. 17–51.

Stone, A.G., Russell, R.F. & Patterson, K. (2003) Transformational versus servant leadership: A difference in leader focus. *Leadership & Organization Development Journal*, 25(4): 349–361.

Sun, B.J., Deane, F., Crowe, T., Andresen, R., Oades, L.G. & Ciarrochi, J. (2013) A preliminary exploration of the working alliance and "real relationship" in two coaching approaches with mental health workers. *International Coaching Psychology Review*, 8(2): 6–17.

Swieringa, J. & Wierdsma, A. (1992) *Becoming a Learning Organization: Beyond the Learning Curve*. Wokingham: Addison-Wesley.

Taylor, E.W. (1994) Intercultural competency: A transformative learning process. *Adult Education Quarterly*, 44(3): 154–174.

Taylor, S.S. (2014) The impoverished aesthetic of modern management: Beauty and ethics in organizations. In D. Elm & D. Koehn (eds), *Aesthetics and Business Ethics*. Amsterdam: Springer, pp. 23–35.

Thornton, L. (2009) Leadership ethics training: Why is it so hard to get it right. *Training and Development*, 63: 58–61.

Tourish, D. (2012) *The Darkside of Transformational Leadership*. Hove: Routledge.

Treviño, L.K., Weaver, G.R. & Reynolds, S.J. (2006) Behavioral ethics in organizations: A review. *Journal of Management*, 32(6): 951–990.

Tsaroucha, A., Kingston, P., Corp, N., Stewart, T. & Walton, I. (2012) The emotional needs audit (ENA): A report on its reliability and validity. *Mental Health Review Journal*, 17(2): 81–89.

Tugade, M.M., Fredrickson, B.L. & Barrett, L.F. (2004) Psychological resilience and positive emotional granularity: Examining the benefit of positive emotion on coping and health. *Journal of Personality*, 72(6), December, 1167.

Turnbull James, K. and Collins, J.S. (eds) (2008) *Leadership Perspectives: Knowledge into Action*. London: Palgrave.

Uhl-Bien, M. (2006) Relational leadership theory: Exploring the social processes of leadership and organizing. *The Leadership Quarterly*, 17(6): 654–676.

Uhl-Bien, M. & Osima, S.M. (2012) *Advancing Relational Leadership Research: A Dialogue Among Perspectives*. Charlotte, NC: Information Age Publishing, pp. 203–225.

Van de Valk, L.J. & Constas, M.A. (2011) A methodological review of research on leadership development and social capital: is there a cause and effect relationship? *Adult Education Quarterly*, 61(1), February: 73–90.

Van Dierendonck, D. (2011) Servant leadership: A review and synthesis. *Journal of Management*, 37(4): 1228–1261.

Van Praag, E. (2004) *Spiritual Leadership*. London: Sage.

Velasquez, M., Andre, C., Shanks, T. & Meyer, M. (1996) Thinking ethically: A framework for moral decision-making. *Issues in Ethics*, 7(1). Available at: www.scu.edu/ethics/publications/iie/v7n1/thinking.html (accessed January 31, 2015).

Vinkhuyzen, O.M. & Karlsson-Vinkhuyzen, S.I. (2012) The role of moral leadership for sustainable consumption and production some theoretical and normative explorations. Proceedings: Global Research Forum on Sustainable Consumption and Production Workshop, June 13–15, Rio de Janeiro, Brazil. Available at: edepot.wur.nl/245635 (accessed February 14, 2015).

Vroom, V.H. & Jago, A.G. (1974) Decision making as a social process: normative and descriptive models of leader behavior. *Decision Sciences*, 5(4): 743–769.

Walumbwa, F., Avolio, B., Gardner, W., Wernsing, T. & Peterson, S. (2008) Authentic leadership: Development and validation of a theory-based measure. *Journal of Management*, 34(1), February: 89–126.

Weaver, G.R., Treviño, L.K. & Agle, B. (2005) "Somebody I look up to": Ethical role models in organizations. *Organizational Dynamics*, 34(4): 313–330.

Weick, K.E. (1993) The collapse of sensemaking in organizations: The Mann Gulch disaster. *Administrative Science Quarterly*, December.

Weinstein, N., Brown, K.W. & Ryan, R.M. (2009) A multi-method examination of the effects of mindfulness on stress attribution, coping, and emotional well-being. *Journal of Research in Personality*, 43: 374–385.

Weiss, C. (1995) Nothing as practical as a good theory: Exploring theory-based evaluations for comprehensive community-based initiatives for children and families. In J. Connell, A. Kubisch, L. Schorr & C. Weiss (eds), *New Approaches to Evaluating Community Initiatives*. Washington, DC: The Aspen Institute, pp. 65–92.

Western, S. (2013) *Leadership: A Critical Text*. London: Sage.

Wheeler, D. (2012) *Servant Leadership for Higher Education: Principles and Practices*. San Francisco, CA: Jossey Bass.

Wong, C.A. & Cummings, G.G. (2009) The influence of authentic leadership behaviors on trust and work outcomes of health care staff. *Journal of Leadership Studies*, 3(2): 6–23.

Zaccaro, S.J., Gilbert, J.A., Thor, K.K. & Mumford, M.D. (1992) Leadership and social intelligence: Linking social perspectiveness and behavioral flexibility to leader effectiveness. *The Leadership Quarterly*, 2(4): 317–342.

Zaccaro, S.J., Mumford, M.D., Connelly, M.S., Marks, M.A. & Gilbert, J.A. (2000). Assessment of leader problem-solving capabilities. *The Leadership Quarterly*, 11(1): 37–64.

Zhong, C.-B. (2011) The ethical dangers of deliberative decision making. *Administrative Science Quarterly*, 56: 1–25.

INDEX

Academy of Management 8
accountability 7, 34, 38, 157, 180, 185–6, 191, 226
ACE FIRST model 13
achievement 93, 122
action 20–1, 25, 44, 70, 78–9; balance 87, 91–2, 95, 98; decision-making 126–7, 129, 131, 133–4, 136, 139, 143, 146, 149, 152; gravitational factors 83–4; plans 134, 156, 165; research 16; role 156–81; self-awareness 99–101; sphere technique 107, 116
Adler, A. 89
Adler, N. 95
administrators 172–3
adrenaline 7
agency 189–90, 215
agenda-setting 21–2, 35, 39, 47, 78, 221–6
Agyeman, J. 39
Akrivou, K. 24–5, 32
alliances 186–9, 196–7, 224
altruism 135, 202
Alvey, S. 192

amygdalae 6
analysis-paralysis 165
Andrews, W. 88
anger 118, 121, 160, 163, 178, 192
Annas, J. 5, 70–1
Apple 8
April, K. 17
Argyris, C. 14
Aristotle 75, 179
Atkinson, T. 139
attention 91
attitude 172
audits 88–94
authentic leadership 200, 203–6, 214, 216–17, 224
authority types 130
autonomy 91–3
Avey, J.B. 64–5
avoidance 64
Avolio, B.J. 11, 201, 210

Bachkirova, T. 2, 97, 202
Bagozzi, R. 12, 87
balance 19, 35, 38, 42, 60; agenda-setting 223; decision-making 126,

139; gravitational factors 72, 82–3; implementation 173; self-awareness 86–104; sphere technique 105, 107–8, 114, 116, 118–21, 123; trust 191
Bandura, A. 57, 62–3, 70
banks 9
Barclay, K. 192
Barling, H. 201
Barnard, J.W. 118–19
Barner, R. 16
Baron, L. 189
Barry, D. 212
Bass, B.M. 201–2, 216
Beck, J.W. 172
benevolence 21, 184, 192–7
Benjamin, D.J. 26
Bennet, A. 124, 126, 128–9, 135, 138, 143, 175, 177
Bennet, D. 124, 126, 128–9, 135, 138, 143, 175, 177
Bennett, R.J. 11
best practice 13
bias 110, 115–16, 132, 150, 157–61, 163–4, 168, 181
Blanchard, K. 36, 208–9
blind spots 19, 80, 132–3, 171, 188, 223
Bluckert, P. 185, 187
Bogardus, E.S. 112
Boniwell, I. 67
boundaries 21, 42, 45, 53, 129, 132–3, 182, 186, 198, 224
Boyatzis, R.E. 24–5, 32, 88
Boyce, L.A. 185
boycotts 8
BP 8
brain 109–10, 137, 139, 164–5
brainstorming 141, 148, 165
Branson, R. 27, 32
brave leadership coaching model 1–22, 41, 43, 59, 104; agenda-setting 221–7; decision-making 126–55; gravitational factors 59–86; implementation 156–81; leadership theories 199–220; pulling factors 41–58; sphere technique 105–25; stories 23–40; trust 182–98
brave point 123, 125
brave sphere 105–26, 144–5, 148–9, 174, 177, 223
bravery 46–7, 52, 57, 59, 68; action 156–81; agenda-setting 221–7; balance 86–104; decision-making 126–55; definitions 1, 3–13, 23, 39; gravitational factors 59–85; ideas of 25–32; positioning 199–220; pulling factors 41–58; self-awareness 86–104; sphere technique 105–25; stories 23–40; trust 182–98
breathing techniques 96, 108–10, 123
bricolage 64
Bright, D.S. 75, 190
Brockbank, A. 39
Brown, K.H. 178–9
Brown, K.W. 96–7
Brown, M.E. 26, 204
Buckingham, M. 72
Bullock, S. 59
bureaucracy 173
Burnett, C.A. 137, 164, 167
burnout 32, 173
Burns, J.M. 2, 35, 202, 206
butterfly effect 128–9

calculus-based trust 183–4
Cameron, K.S. 38, 60, 67, 75–6, 190
Camillus, J.C. 143–4
Carr, A.E. 172
Carver, C.S. 99–100
Caza, A. 75, 190
challenges 1, 10, 18, 22, 38; agenda-setting 221–2, 226–7; decision-making 144–5; gravitational factors 60–2, 65, 72–3, 77, 79; implementation 157–68, 174, 176–8, 181; pulling factors 43, 45, 47, 51, 56–7; self-awareness 87, 90, 97, 101, 104;

sphere technique 106, 108, 118, 122–3; trust 183, 186–7, 191, 194, 196–8
character strengths 60–1, 67–84, 122, 187, 191
Chartered Institute of Purchasing and Supply 78
Checkland, P. 142
Chevalier, R. 209
China 7–8
Choi, J.J. 26
Churchill, W. 30–2, 34
Churchman, C.W. 128
citizenship 76, 180
Ciulla, J.B. 206–7
Claxton, G. 138–9, 164
Clifton, D. 72
climate control 1
closed-eyes exercises 145
Clutterbuck, D. 2
coaching models 11, 13–18, 23, 25, 39–40; agenda-setting 221–7; decision-making 127, 130–4, 138, 140–54; definition 1–3; gravitational factors 62, 64, 67, 71–3, 77, 79–82, 84; implementation 158–64, 167–74, 177–80; leadership types 179–81; pulling factors 43, 45–7, 52, 57; role 174–81; self-awareness 87, 89–94, 104; sphere technique 108–9, 113–14, 117, 119–22; trust 182–97; types 199–213
cognitive behavioural therapy 87
cognitive processes 126–7, 137, 139–40, 165–6, 168, 180, 184–5
Collard, P. 97
Collins, J.C. 45
Collins, J.S. 199–213, 220
comfort zones 12, 180, 216
command-and-control 179–81
communication 171–4, 179–81, 185, 210, 224
company culture *see* organizational culture

competence 93, 100–1, 135, 199, 208, 219
complex problems 8, 20, 22, 31, 34; decision-making 126–9, 131, 135, 138, 140–54; implementation 161, 174–5; pulling factors 41–3; sphere technique 110, 112, 124
complex responsive approach 157, 174–81
Conan Doyle, A. 82
conferences 8
confidence 62, 123–4, 139, 158, 187, 194, 203, 208
confidentiality 90, 187, 189–90, 192, 196, 226
Confucius 93
connections 92, 127, 142–3, 151–3
consequences 156, 168, 181
Constas, M.A. 219
contingencies 142, 167
contracts 47, 76, 183–4, 186, 188–9, 192, 202
control 91–3, 99–100, 119–21, 141, 167, 177, 179–81
Copeland, M.K. 8, 203
Copland, M.A. 115
core strength 86–7, 103, 223
corporate leaders 7–8, 15, 22, 51, 111, 143, 225
corporate social responsibility 8, 32, 34, 76, 152, 169, 176
corporation tax 8
corruption 9, 12
cortisol 7
counselling 3
courage 3–6, 10, 14, 57, 68–70; balance 87–8, 95; gravitational factors 72–3; implementation 156, 179; self-awareness 98, 101; trust 182, 196
Coutu, D. 64
Covey, S.R. 36
Cox, E. 2, 40, 66, 97–100, 111, 136–7, 139, 156, 165–7, 179, 183–4, 186, 189

credibility 21, 29, 149, 184–8, 192, 197, 211, 224
Cresswell, J.D. 96
critical problems 129–30, 135
critical thinking 15, 68, 126, 138, 146, 157, 163, 165–7, 180–1, 206
Croskerry, P. 137, 161, 163–4, 166
Cummings, G.G. 204

Dahlsgaard, K. 69
Dane, E. 136–7
Day, D. 14, 200, 202
Day, P.S. 141
De Haan, E. 187–9
De Martino, B. 161
De Wolde, A. 207
Deci, E.L. 96
decision-making 2, 5–6, 9, 11–12, 14–15; agenda-setting 221, 223; balance sheet 147; brave 126–55; challenges 20; gravitational factors 70, 73–4, 82–3; implementation 156, 158–61, 163, 165–9, 171, 173–81; leadership theories 219; pulling factors 42–3, 46–7, 51–2, 54, 56–7; rational approach 131–4; role 126–55; self-awareness 86–7, 91, 93, 95–6, 98, 103; sphere technique 106, 110–12, 114–15, 117–19, 121–5; stories 28; techniques 141–54; trust 190–1; types 154
deliberate intuition 164–5
delusional optimism 120, 158
Densten, I.L. 177
depression 118
deregulation 7
desensitizing 122
Dessler, G. 208
detachment 20
devil's advocate technique 158, 165, 178
diagrams 47
dialectics 117
Diaz, F. 97

Dibben, M.R. 183–4
disorienting dilemmas 110–11, 190
doing right 77–9, 101, 124, 136, 139, 154, 167, 181, 217, 225
Dolan, S.L. 34–5
Doris, J.M. 70–1
Doval, H.C. 81
Drake, D. 39
Drucker, P.F. 127, 131–4, 147–8, 154
Dual Strategy 44
dual-process system 137
Dufault, K. 62
Dutton, J.E. 216

Eagly, A.H. 205
Earhart, A. 31
East 69, 96
Echols, M. 39
ego-system awareness 118–19, 193–4, 202, 226
Eley-Morris, S. 183
Elston, F. 67
Ely, K. 185, 196
emergence 128–30, 141
emotional intelligence 14, 19, 129, 132, 136, 139, 156, 160–3, 167, 181
emotional needs audit (ENA) 88–94, 103
emotional self-awareness 86–104
engagement 126
enhanced intuition 163
Enron 190
environment 7–8, 19, 22, 28, 38; agenda-setting 221–3, 226–7; decision-making 128–9, 131–2, 140, 142–5; gravitational factors 72, 78, 80, 82; implementation 157, 169–70, 176; pulling factors 43, 46–7, 51–2, 55, 57; self-awareness 87, 94, 98–100; sphere technique 106, 111, 113
equilibrium 46, 53–7, 86, 89, 103, 117, 128, 223
ethical leadership 200, 205–8, 214, 216–17, 219

ethics 1, 5–6, 8, 12–14, 17; agenda-setting 221, 224; challenges 19, 21; decision-making 133, 135–6, 147, 149–50, 152, 154; gravitational factors 72–3, 75–6, 78; implementation 170, 176; pulling factors 51–2; self-awareness 87, 98, 101, 103; stories 26, 34–6; trust 189–90, 198, 203
euphoria 159, 167
Evans, J.S.B. 137
execution 126
executive development 13, 21, 47, 67, 199–213, 218, 220, 224–5
expediency 15–16
external barriers 156–7, 181

fair play 74, 91, 118, 123, 158–9
fear culture 28, 57, 73, 88, 97; balance 104; decision-making 152; implementation 156, 163, 167; sphere technique 118, 120–3; trust 195
feed-forward orientation 144
feedback 70, 72, 99, 104, 118; decision-making 129, 134, 142, 144; implementation 171–2, 174, 179; leadership theories 219; self-awareness 104; trust 185
Fiedler, F.E. 208
Flavell, J. 167
focus 100, 115–17, 143, 148–9
focused convergence 164
Follini, B. 44–6
followers 2, 11, 21, 112, 177, 181, 203, 208–12, 214–16
force-field analysis 42, 105
Foxconn 8
frameworks 1–3, 11, 13, 16–17, 21; action 167; agenda-setting 223; decision-making 134, 153; gravitational factors 64; leadership theories 209, 211; sphere technique 105–6, 120; stories 23–5, 32, 40; trust 182

framing effect 161–4
Francisco, J.M. 137, 164, 167
Fredrickson, B. 76
friendships 92–3
Frisch, M.H. 192
Fry, L.W. 209
Fryer, M. 203
Full Range Leadership (FRL) model 202–3
Fulop, L. 131
future generations 227

Galinsky, A.D. 180
Gallwey, T. 195–6
Gandhi, M. 28, 32, 103–4, 160–1, 178
Gardner, W.L. 204, 206
Garland, E.L. 88
Garratt, B. 9
Gates, B. 27, 32
generic problems 131–2
George, B. 203
Gestalt psychology 14
Gillespie, D. 178–9
Gjerde, S. 3
Gladwell, M. 162
globalization 7, 118
Glunk, U. 44–6
goals 2–3, 12, 19, 62–6, 72; agenda-setting 223; decision-making 126, 130, 132, 146, 154; ethics 206; gravitational factors 80; implementation 156, 166–7, 169, 172, 176; leadership theories 208, 211–12; self-awareness 87, 98–100; sphere technique 125; trust 185–6
Goleman, D. 37
Graber, D.R. 36, 173
Graen, G.B. 212
Gravenstine, K. 39
gravitational factors 19–20, 43, 59–85, 103, 105; agenda-setting 222–3; decision-making 126, 132, 144–5; implementation 156; self-awareness

87; sphere technique 113–14, 116–17, 123
Gravity 59, 148
Gray, J.H. 177
Grayson, K. 192
Greenleaf, R. 209–10
Gregory, J.B. 172
Griffin, J. 88–9
Griffin, M.A. 201
Grint, K. 32, 112, 127–31, 147, 154, 175, 213, 222
groupthink 10, 13, 132, 140
Guignon, C.B. 204–5
Gulf of Mexico 8
gut feelings 86, 136, 140, 149, 164–5, 167–8

habits 19, 75, 80, 87, 95–8, 107; action 157, 164, 169; decision-making 132–3, 146; sphere technique 110; trust 190, 197
Haidt, J. 136
Halpin, S.M. 14
Hannafey, F.T. 189–90
Hannah, S.T. 3, 11, 70, 221
Harder, M. 169
Harris, J.C. 212
Harrison, M.M. 14
Harvey, M. 173–4
Hayward, M. 120
Heal, G. 7
Heffernan, T. 183, 188, 192
Heifetz, R.A. 112
helicopter view 111–12
Helsdingen, A.S. 179
Heracleous, L. 44
Hersey, P. 208–9
Higgins, J. 16
Hill, F. 219
Hofstede, G. 34
Hoover, E. 169
hope 60–3, 65–7, 69, 84, 88
House, R.J. 208
Huffington, C. 186

Human Givens 19, 88–9
humanity 68–9
humiliation 121
hunches 136–41, 161

ideal self 24–6, 32
identification-based trust 183
identikit approach 224–5
identity 18, 23–4, 26, 39, 64, 143, 204, 206
ideology 115
implementation 37–9, 126–7, 130–1, 146, 149, 156–69, 171–81, 224–7
imposter syndrome 122
improvisation 64, 130, 178
influence traps 118–23
information overload 165
Ingham, H. 191
innovation 10, 18, 54–7, 62, 106, 117, 128, 152–4, 171–3
insight 79–84, 141, 143, 162, 192
instinct 124, 136, 141, 163, 165
integrity 5, 21, 87, 149, 184–5, 188–91, 196–7, 203, 207–11, 224
interdependencies 18, 42, 44–6, 49–53, 118, 179, 222
internal barriers 156–7, 181
Internet 7, 31, 141
intimacy 92–3
intuition 10, 86, 122–4, 127, 135–41
Ireland, R.D. 136
Irving, J.A. 69, 75
isolation 43, 91–2, 190–1
Ives, Y. 66, 99–100, 186

Jackson, R.J. 185
Jago, A.G. 131, 155
Jensen, S.M. 64
Jessop, B. 81
Jobs, S. 32, 134
Johnson, D. 44–5, 158, 192, 209
journals 95
justice 68–9

Kahneman, D. 120
Kaiser, R.B. 72
Karlsson-Vinkhuyzen, S.I. 38–9
Katoch, D. 5
Kaufer, K. 118
Kelloway, E.K. 201
Kemp, T. 191, 195
keywords 106, 111, 116
Kilpatrick, A.O. 36, 173
King, M.L. Jr. 1, 32–3, 221
Knapp, M.S. 115–16
knowledge-based trust 183–4
Kohlberg, L. 135, 207
Kollmuss, A. 39
Kouzes, J.M. 24
Kowalski, R.M. 3, 156
Krishnan, V.R. 202
Ku, G. 180
Kukard, J. 17
Kyngdon, A.S. 192

LaBier, D. 218
Ladegard, G. 3
Lanctot, J.D. 69, 75
lawyers 28
Leader-Member Exchange (LMX) theory 212
leadership theories 179–81, 199–220, 224
Lean, M.E.J. 183
Lee, G. 13–14
Lee, R.J. 192
legislation 7–8
Lester, P.B. 3
Lévi-Strauss, C. 64
Lewin, K. 42
LIBOR lending rate 9
life space 42
light box technique 141, 147–55
limbic brain 110
Lincoln, A. 30, 32
Linley, P.A. 69–70
Linsky, M. 112
Lipman-Blumen, J. 9

local traits 70–1
Lofting, H. 41
Loughlin, C. 201
Lovallo, D. 119
Luft, J. 191
Luthans, F. 61–2, 64–5, 67, 72, 210

Maak, T. 176
McCarthy, J.D. 12, 87
McGill, I. 39
McLaughlin, M. 89
managerialism 146
Mandela, N. 29, 32
Marianetti, O. 97
Mark, A. 131
Markovic, J. 184–6, 188, 192
Martocchio, B.C. 62
Maslow, A. 89, 207
Massey, G. 192
Mayer, R.C. 36, 183, 207
MBAs 13, 17
meaning-making 93–4, 115–16
Médecins Sans Frontières 31
media 8
mentors 9, 27, 93, 133, 146, 182, 185
metacognition 165–8, 179
Mezirow, J. 110
middle management 10, 180
Miller, C.C. 136
Miller, W.I. 70
mindfulness 19, 88, 96–8, 103, 106–7; action 163, 166; agenda-setting 223, 226; sphere technique 111, 123
mindware 163
mission statements 51, 133, 171, 173
Mitchell, J.R. 167
Mobley, S. 39
Model I 14
moral self-awareness 86–104
Morin, D. 189
Morin, L. 189
multi-pass approach 52
multi-tasking 94

Mumford, M.D. 41–2, 106, 113, 169, 176
Murrell, K.L. 212

narcissism 118, 120
narratives 16, 27, 40, 122
Neal, D.T. 99
Neal, L.J. 185
neocortex 110
networking 92
Northouse, P.G. 206
Nyberg, D. 204–6

observation sphere 20, 105–6, 111–16
O'Connor, M.J. 36
online tests 67, 72
open-door policy 28
Ophir, E. 94
optimism 60–3, 65–7, 84, 101, 118–21, 158
options 125, 127, 132–3, 141, 143, 146–52, 154–5, 166, 223
organizational culture 10, 25, 31, 34, 38; decision-making 143, 150; gravitational factors 67, 76, 79; implementation 169, 171, 173, 175, 180; leadership theories 213; pulling factors 47, 50–2, 54; sphere technique 110, 114–15, 117; trust 193–4
organizational failure 2
outcomes 2, 16, 45, 63, 66; balance 99–100; decision-making 127, 131, 133, 148, 155; gravitational factors 76, 78–84; implementation 162, 166–8, 173, 179; leadership theories 210; trust 183, 186, 191, 195
over-confidence 158, 187
over-optimism 118–21, 158
Overfield, D.V. 72

Pankhurst, E. 31
paradigm shifts 39
Park, N. 63, 67, 69

Passmore, J. 97
pathologies 118
Pawar, B.S. 202
peer pressure 73, 86
performance indicators 8, 10, 12–13, 62, 66; balance 86; gravitational factors 75–6, 80; implementation 172; self-awareness 99–100; sphere technique 118
perspective transformation 110, 113, 116, 118, 132, 177
Peters, K. 17
Peterson, C. 4–5, 63, 67, 69, 74–5
philosophy 8, 24, 67, 71, 116, 173, 203, 205, 217
pilot schemes 144
Plato 75
Pless, N.M. 176
polarity traps 44–6, 49–53, 168–71, 181, 222
politicians 7–8, 30, 225
Porras, J.I. 45
positioning 21, 199–220
positive deviance 11–12, 76, 78
Posner, B.Z. 24
post-decisional process 126–7
Poulter, J. 142
power relations 174, 190, 212
Pratt, M.G. 136–7
pre-decisional process 126
priming 26
privacy 94
privatization 7
pro-social 12
problem-solving 20, 41–2, 44, 72, 184; agenda-setting 223–4; implementation 163, 175, 177, 179–80; role 127–31; sphere technique 106, 110, 113, 115, 124
professional development 190–1, 198, 224
profit 8, 21, 76, 79, 152–3, 168–9, 226
prototypes 144
Proust, M. 175

psychological capital 19, 60–2, 64–7, 75, 84, 222–3
psychological challenges 157–68, 181
pull-push theory 42
pulling factors 18–20, 41–59, 80, 86, 103; agenda-setting 222–3; analysis 46–57; decision-making 126, 132, 142–5, 154; implementation 156, 160; self-awareness 87, 104; sphere technique 105, 113–15, 117, 119–20, 123
purpose 93–4
Pury, C.L.S. 3, 156

qualifications 13, 185
quick fixes 148
Quinn, J.M. 99
Quinn, R.E. 216

Rafferty, A.E. 201
rapport 89–90, 186–7, 195–6
Reagan, R. 7
Reave, L. 207
reeve, C. 29
reflective pause 87, 94–6, 101, 103, 105–6; agenda-setting 224; decision-making 126, 131, 141; ethics 207; implementation 156, 166–7, 177; sphere technique 108, 110–12, 116–18, 122, 124; trust 184, 187, 190–1
rehearsal processes 101, 154, 178–9
relational leadership 179–81, 200, 205, 211–19, 224
relaxation 108–9, 113, 121
reptilian brain 110
resilience 33, 60–5, 67, 84, 87–8
resourcing 172–4, 178, 181
respect 21, 28, 33, 35, 195, 211
retroductive analysis 79–84
rich picture technique 141–4, 154
Riddle, D. 2
Riggio, R. 201
Robbins, B. 86

Robinson, S.L. 11
role models 23–4, 26, 32, 36–7, 39; agenda-setting 222; balance 100, 102; gravitational factors 65, 83; sphere technique 117; trust 195
role play 178–9
Rubicon metaphor 157–61, 168, 181
Ruch, W. 67–9
Ruedy, N.E. 98
Russell, R.F. 210
Ryan, R. 96–7

Sadler-Smith, E. 138–41, 165, 167
safe distance 19–20, 112, 123, 223
sanctuary sphere 20, 106–11, 123, 132, 223
scenario development 129, 141, 144, 148, 154, 178–9
Scharmer, C.O. 118
Schaubroeck, J.M. 207
Scheier, M.F. 99–100
Schein, E. 2, 221
Schoemaker, P.J. 141
Schweitzer, M.E. 98
security 90, 121
seeding 129
Sekerka, L.E. 9, 12, 87–8, 95, 98–101
self 57, 71–2, 98, 103, 192–4, 205–6
self-awareness 19, 24, 72, 74, 86–104; agenda-setting 222; implementation 167; leadership theories 210, 214–15, 218–19; sphere technique 119, 121
self-efficacy 60–2, 65–7, 84, 100
self-regulation 87–8, 95–101, 103–5, 110, 126, 166
Seligman, M. 4–5, 61, 67, 69, 74–5
Senge, P. 24, 36, 93
sensing gaps 164
servant leadership 179–81, 200, 209–11, 214–16
Shefy, F. 138–41, 165, 167
Shelp, E.E. 4
silence 106

Simmons, A.L. 111, 117
simplification 129
Singapore Airlines 44
Singh, N. 202
situationalism 70–1, 73, 200, 208–9, 214–18, 224
Snyder, C.R. 63
social capital 157, 219
social cognitive theory 57, 70
social construction 16, 23, 130, 204–5, 212
social skills 179–81, 185
socialization 34
Sones, E. 219
Sower, V.E. 111, 117
Spears, L.C. 210
sphere technique 20, 105–25
Stacey, R. 174–5
Stajkovic, A. 62
stakeholders 2, 8, 20–1, 25, 49; agenda-setting 224; decision-making 128, 133, 142–3, 146–7, 149, 154; implementation 157, 168–76, 179, 181; sphere technique 110, 115–16, 123; trust 182, 185, 190
Stanford Graduate School of Business 218
Starbucks 8
status 93
Stephens, C. 219
Stephens, J.P. 64
stepping method 64
stewardship 17–18, 210
Stober, D.R. 186
Stone, A.G. 210–11
stories 16, 18, 22–40, 43, 47, 94, 104, 222
stress 10, 19, 32, 60, 64; balance 87, 89, 93, 97, 103; decision-making 146; sphere technique 110
Strickland, A.J. 26
sustainability 38–9, 83, 87, 106, 125; agenda-setting 222, 226–7;

decision-making 152; implementation 157, 169, 171, 180
Sveningsson, S. 204–6
Sweeney, P.J. 3
Swinnerton, J.A. 115
synergies 18, 42, 46, 49–53, 104, 213
System 1 coaching 165–6
System 2 coaching 165–6
systems theory 16, 142

tame problems 125, 128–31, 135, 174
taxes 8, 79
Taylor, S.S. 114
technology 8
temperance 68–9
Thatcher, M. 7
Thornton, L. 219
thought exercises 106, 113, 123
Tierney, D. 158
timing 78
tipping points 128–9
Tourish, D. 9, 203, 205
toxic leaders 9–11, 226–7
traditional leadership development 199–213
transactional leadership 202–3
transcendence 69
transformational/heroic leadership 200–2, 214, 216–17, 224
transparency 8, 10, 33, 204
Trevino, L.K. 26, 204
triple-loop learning 15
true exceptions 131–2
trust 21, 124, 136, 140, 150–1, 162, 176–7, 182–98, 209–11, 224
Turnbull James, K. 199–213, 220
Tyrrell, I. 88–9

Uhl-Bien, M. 211–12
United Kingdom (UK) 8–9
United States (US) 32, 63, 186

Values in Action (VIA) Institute 67, 72
values elicitation 18, 25–7, 33–9, 73

Van de Valk, L.J. 219
Van Dierendonck, D. 209–10
Van Gog, T. 179
Van Merriënboer, J.J. 179
Velasquez, M. 149
Vinkhuyzen, O.M. 38–9
virtues/virtuousness 60–1, 67–84, 149, 179, 205
Vitulano, L.A. 189–90
Vroom, V.H. 131, 155

Walsh, J. 97
Walumbwa, F.O. 11
Wang, C.S 180
websites 89
Weick, K.E. 64
Weinstein, N. 97

West 7, 69, 96
Western, S. 200, 210
wicked problems 20, 41, 106, 110, 124–5; agenda-setting 223; decision-making 128, 130–5, 138, 143–4, 147, 154–5; implementation 174–5; leadership theories 220
Wirtz, J. 44
wisdom 68, 113, 177
Wong, C.A. 204
Wood, W. 99

Zaccaro, S.J. 112
Zhong, C.-B. 135–6
Zigarmi, D. 208
Zigarmi, P. 208

eBooks
from Taylor & Francis

Helping you to choose the right eBooks for your Library

Add to your library's digital collection today with Taylor & Francis eBooks. We have over 50,000 eBooks in the Humanities, Social Sciences, Behavioural Sciences, Built Environment and Law, from leading imprints, including Routledge, Focal Press and Psychology Press.

ORDER YOUR FREE INSTITUTIONAL TRIAL TODAY

Free Trials Available

We offer free trials to qualifying academic, corporate and government customers.

Choose from a range of subject packages or create your own!

Benefits for you
- Free MARC records
- COUNTER-compliant usage statistics
- Flexible purchase and pricing options
- 70% approx of our eBooks are now DRM-free.

Benefits for your user
- Off-site, anytime access via Athens or referring URL
- Print or copy pages or chapters
- Full content search
- Bookmark, highlight and annotate text
- Access to thousands of pages of quality research at the click of a button.

eCollections

Choose from 20 different subject eCollections, including:

- Asian Studies
- Economics
- Health Studies
- Law
- Middle East Studies

eFocus

We have 16 cutting-edge interdisciplinary collections, including:

- Development Studies
- The Environment
- Islam
- Korea
- Urban Studies

For more information, pricing enquiries or to order a free trial, please contact your local sales team:

UK/Rest of World: **online.sales@tandf.co.uk**
USA/Canada/Latin America: **e-reference@taylorandfrancis.com**
East/Southeast Asia: **martin.jack@tandf.com.sg**
India: **journalsales@tandfindia.com**

www.tandfebooks.com

An environmentally friendly book printed and bound in England by www.printondemand-worldwide.com

PEFC Certified

This product is
from sustainably
managed forests
and controlled
sources

PEFC/16-33-415   www.pefc.org

This book is made of chain-of-custody materials; FSC materials for the cover and PEFC materials for the text pages.

#0214 - 061115 - C0 - 229/152/15 - PB - 9781138786028